From 8,000 feet, the Flying Dutchman flew his chopper into a high-nose altitude and peeled off into a single-ship approach. His passengers were looking straight down at the ground from the open doorway. Before anyone could blink, they were diving toward the ground at 4,000 feet a minute, about as fast as a helicopter can come out of the sky with its main rotor still attached. The 12.7's opened up. Tracer rounds looked like basketballs zooming by. The supersonic bullets popped as they passed, breaking the sound barrier. When a bullet found its mark, it felt like someone smacking the ship with a baseball bat.

As soon as the troops on the ground had hefted the two critical cases into each side, John blasted out low level, now taking fire from the ground. He knew the Huey didn't have long before it became so much battered magnesium. . . .

JAY and DAVID GROEN

HUEY

BALLANTINE BOOKS • NEW YORK

 Published in the United States by Ballantine Books, a division of Random House, Inc., New York, and simultaneously in Canada by Random House of Canada Limited, Toronto.

Library of Congress Catalog Card Number: 83-91127

ISBN 0-345-31253-8

Manufactured in the United States of America

First Edition: February 1984

CONTENTS

PROLOGUE

"THIS IS LUCKY STAR BASE, WE NEED YOU TO FLY SOME artillery specialists and advisers to the top of 822."

"Roger. It's getting late, though."

"You're to spend the night on the mountain with them and come back in the morning."

"Roger."

So he was not quite done. John Vanvorden had one more day before he could take the short timer's chair in the officers' club for his last week and a half in Vietnam. He stopped thinking about short time until he had safely flown the specialists and advisers up to the fire base just recaptured by South Vietnamese forces. By the time he shut down the helicopter, it was sunset.

To the east lay a lower mountain, to the west a ravine. The fire base seemed to sit on top of the world. The setting sun outlined strips of clouds in red and gold. Below was the deep green jungle, strange and foreign.

A team of four F-4 Phantoms started working the mountain to the east with 20-mm. cannon. All the Americans lined up as if they had 50-yard-line seats in a football stadium. The F-4s were running directly overhead. Fire streamed from the fighters' guns, and the sound, an unbroken *brrrrrrr*, was accompanied by enthusiastic cheering from the onlookers. A crackling noise echoed back from the target area. The men cheered harder. Then brass casings from the F-4s came crashing down around them. The veterans, without taking their eyes from the spectacle, reacted automatically to the *pang pang pang* by reaching for their steel pots.

John sat back against the skid of his helicopter, watching it all: the men, the air-to-ground gunnery, the South Vietnamese soldiers, working to get the base cleaned up. In half an hour, the Phantoms disappeared, and silence throbbed in his eardrums.

As the men began to prepare bedrolls or heat up C rations, John rigged his hammock inside his helicopter. He was too tired to eat, but sleep did not come immediately. What good ships the Hueys were, he thought. How many times had this one held together to get him out of hostile situations? Remembering a close one, he recoiled involuntarily in his hammock. Damn, he was glad to be getting out. The Vietnamese could have the whole job. At twenty-one, he was too old for this war.

It took him a minute to wake up when the crew chief shook him at first light, calling his name.

"I'm sorry, sir. They woke me looking for the aircraft commander."

"Okay, chief. What's up?"

"There's an LRRP team out here needs you," said the chief, referring to a U.S. Army long-range reconnaissance patrol.

John slid out of his hammock and began to pull on his boots. It was just five-thirty. He could have slept twelve hours. "Shit! What do they want?"

"I don't know, sir," said the chief.

"We want to talk to the AC," said a voice outside.

"Well, hold your horses," said John warily. He jumped

out of the helicopter. In the dim light, he could hardly make out the two men waiting for him, camouflaged as they were with black and green face paint and wearing black and green fatigues.

They introduced themselves as Sergeant Gates and Corporal Carlson. They were attached to the 173rd Airborne. "We got a buddy out in the bush, wounded," said Carlson.

"Where?"

"Northwest."

"How the hell did you get there? This whole area's under a special ARVN operation."

"We know that, but we got surprised by a company of NVA come down off this hill." NVA were North Vietnamese army regulars. "They shot one of us, broke his leg. We got away and weren't chased, but we had to leave him off. Down that way." The whites of the man's eyes flashed as he looked in the direction where they had left their companion.

"You sure you know where he is?"

"We know," said Gates.

John believed that. It never failed to amaze him how good these men were in the bush, how they could turn up anywhere.

"Well, we have to wait until it gets lighter, and I have to get it cleared."

An hour later, they were on their way. The place the LRRPs indicated was under two minutes' flying time away, but it took them ten to find it. The spot was little more than a hover hole in the jungle canopy.

"Gotta cut that one limb out of there and we'll have enough room," said John to his peter pilot, a newby to Vietnam named Rosen.

"What limb? Where? How?" Rosen had obviously never seen a helicopter used as a cutting tool. John did not answer. He slid the rotor in sideways under the limb and hacked it off, making a hell of a racket and causing the ship to shudder each time the blade hit wood. It worked. "Now we go down."

The LRRPs had their buddy in the helicopter in two minutes. "All set, Dutchman," shouted the crew chief over the intercom.

"Give us some covering fire, gunners," ordered John.

As the two gunners sprayed the trees, John eased the ship out of the hover hole. He tilted forward to zoom away at low level.

Then the lights went out.

In that instant, as they hung above the trees, the enemy had opened up with a heavy machine gun, and an armor-piercing round came up through the floor. A bullet pierced John's chair in the groin area and was stopped by the Colt .45 automatic he wore between his legs under the chicken plate. Fortunately, the heavy chair had taken most of the bullet's force. As it was, he needed emergency help. Besides mashing both testicles, the pistol split in half, cutting into the big arteries inside both thighs. The top of his helmet had punched a hole in the greenhouse window in the ceiling as his chair was blown completely off its height-adjustment tracks.

Rosen, with his hands on the controls as John had taught him, recovered quickly and continued to fly out low. "Chief, give me some help! The Dutchman's hit. I'm heading for the MASH."

The crew chief knew what to do. He was already disengaging John from the wreckage of his chair, and as soon as he had him lying flat, he began applying pressure above the wounds to stop the blood that was pumping out in rapid spurts.

No longer conscious of his surroundings, the wounded aircraft commander drifted, as in a dream, back to his first days in Vietnam, only twelve months before on any calendar but a lifetime ago in a war zone.

1

ARRIVAL

WARRANT OFFICER JOHN VANVORDEN WAS ONE OF ONLY four officers on the DC-8 packed with soldiers. Young for a helicopter pilot but no rare exception at twenty, he was on his way to Vietnam in July 1970. The grunts—infantrymen—sat three abreast on either side of the aisle. They all looked identical, with closely cropped hair, in new green jungle fatigues. As if to assert their individuality, they had talked much about themselves between naps on the long flight.

John had not. Before the army, John had prided himself on his physical strength, although he was of average height. His thick blond hair had often brought comments from girls. But in the army there was always someone bigger and stronger, and as for girls, he had shelved that subject for the time being. He wanted to think only about piloting Hueys, the UH-1H Iroquois, which he loved to fly.

Also known as slicks, the UH-1Hs were mainly used in Vietnam for troop and cargo transport, command and control, VIP flights, and reconnaissance. John could only guess about combat flying, but up to then, flying helicopters was fulfilling a dream. The dream had started years before when he sent away for a comprehensive set of plans to a home-built autogyro, a machine much like a helicopter, advertised in *Popular Mechanics*. Although the autogyro never got built, the blueprints wore out from years of unfolding and folding while John planned with his friends in the back of his dad's garage.

Now John was finally getting his helicopter, and in Vietnam, the helicopter was a great equalizer. While flying, no one was more free, more powerful, than a Huey pilot. In the air, John felt in control, supreme.

When the DC-8 began descending to land at Bien Hoa Air Base, the soldiers came wide awake and stopped talking. The ones by the windows held their heads back so the others could see out. There was a stir as the plane turned off the taxi strip, but no one seemed eager to get out. It was as if sudden fear of the unknown held them immobile. How many fighting men in how many wars had felt that fear? John wondered. Did they all ask before battle, "What will it be like? Will I ever get back home?" This was their generation's war. This was Vietnam.

The doors of the DC-8 swung open. John pushed toward the exit. As he took his first breath of air in "Nam," heat, humidity, and an indescribably foul smell hit him. The extraordinary stink made him feel like a newby, a new boy or FNG, fucking new guy, as the instructors in Texas told him he would. He remembered one saying you got so you didn't notice the odor made by a twenty-four-hour latrine detail of enlisted men collecting human sewage to burn in fifty-five-gallon drums that had been cut in half. Jet or diesel fuel was mixed with it. The army had to burn it that way because the water table was too high to bury it. How could you get used to a stink like that?

In the passenger terminal sat more grunts waiting to return home. They were mud stained and haggard, just as they had walked out of the war. Within five minutes, the new soldiers' jungle outfits were sweat soaked, but compared to the returnees, they looked immaculate. Fearing to look stupid, the newbys asked very little advice from the returnees.

John spotted a chief warrant officer in the terminal and went over to him. "Sir, do you know where I find out where I will be assigned?" he asked the CW-2.

"Listen, newby, in Nam you don't call warrants sir, don't call lieutenants sir, and damn few captains. Stand over there." He pointed to a corner of the terminal. "They'll call your name. Sometime."

Afraid of another contemptuous look, John walked over to the corner without a word. He waited. All around were faceless soldiers, clean new ones like himself and battered ones going home. He thought back to his parents in Salt Lake City. His room still had its closetful of clothes. He remembered his athletic trophies, skis, weights, and other sports equipment now stored in the garage.

An hour passed. Then a staff sergeant began calling names on another list. "Sims, Thomas, Vanvorden . . ."

John started out of his daydream and went over to the sergeant. "Did you call Vanvorden?"

"Yes, sir. Okay, everybody I called, follow me," he shouted above the noise in the terminal.

The bus had wire mesh on the windows—to deflect hand grenades, someone muttered. A guard in the doorway toted a machine gun. John was taken to an officers' barracks in a holding company to wait for his permanent assignment. The raw wood structure was no comfort station. There were no sheets or blankets on the bunk beds, and nobody spoke to him. Everybody else seemed to have a weapon, but he was given none. Actually, the base was quite safe, but nobody told him so. Nobody asked, either. Rather than look like FNGs, fucking new guys, including officers, suffered their anxieties quietly.

He was there for three days, feeling like a zombie. Waiting alone as a transient was even more depersonalizing than being with the plane load of GIs coming over.

It was a relief when he got his orders assigning him to the 155th Assault Helicopter Company, Tenth Combat Aviation Battalion, Seventeenth Group, First Aviation Brigade. From brigade in Long Binh, he picked up some of his clothing issue and then was flown to group at Nha Trang. Part of the base there was under mortar attack and ground assault, he had gathered, although nobody had told him anything directly. When the C-130 wheeled onto the runway, the pilot spun it around. The wide tail ramp slammed open, and airmen began shoving off cargo and baggage. The aircraft commander came aft, yelling at John and two other troops disembarking at Nha Trang. "Git off my fuckin' airplane," he ordered, his voice booming over the engine noise. "Git off. C'mon, Git! Git!"

The three men stumbled down the ramp and were pelted with sand and gravel blown by the tremendous prop wash from the four turboprop engines as the huge plane roared away. His two companions had been in Vietnam awhile and seemed to know what to do, so John followed them. Nha Trang was a ghost town, rows of buildings but no people. The base, said one of the officers, was on red alert, and anyway, said the other, the U.S. share in it was winding down. In the deserted air terminal, there was a row of telephones on one wall and a long list of numbers classified by branch of service with unit designators.

John located the Seventeenth group and made his call.

"Headquarters," answered a tinny voice.

"Is this Seventeenth Group?" John asked.

"Yeah, it's the Seventeenth Group."

"This is Mister Vanvorden. I'm at the airport."

"Yeah, which one?"

"How the hell would I know?" asked John. "I just got here. I'm fresh in country. Whatever one they come in at, I guess."

"We'll send someone to get you," said the voice, and the phone clicked off.

The other two officers were picked up after a few minutes. John waited. It got dark, and he got nervous. A few Vietnamese soldiers, ARVNs, grunts in the Army of the Republic of Vietnam, came by. They paid no attention to him. After two and a half hours, a driver arrived, a specialist Fourth class, who took him to group headquarters and showed him the barracks there.

"If we get hit," he said, pointing to a sandbag-covered trench just outside the door, "this is your bunker."

"How do I know when we get hit?" asked John.

"Don't worry, you'll know. We got hit today."

"Do we get guns?"

"No guns," the specialist said, shaking his head.

"What do I do if they come in?"

"They don't come in."

The spec 4 drove off, leaving John to go inside, stow his duffel bag, and find a bunk. Only four or five bunks in the whole bay looked as if they belonged to anybody. There were no sheets or blankets there, either. He threw his bag on one of the lower bunks and walked out to find the officers' club.

There he had a snack and two beers while he studied a near-naked troop of Australian girls passing themselves off as dancers. They had homely faces and no talent but beautiful bodies. After two hours, he went back to the barracks. The lights were off, and a half-dozen men were sleeping. Nha Trang, hot and humid by day, could get very cold at night. John kept his clothes on and got between the baggy mattress cover and the mattress. Trying to sleep, he had lain there only a few minutes when explosions shook the barracks. Dust sifted from the rafters. He jumped out of bed ready to head for the bunker, but no one else moved except for one guy who turned over in his bunk.

Doggone, thought John, they must not be hitting close enough to worry about. He contained himself, as he had learned to do during flight school with constant harassment from the instructors and even fellow trainees. He had learned the most important quality of a good pilot is a calm mind, the ability to think and act under pressure.

Military training rushes back at you in times of need. John now remembered vividly an incident only obliquely related to his training in flight school but responsible for much of his resolve in getting through successfully.

A face and a voice, as clear as when it first spoke, came to mind, as did an index finger thumping him on the chest.

"Vanvorden, I've seen your type before, too wet behind the

ears. You'll never make it through this, let alone Vietnam.'' It was an older student pilot back in Texas, Capt. Cortland B. Hayes.

In flight school, warrant officer candidates and regular officers were segregated except for training on the flight line. John never could understand it, but this Captain Hayes singled him out for abuse whenever he was around. He was the youngest in his class. He was told later by another candidate that Hayes thought the army was wrong to recruit trainees as young as John. It hurt the chances of older, better men. Hayes was old for a student. Following a successful tour in Vietnam, he was cross-training into helicopters. John was not afraid of the man, but he had said nothing, not knowing what kind of influence Hayes had on the instructors, many of whom Hayes outranked.

The statement, punctuated by the thumping index finger, grated on John all these months and even now took away the fear of the explosions outside. The explosions stopped, and he fell asleep until he was awakened again by more. The ground shook. Again he was the only one on his feet, but they sounded so close. This happened at intervals all night, and he had nightmares that the barracks was being overrun by NVAs, the North Vietnamese Army.

In the morning the sun poured through the windows and everyone began getting up. John was no longer afraid, but he was amazed that no one had gone for the bunkers during the night. Affecting nonchalance, he approached several of the others from nearby bunks. ''Hey, did you guys hear any loud booms last night?''

''What d'ya mean?'' one of them asked, scratching his head.

''Well, I don't know, some loud explosions woke me up a couple of times. Sounded like incoming or something.''

''Oh, that,'' said another. ''Heck, all that is is the artillery battery right over there.'' He pointed out a window. ''They're shootin' out. Don't worry. You get incoming, you'll know!''

John had to attend a series of briefings at Group. G2, intelligence, was in a large concrete building with double steel doors. After the doors shut behind him, John was led into a darkened room with an immense wall map rigged electronically and magnetically to show the latest battle action. A huge panel of buttons and lights controlled the map while officers and enlisted men explained the scene in lowered voices, impressing on newcomers that the United States was firmly in control. Like most FNGs, John did not understand much of what G2 had to say, but the main idea was that the United States had its shit together.

After a short trip through Battalion in Dong Ba Thin, near Cam Ranh Bay, John was flown to his final destination, the 155th Assault Helicopter Company in Ban Me Thuot. The Camp Corriel compound included a runway, two large parking ramps for helicopters, a maintenance hangar, control tower and billets, mess hall, and offices. The perimeter was shaped like a large, narrow triangle, with the narrow point facing west.

Quarters for officers and enlisted men took up the east part of Camp Corriel. Narrow cement sidewalks ran through coarse grass between the buildings. In the middle of the base were the PX, NCO club, underground hospital, and the theater. The perimeter was fortified with guard towers and machine-gun bunkers. Beyond them was a ten-foot cyclone fence surrounded with concertina barbed wire, and outside of that were land mines, trip flares, Claymore trip, and command-detonated Phugas mines. It seemed well protected.

John's company was top-heavy with officers, eighty of them to two hundred enlisted men, because it was a flying unit and all pilots were officers. Twenty-four operational helicopters were maintained on the average, including Huey "C" model gun ships. They did not get the slender-bodied AH-1G Cobra gunships, though, the ones called "snakes." Those went mostly to cavalry units, like Custer's old outfit, the First Cavalry Division. Their sophisticated firepower was used for aerial rocket artillery.

Joining a new outfit was never easy. In Vietnam, it was a bitch. John had to spend five days sleeping in a utility room until a man rotated out of his platoon. In the meantime, he was issued his clothes, flight gear, and a .45 caliber automatic pistol. It would be awhile before he was allowed to fly.

He was more comfortable after he moved into one of the barracks, which were built out of wooden ammo boxes and had corrugated tin roofs. The windows and doors were screened. By Vietnam standards, he would learn, these buildings had class. Each officer lived in his own eight-by-ten cubicle, called a hootch. Hootches were furnished with single beds and double-doored wooden wardrobes; over the months, men added things like tables, chairs, and fans. Some even had rugs on the floor instead of rice mats, and art work rather than *Playboy* foldouts on the walls.

Hootch maids did the housekeeping and took the laundry. They were allowed on base in the daytime along with other Vietnamese workers for the menial tasks. John's hootch maid looked not a day under fifty, and her teeth were black from chewing mildly narcotic betel nuts. She could not stand up straight after years of planting rice, but she smiled constantly, thus earning the nickname "Happy."

New arrivals like himself were only called "newby" or some derivative of FNG. After a month or so, usually after a screw up, you got a nickname.

One of his instructors, back in the real world, had liked the way John was shaping up as a pilot and had told him something. A twelve-month tour in Vietnam, he said, was like a lifetime. For the first three months, you were young and unreliable. You figured you were well trained for war, but the veterans knew you were not. The youngster, the newby, either learned what only experience could teach, or he simply did not make it. From the fourth to the tenth month, you were a veteran. The war was your private joke, and you were its mainstay. Then the veteran got old. For the last two months, he was unreliable again, because he looked forward to getting out and back to the world.

John intended to become a veteran fast. Right now, he was moving in with a group of men who had been through a lot together in a country with few ties to the United States. Such simple acts as being considerate of FNGs were unimportant. That's how it is, he told himself.

2
FNG

THE ENEMY, THE VC, MORTARED THE BASE AT THE END OF John's first week in camp. The first shell hit and he was out of his bunk yelling, "This is it! This is it!" It had not taken the siren to let him know. He put on his fatigues and pulled on his boots. More mortars fell as he slipped into his flack vest and got his weapon. With his steel pot on his head, he made it to the bunker just in time to hear the all-clear. The rest of the officers in his platoon were already coming out. Most were in shorts; one was naked. They looked at John and hooted. "Fucking new guy! Who do you think you are, John Wayne?"

The biggest man in the platoon, who must have weighed 240 pounds, slapped him on the back, laughing as he went by. It was Frank Arata, an Italian from Brooklyn. John heard he had played defensive tackle for an upstate New York school until he flunked out. Arata was very much respected. The men listened to him as if he were the platoon leader.

Mortar attacks were rarely heavier than a dozen shells, and John now knew that he could get out of bed, into the bunker, and back into bed and asleep again within forty minutes. Okay, shit, he thought, I won't make that mistake again.

Two nights later, when the base was shelled again, John leaped from bed and ran out into the hall. He was immediately run over, hitting the floor like a spare tenpin. It was Arata. Everybody else knew that at the first sound of incoming, Arata blasted headlong down the length of the barracks and dove into the bunker without even waking up. Anyone in his way was mowed down. When John got to the bunker, with a bloody nose, Arata was sitting there, eyes closed, snoring. John, five feet ten and 170 pounds, had not caused Arata to shorten his stride. After that, John waited like the others for Arata's charge down the hallway.

Every day John watched the helicopters taking off without him. Gunnies, Charlie-model gunships, stayed aloft, providing covering fire for troop carriers. H-model Hueys, the slicks, were the workhorses of the 155th. A beautiful aircraft, as powerful and maneuverable as any of the Vietnam-generation helicopters, its missions were as variable as it was versatile. The real danger was when they were sent to land in hot LZs, the landing zones staked out in disputed territory.

He itched to fly again. Nothing in his life had compared to flying helicopters. Leaving the ground at high speed, being up there, was an emotional high. No home run, no touchdown, not even a downhill ski run, was comparable. As he mastered the art of flying a chopper, the machine ceased to be a thing apart. It became an extension of his body, responding to his hands on the controls so that he lost awareness of anything but his own will transporting him through the air like some giant hummingbird.

It was two months since he had flown, what with home leave and all the waiting around in Vietnam. As the day approached when he would take his check-out flight with the company flight safety and standardization officer, he felt stirrings of anxiety. Although he had forbidden himself to think about it, he was reminded of his twelfth-week flight test in flight school. If you flunked that test, that was it. You washed out. No second chance. Instructors warned you about check ride-itis, the fear that kept you from doing as well as you were able.

It had been a typically clear Texas morning with its typically giant sky over the flat land. Perfect flying weather. In the flight shack, waiting for his turn, John tried to hang on to his confidence as he watched his classmates go out and come back. Some were ecstatic, some destroyed. He avoided the eyes of the rejects. He walked to the cooler for a Coke, but as he reached for the last can, another hand grabbed it away.

Thinking it was one of his classmates, John protested, "You son of a bitch, you took the last fucking Coke!"

The hand hesitated, and the knuckles around the can turned white. "Who you calling a son of a bitch, candidate?"

The hand belonged to his check pilot. John went pale, and his card-house confidence tumbled. "I—I didn't think . . ."

"Right! Well you better think now because just as soon as I drink this last fuckin' Coke, we're going for a little ride." He sat down near Captain Hayes, who had already passed his check ride. Hayes would look over at John and then talk in hushed tones to the check pilot. Hayes looked smug.

John walked in silence with the check pilot out under the perfect sky and climbed with him into the tiny TH-55-A training helicopter. The check pilot took it up to a hover, the single most difficult maneuver in a chopper. Then he turned the controls over to John.

"Okay, set it down and then pick up and give me a clearing turn for a max-performance takeoff."

"Yes, sir," said John, trying to hold the hover and to recover his confidence.

John set the ship down, but he failed to throttle back slightly while reducing the pitch of the rotor blades. He hoped the check pilot hadn't noticed and that he had not oversped. After an overspeed, a helicopter needed to be inspected by a mechanic before it was flown again.

The pilot wrenched the controls from John. "You know what you just did? You oversped the engine!" He pointed to the rpm needle, which must have gone past the red line. Then he cut the engine. "If you'd done that after picking up, the ride would be over right now."

"No!"

"That's right, but since you never even started, I got to take you up again."

By the time they were back hovering in another helicopter, John was sweating so much he began to fog up the bubble. Sweat got into his eyes and fogged up his face mask.

"Here, you take it a minute," the check pilot shouted at him and wiped the bubble on his own side. Then he took back the controls and gave the cloth to John to wipe off the other side.

"You son of a bitch," yelled the pilot when his side fogged up again. "You knock that off or we'll never get out of here."

John tried not to sweat. He began shaking. The test pilot landed back on the ramp and said, "Get out and give me twenty!"

The students and instructors back at the flight shack, including Captain Hayes, watched the odd sight. They agreed that John Vanvorden was in deep shit now. Hayes stood in the doorway laughing. "I knew that dumb Dutchman wouldn't make it. What'd I tell you?"

But the push-ups did the trick. John settled down and passed his first check ride.

Would they give you a chance to do push-ups in the middle of a war? he wondered. John resolutely refused to think more about that first stateside check ride as he sat on a bench in the 155th operations building the morning his test was scheduled. Nearby, two Vietnam air force pilots were arguing about something.

"Vanvorden!"

"Yes, s . . ." He had almost sirred a W-2.

"C'mon outside here," said a chief warrant officer who was standing in the doorway. "I'm the flight safety officer. Get in that helicopter with that captain. Hurry!"

John figured some other guy was going to give him the check ride. He hurried out to the flight line and jumped into the helicopter, trying to act cool and not look like an FNG as he buckled in. When he had put on his helmet, the captain started the engine. Five U.S. soldiers got on board with a bunch of gear, coils of rope, cable, strap harnesses, and guns.

The captain was his platoon leader. John decided the captain was taking the soldiers somewhere before he gave him the checkride. Over the intercom, the captain said, "You ready to go?" and took off without waiting for the answer. He didn't say anything to John about watching the instruments. For fifteen minutes or so, John enjoyed the view of the jungle. The helicopter began to descend and slow down before John saw a flight of eight others in formation also going in. He looked farther and saw a landing zone, an LZ, with a Huey lying on its side burning. Next to it was another Huey shot full of holes. Several troops on the side of the LZ were headed into the jungle. "We're going into combat!" he exclaimed involuntarily without pushing his mike button. For the first time, he noticed that everyone inside his helicopter wore flack vests and was heavily armed. The captain had on his chicken plate, and his armored side plate was in position. The chicken plate, made of hardened steel with a thick layer of porcelain on the outside and held in place by a vest, protected you from chin to lap. John was not wearing his, and nobody had slid his side panel in place for protection on the outside of the armor-plated seat. It had to be done from behind.

Wholly exposed, he suddenly realized what was happening. He was a newby, just so much cannon fodder. The captain had to have a peter pilot in the right-hand seat according to regulations, and if he had really thought he might have to rely on his peter pilot to get the ship back in the event he was wounded, he would never have taken John. From conceit or apathy, an FNG had been stuck in as copilot, and nobody gave a damn about his safety. That was how most of the seasoned troops felt about newbys. They had lost so many friends, they were reluctant to make new ones. If someone new got blown away, it hardly mattered. His death had no effect on you.

The AC, the aircraft commander, said to John as they went in that newbys should be seen and not heard. John kept quiet and watched. He did not know how hot the situation was, but there was very little ground fire. It must have been suppressed. Gun ships zoomed overhead. The burning ship on the ground disintegrated. John's helicopter went in to rig the other downed Huey for sling loading back to base by a CH-47, a Chinook cargo helicopter, affectionately called a shit hook.

Rigging for extraction took skill and courage. The riggers jumped out of John's ship and climbed on the crippled Huey. They secured the rotor system and attached a sling. Then the shit hook came in. It was a matter of split-second timing. The Chinook flared into a hover. One man waited with the doughnut, a rubberized steel ring on the end of the sling. He slammed it hard onto the Chinook's belly hook to let the pilot know it was hooked up. As the shit hook picked up, the rigger dived for the ground to avoid earning a 160-knot ride back to base clinging to the disabled Huey's rotor mast.

John could not see it all, but he knew what was happening. As soon as the men and the rigging had been dropped off, the captain headed back for Ban Me Thuot. All the captain said when they arrived was "Get out."

He took his check ride in the afternoon. It was a good test of his ability. While he hovered, made engine-off approaches, simulated tail-rotor-failure flying, and performed various other emergency procedures on command, he had to be continuously aware of the readings on the gauges. This would be particularly important if the helicopter was taking fire from the ground.

John's skill was still there, and he carefully monitored warning lights and the six-pack, as the main gauges were called. These were for transmission and engine oil pressures and temperatures, fuel pressure, and amp meter. There were warning lights on the console for fire, high or low rpms, and a master caution light for indicating that a chip light was lit on the warning panel below. The chip-light system is an ingenious way of detecting loose metal fragments, no matter how fine, in places where there are moving parts. If the ship got hit by ground fire, the lights would tell the pilot where. John passed easily, and after an oral exam, was checked out to fly slicks.

His first missions as a peter pilot, sitting in a Huey side by side with the aircraft commander on his left, were "ash and trash" flights—flying top brass from one point to another or picking up supplies. After he had been a peter pilot for a few months, John would be tested again and certified, if he passed, as an AC.

Initiating a newby was the favorite amusement of the veterans. Otherwise, they left an FNG pretty much by himself. John preferred solitude, and his Dutch inheritance stood him in good stead. He seemed self-contained and rarely gave away his ignorance or his vulnerability. Perhaps, like that guy named Roger, who had become a legend in the company because he had escaped every initiation planned for him, John could escape the worst.

In the officers' mess, they talked about Roger. He was tall, wiry, a very fast runner, and a crazy bastard. Once, to escape getting threaded on a tail stinger, he had jumped through concertina wire and stood in a mine field. Getting threaded was no fun for the victim. The bar on the tail of a Huey extended about three feet, protecting the tail rotor blade from hitting the ground on landing. When a pilot came in at an exaggerated tail low angle, the stinger caught the ground first and leveled the ship. A man was threaded onto a parked Hueys tail stinger through one pant leg all the way up to his belt. That left him hanging in midair about five feet off the ground. He had to figure a way down or wait until his pants tore off. John was sure he would rather live through that than stand in a mine field, though.

John thought part of his own problem was that he looked new. Experienced pilots wore flight caps that, unlike army issue, were collapsible and easy to carry indoors. There must have been someplace among the shops off post selling them. One night, he stopped by Arata's hootch to find out where. The poker game was going on as usual. At the doorway, John asked if he could come in and watch.

"Your money's as good as the next guy's, I guess," said a mousy-looking pilot nicknamed, for obvious reasons, Shorty.

"Hey, newby," boomed Arata, who was surrounded by empty beer cans. "I hear you fly pretty good. Maybe I'll let you fly with me on 'A' team sometime."

John waited for the laughter. It did not come. Maybe he meant it, thought John, suppressing his excitement.

"Ain't no seats open right now," said Roger, who was next to Arata.

"Well, I don't want to play just yet, anyway," said John.

"Whatsa matter, scared of losing a little change?" asked Shorty.

"Nah," said John, who had been afraid of shoving into the game.

"Last card, down and dirty," said Roger, dealing seven-card stud.

"Hey, where'd you guys get those flight caps I see all over the place?" asked John as Roger swept in the chips.

"You fuckin' new guys don't know nothin'," said Torch, a dark-faced pilot on the other side of the table. He was called Torch because when he was a newby, he had set his bed on fire while smoking. A day later, he had caught his boot on fire walking clear of the refueling area. Some spilled fuel flashed when he stepped on a match after lighting a cigarette. From then on, he was Torch.

"Ya get 'em at the Slope Shop,"said Roger.

"Where's that?"

"Off post. Next to number-one laundry," said Torch. John knew that all laundries were called number one. "Call you, sucker; let's see what you got."

"Three bullets."

"You unconscious bastard!" Torch stood up to leave. Roger raked in more chips.

"Can I take your seat?" asked John.

Torch slammed out of the room. "No fucking class, that guy," said Arata. "Sure, sit down, newby."

John bought in. These guys were pretty nice. "Which number-one laundry is the Slope Shop next to?"

"Look," said Roger, "you go about a block off the main gate, you see the stump of a big tree where kids are all the time playin'. The laundry there is the one we're talking about. The Slope Shop is on the left."

"Okay, you guys. A little baseball, no peeky," said Arata, the cards buried in his big hands.

John lost all his chips in half an hour.

Next day, after flying, he went to look for the Slope Shop. Slope sounded like something to do with skiing, and he had a mental picture of a ski shop, but when he found the place, which he recognized because different unit patches were nailed to the door, it was just a shack like all the others lining the street. Anyway, it was closed. There was no sign out front saying Slope Shop, either.

He tried again on three different days. It was always closed. John was determined to get his cap, but he did not feel like asking the others any more about it. A Vietnamese probably could have helped him, but he did not want to ask a gook. Gooks were just not cool. Their pilots were always walking around wearing their flight helmets with the smoke-colored visors down, looking goofy. The U.S.-made helmets were too big for them, so they stuffed newspapers in the top to make them fit.

Arata, like most of the men on the base, didn't think the Vietnamese were worth a damn as fighters. He had once talked about a gook who was with him as copilot on a combat assault mission. They took hits in the LZ, and afterward Arata noticed a bullet hole in the back of the VNAF helmet. "You okay?" he asked. The gook nodded. "Take a look at your helmet." The copilot took it off, and when he saw the hole, he passed out. Arata thought he really had been hit, but it turned out the bullet had missed his head and had gone through the newspaper and out the front. "Fucker fainted," Arata had said disgustedly.

The day John had made his third unsuccessful trip to find a cap, the commander of the Twenty-third ARVN Division, General Kahn, and his aide were to be ferried to another base in a company helicopter. While the AC and his peter pilot waited with the blades turning, the general and his aide got on board and hooked up the intercom, but the AC had not noticed them. On the intercom to the peter pilot, the AC said, "Where's that fucking gook Kahn and that other little dink that runs around with him?"

General Kahn, who spoke perfect English, stormed off the ship and reported to Major Smith, who then invited him to come to the safety briefing that evening and hear him give the eighty American officers hell.

Major Smith, the new CO, had tried to clamp down on racial slurs by ordering the men to stop using derogatory names for their allies. Civilians were to be called Vietnamese, and soldiers were ARVNs. Except in front of the CO, the old usage remained the same.

Kahn was no one to cross. He had been a colonel in the Viet Minh army when they shelled into submission a French division in the Mang Yang Pass. The story was that Kahn took the remaining French troops, several thousand, up on a hillside, had the prisoners dig vertical graves, and then killed every one. Kahn himself had pulled the trigger on all the high-ranking French officers.

That night, in front of Kahn, Major Smith raked the American officers over the coals. "I'll take your wings," he said loudly, "unless you understand that the Vietnamese are not gooks or any other slang name. You understand?"

Kahn looked smug. He was big for a Vietnamese, almost fat. John thought he probably had Chinese blood in him. Major Smith looked like what he was, a career officer. He was not going to allow anything to stand in the way of his silver leaves. He ignored the atmosphere in the room. His officers, used to dozing through safety briefings, were sullen and tense as he threatened them with courts-martial.

"Now," the major concluded, "do you have any questions?"

There was silence. The major glared. "Come on. You new guys out there. You must have a question."

He was looking at John, who felt compelled to ask a question, but he could not think of one.

"Any question at all!" demanded the CO.

John raised his hand. "Well, this is kind of unrelated, sir, but do you know when the Slope Shop is going to open up?"

The place got so quiet, John heard his heart beating. The look on the major's face was one of incredulous disbelief. The officers looked stunned. Then a wave of hysterical laughter broke the silence. "Way to go, newby!" one man shouted.

General Kahn stamped from the room, and the major charged at John, who immediately stood to attention. He had no idea what was the matter, but he was laughing because everyone else was.

"You think you're pretty funny?" the major yelled in his face above the raucous laughter. "You are in a lot of trouble, boy! You got a lot of balls, boy!"

John racked his brain for an explanation. "Heck, I don't even know what I said!"

The major turned brick red with frustration. He knew John was innocent. "Damn, that fat ass is sure to go to battalion now," he said furiously.

John felt sorry for the major. He also felt sorry for himself, for the inexperience that had made him look so foolish. Arata walked up behind John and put a big hand on his shoulder.

"Newby, you're all right. I'm gonna show you how to fly."

3

PETER PILOT

THE PILOTS SPOKE WITH JOHN MORE OFTEN AFTER THAT MEMorable briefing, but he avoided the CO.

Though most of John's flights were still ash and trash, he was taken as peter pilot on a few combat flights. It was his job to monitor the instruments, or if he took the controls, to fly where and how the AC told him to. Both pilots had control panels for the radio, but only the AC talked to the ground.

John tried to fly with as many ACs as he could to learn about combat flying. At altitude, you had to stay above two thousand feet, the effective limit for small-arms fire. When down low, you kept right on the "deck" so the enemy would not spot the ship and anticipate a shot at it. Treetop flying was tricky. It required skill at map reading plus a sort of sixth sense, an inertial navigation system inside your own head, which John seemed to have naturally.

John flew with Blacky for the first time on a mission to supply a compound on Lac Thien island. Blacky was a warrant officer with a reputation for his skill at buzzing elephant herds. It was amusing to see the huge pachyderms stampede. One elephant had been nicknamed Mohammed. He hung out in the area of Lac Thien, a lake southeast of Ban Me Thuot, where Teddy Roosevelt used to hunt. Roosevelt had built a two-story villa on an island. The villa was now a whorehouse, but men who had been there said the plaques commemorating big-game trophies still hung on the walls. Mohammed was a big black bull that refused to run. Instead, he would try to knock a Huey out of the air. If the chopper got too close he would push off with just one hind foot on the ground and slash wildly at the ship with his trunk.

First they chased elephants, and John saw the famous Mohammed, his head up and his ears out wide. If the magnificent black beast had ever hooked a skid with his trunk, that would have been it. Afterward, they headed on for the compound and were on final approach when Blacky unexpectedly aborted the landing. John was not tuned in to the radio conversation between the AC and the ground, so he had no idea why.

"Okay, listen, newby," Blacky said. "We got to go medivac some Vietnamese that got blown up. They're probably gonna look real bad, so don't you get sick."

"You get sick, you get to clean it up," the crew chief added.

He was the left-hand gunner in the air, an old guy, over thirty, on his second tour. It was his job on the ground to make sure the helicopter was clean and mechanically maintained. Old crew chiefs were tough as nails with new officers. If a newby peter pilot screwed up, flew out of trim or anything, the crew chief would sneak up and smack him on the back of his helmet with a big screwdriver. Flying out of trim put a wind of hurricane force in the face of one of the gunners; the doors would always be open or off the ship completely, and the gunners, aft of the passenger compartment, were completely exposed.

As they set down, John could see a French-built truck lying on its side, split in half. A VC mine had blown it up. Bodies were everywhere, a lot of women and children, babies. Those trucks were always jammed. The wailing was continuous. John reminded himself that he must stay cool, not let it bother him. He had to take on a detachment about others who got wounded, even close friends, to be of most help to them. But this act against helpless women and babies caused a sick feeling of anger and outrage to rise and lodge in John's throat. Speaking was difficult.

As they loaded the dirty, burned, broken-up bodies, they could not tell which were dead. About half of them, it turned out. John noticed one woman with no foot and a shinbone sticking out of her flesh. Other people had arms missing. It took two trips to medivac the lot, leaving them at a Vietnamese aid station near the base in Lac Thien.

After delivering the last of the wounded, John could only think, How useless. He was also struck by the inferiority of their aid stations.

He had little time to reflect upon this experience, because command began assigning him to ever more dangerous missions, mostly into Cambodia to interdict NVA supply lines and drop surveillance teams. They were called FOB, fly over the border, missions. The Hueys that went over were unmarked, and the crews wore civilian clothes. That was to give the generals what they called ''plausible deniability,'' meaning that the American public had not been informed of this particular escalation in the war.

The objective was to secretly insert or extract handfuls of troops in Cambodia. Special forces body snatchers or LRRP snipers went in, but mostly they inserted seven-man teams of ARVN soldiers dressed as NVAs. They would observe troop and supply movements along the Sihanouk Trail, which ran northeast along the South Vietnam border, up to O Rang in Cambodia, the southern terminus of the Ho Chi Minh Trail.

The ARVNs wore the same pith helmets, tan uniforms, and tan sneakers as the NVA and carried the same rifles. When it was time to pick them up, they put color-coded scarves around their necks and carried the rifles in their left hands to distinguish them from the enemy.

Flying FOB were four Charlie model Hueys, three F-4 Phantoms and a forward air controller, usually an O-2 Cessna Skymaster. Getting the contingents in was not bad, but getting them out of a fire fight could be nasty.

The Hueys were manned with A, B, C, and D teams. A team went into the hole, and if their Huey was shot down or disabled, B team extracted them, and C team pulled the ARVNs out, while D team covered for B and C. Alpha One was A team's AC.

Nobody in Second Platoon liked flying A team except Arata and John. Arata loved being Alpha One, and everybody thought he was crazy. He sometimes talked about his Mafia connections, and whether they believed him or not, nobody laughed at him. He said he was a killer, and they believed that. In Vietnam, he was staying in practice. The other ACs in the platoon loved Arata because he would take on the dangerous spot. When the platoon drew straws for A team, the AC with the short straw could usually trade with Arata. Then Arata would yell, "Utah! Come on." John acted as if he did not like being chosen, but he did. He felt safe with Arata, who was the best he had seen at single-ship approach, and he was getting good himself by flying with the big Italian.

After inserting troops, the slicks and gunnies would fly back a short distance into South Vietnam. It was usually three or four days before they were called back to Cambodia for a pickup. Catching sun or horsing around was a break from the war except that one time when John got threaded onto a tail stinger. The gang of ACs who grabbed him damn near skewered him. There was a long scrape on the inside of his leg and a bruise on his tail bone.

While he was hanging by his pant leg, they popped smoke grenades nearby. He knew the easiest way down was to unsnap and unbuckle his pants before the stinger took his full weight. Then you could pull your pants down, do a hand stand, and slide them off. Unfortunately, he did not manage to undo his buckle, and he ended up bouncing up and down until the trouser legs ripped apart and he dropped to the ground head first.

The crews cheered and awarded him his "purple gang scarf." Each platoon had its own color, and seasoned crews wore their scarves into combat.

When the call came to extract the ARVNs, there was a scramble to get the ships started and get dressed at the same time. If no convenient LZs were nearby, the triple-canopy jungle was broached by a rope ladder or jungle penetrator. The ARVN spies were flown away clinging for dear life. If too many got on the ladder, the ones on the bottom were picked off by the door gunner. Enemy soldiers often made suicidal tries at blowing a helicopter out of the air by climbing on board with a hand grenade.

Sometimes the LZ was nothing but a hover hole in the jungle's canopy. The pilot could widen the hole by sawing off the tops of trees with the rotor blade, but the underside of the blade could be torn up if care was not taken to slip in sideways instead of going vertically down. Sawing through a four-inch branch shook the ship and sounded like all hell breaking loose, but it worked.

Extraction was paramount. The ARVNs might have intelligence vital to a B-52 mission. The four gunnies provided heavy firepower for cover, and the air force F-4s, guided by forward air controllers, laid down a wall of napalm or got in close with smart bombs and missiles. On a single-ship approach, it was important to stay directly above the LZ, because with friendlies on the ground suppressing fire, it was the safest place in the sky. You came over the top at two thousand feet or higher, pulled the nose back to zero-out air speed, and got into a high nose-up attitude with reduced power and flat rotor-blade pitch. Then the pilot lay the aircraft over on its side in a very steep bank, 135 degrees maximum, which took real technique. Anything beyond ninety degrees is inverted, so you had to bank quickly to maintain a positive G load.

Otherwise, the rotor blades would eat up the ship and everybody in it. You could lose two thousand feet in one full revolution of the ship, spiraling toward maximum air speed, and halfway through the turn, you were already going as fast as the helicopter could go and still stay together. By the end of a full revolution, power was all the way in, the nose coming back, and the forward movement slowed. You kept coming back on your nose and set it down on the ground.

Climbing back up was much slower than descending. Beating it out of there, you stayed low level, right on the deck, for about five or ten miles, before climbing out.

John was getting to be an old newby and gaining respect from the others for his flying skill and for spending so much time with Arata on A team. He saw the arrival of new guys, and as pilots rotated out, he moved up in the hierarchy. Short timers began acting very cautious as their date to leave got close. When Vinny, a short timer in Second Platoon, had only two weeks left to go, he got so dangerously cautious he made the whole platoon nervous. Vinny was a chief warrant officer and had been through Tet of 1968. He ate and slept in his armor, wearing the whole lot twenty-four hours a day, steel pot, flack vest, and chicken plate. Most pilots are superstitious, and Arata refused to fly A team while Vinny was around, wearing his armor all the time. Command finally relieved Vinny of his flying duties.

John, Arata, Vinny, and some others were playing poker late one night during yellow alert. Vinny sat there sweating under all that armor. The rest of them were in underwear and thongs.

"Hey, Vinny, you a muthafuckin' cow'ad," jeered Arata in his New York-Italian accent.

"You know they don't never hit us during yellow alert," said Blacky, "so what d'you need all that stuff for?"

When the base was on yellow alert, it meant that an attack was supposed to come sometime that day or night. Everybody breathed easy during yellow alert. The Viet Cong knew that they were expected to attack, so they almost never mortared the base, and if you were not hit by midnight, you could go to bed because the VC also followed the midnight rule and went to bed.

At 2400 hours, John spoke up. "See that? Safe as church. How many cards you want, Vinny?"

"Goddam it," said Vinny. "I fold this hand." He walked over to the bunk, took off his pot, chicken plate, flack vest, and shirt, and scratched himself.

"Yeah, Vinny!" John cheered with the others. Just as Vinny turned around, a lone mortar shell landed at the end of the barracks, not thirty-five feet from them.

John was sitting halfway into the hallway and saw the flash. It was the first time he got to the bunker before anyone else, and he was all alone. It didn't feel right. He started back for the stairs just in time to get run over by Arata, followed by everybody else. No other shells were fired. Maybe the VC had lobbed that one in as a practical joke before calling it a night. Vinny was so mad he started to go for John but stopped when somebody yelled, "Hey, Utah, you're bleeding!"

John looked down and saw a trickle of blood from the middle of his chest. Lifting his shirt, he discovered a tiny piece of shrapnel barely hanging in. "Oh, great," he said, "I get a Purple Heart."

He took off for the medic station to claim the decoration, but the shrapnel fell out on the way, and he could not find it in the dark. He went on, anyway. The flight surgeon took one look and said, "Fuck you. Get outta here!"

Vinny was back in armor when John returned from the medics. He was still mad and stayed that way until he left. That day, an FOB mission came up. "Never mind choosing A team," said Arata, grinning. "Me and Utah are takin' it. C'mon, Utah." Everybody looked happy. Arata's refusing to fly A team had scared the shit out of the whole platoon. Now everything was back to normal.

Arata liked having John as peter pilot. He figured he was a strong and skilled pilot and could haul him out if need be.

Arata wasn't afraid of death, but he did not want to die in Cambodia.

The insertion of ARVN spy troops ten miles southwest of O Rang went like clockwork. After they left the LZ, John could forget monitoring the instruments for a bit. He looked down at the terrain. There was a crystal waterfall trickling down an emerald mountain. It was hard to believe a war was going on down there. His mind drifted back to pre-army days. . . .

"Hey Utah, whatta hell you lookin at?"

John's head snapped back. "Instruments . . ."

"Goddam right!"

They flew back into Nam to wait out the mission.

4

SHOT DOWN

THE FAC, THE FORWARD AIR CONTROLLER, CALLED JUST TWO days later, sounding excited. Transmitting on the preassigned channel, he ordered, "You guys hightail it back here. It's going to get real hot."

John was napping inside the helicopter when the call came. "Roger Oscar Charlie. We're coming," he replied, beginning the start procedure. Arata threw on his survival vest and chicken plate and got into the ship with the gunners. When the crew chief had shoved the AC armored panel into place, Arata took off—balls to the wall.

"Goin' in hot," Arata shouted over the intercom. John nodded. Flying combat, chatter was minimal. The AC had to be in contact with all the slicks, all the gunnies, the FAC, and sometimes the ground.

Fifteen minutes later, A team was two thousand feet above the LZ. Dropping out of the sky in a spiral approach, Arata pulled such a heavy G force that John knew it must be serious, and he concentrated hard on the instruments.

When they touched down, John could hear automatic fire

and some explosions. He stayed glued to the panel, giving his AC the necessary engine and power readings. The ARVNs, uniformed like NVAs, were frantic as they climbed aboard. Arata was lifting off just as a big explosion hit the left side of the helicopter and blew the ship apart.

John managed to unbuckle and get clear. What was left of the Huey began burning fiercely. The door gunner ran toward him and jumped for cover. John saw Arata crawling away from the wreckage. No one else emerged.

Hardly aware of what he was doing, John got to Arata, who was obviously badly hurt. He could not lift the enormous man, so he grabbed his shirt and dragged him toward the door gunner, who was hiding at the tree line.

He crouched with the door gunner beside Arata and looked back. In the LZ, in front of the burning Huey, were gooks shooting at and taking cover from the circling gunships. The noise was deafening. John unholstered his .45-caliber automatic pistol, the only weapon he had. Farther to the right, the Phantoms dropped napalm. He could feel his breath going short in the tremendous heat. The green jungle turned orange.

From behind the tail of the Huey, a dozen NVA soldiers emerged, shooting and running. John emptied his pistol at them as tracers and bullets flew overhead. Just fifty feet away, still in the open, a gunship caught them with minigun and fleshette rockets. The NVAs disintegrated in a cloud of dust, as if they had turned to powder. The combination of 2,200 individual darts per rocket and 4,000 rounds per minute from the minigun was devastating.

There was no way the three Americans could be picked up soon. The burning helicopter obstructed most of the LZ. Plenty of NVA were still shooting. John motioned the door gunner, a Private, named Brown, to help him. They would have to hide in the jungle, dragging Arata with them into the thick, swampy underbrush.

Arata's left leg was charred to the bone. He was unconscious. When they had to rest a second time, the big man regained consciousness.

"Hey, Utah, you still here?" he asked in a weak whisper.

"Still here, buddy," said John, keeping his voice very low. It was important they not be heard.

"Look, Vanvorden, if I'm too heavy . . ."

"It's okay. It's okay, Frank. There's three of us. You'll be okay." Brown tried to speak, but John told him to shut up. He wished to hell they carried morphine, but it was forbidden because of drug abuse in Vietnam. All they had with them was aspirin.

"Madonna Maria, not Cambodia," whispered Arata, and passed out again.

As they fought their way through the tough jungle, John kept Brown quiet by waving the .45 in his face. Silence was the survival rule. Brown was terrified, of John, of the jungle, of the enemy. John was scared, too, but he had to take command.

At the point of exhaustion, John figured they had clawed their way as far as they could go. He selected some heavy underbrush to hide in and lay down with Arata's head in his lap. Brown, numb with fright, stayed near Arata's feet. All three found themselves nearly submerged in eight to ten inches of swampy water.

John figured once the NVA had counted the dead crew members, they would look for any survivors. Sounds he could hear under the continuing noise of gunnies and F-4s convinced him the NVA had already begun to look for them.

The portable waterproof survival radio John took from Arata's vest had a silent switch that kept the speaker noise from traveling far.

"Mayday, Mayday," he whispered over the guard channel. "This is Alpha Team Two transmitting on Guard. Any station read?"

"Alpha Two," replied an F-4 pilot overhead. "This is Cowboy One Six. Go ahead."

"Cowboy One Six, Alpha Team is down and dirty. Survivors are Alpha One, Two, and Four. We are requesting pickup as soon as possible."

"Alpha Two, there's no way we can get you tonight. Call Silver King Three Five at 0800 hours tomorrow. Good luck. Cowboy One Six out."

That was it. They were spending the night. For the rest of the afternoon and into the evening, they could hear gunnies, F-4s, and reinforcement aircraft coming again and again. Then the weather turned bad, and it began to rain.

Brown was slumped over sobbing. John kicked him lightly and looked at him threateningly until he shut up.

During the night, Arata died in John's lap. The invisible cord that attached the two pilots since the emergency started was broken. The loss was heavy. Arata had seemed like his guardian. John had already seen plenty of dead men in this war and had built a wall around himself, but now the wall began crumbling. Arata. One minute alive, the next a corpse. Why? What the hell were they doing in this strange country? He felt sad, abandoned, and somehow responsible. Propped up on his helmet, John closed his eyes. It was all so futile.

"What was that noise?" Brown whispered, wrenching John from his thoughts.

"Shut the fuck up!" John hissed. He hardened to the reality.

The noise in the dark was the NVA beating the bushes to find the missing crew. It sounded like several platoons out there, splashing through the swamp. Sometimes the splashing was very close.

The sloshing and brush beating, calling back and forth in Vietnamese, went on all night. When it got really quiet now and then, John figured the NVA were listening for them to make a sound. He hoped like hell Brown would stay quiet. Now and then, he felt himself napping. He was numb, and the helmet was uncomfortable to lie on; Arata's corpse was heavy.

The hot, wet climate meant rapid decomposition. By morning, Arata's body had begun to stink, and the smell of rotting flesh was almost unbearable. But there was no way to leave their hiding place while they could still hear the NVA.

Brown was huddled up now, not making a sound. He was afraid that John was crazy and would shoot him if he moved. He leaned over to drink from the swamp. John was repulsed but knew that he himself would have to drink sooner or later. When he dared a small taste, the water tasted like the smell. He held his nose until he tired of leaning on one hand.

When 0800 hours arrived at long last, John whispered into the radio, "Silver King Three Five, King Three Five, this is Alpha Team Two. Do you read?"

A C-130 flying communications station was waiting. C-130s could orbit for ten hours at a time, and one was immediately replaced by another. There was twenty-four hour coverage for directing rescues, strikes, and other missions. "Roger, Alpha Two. This is King Three Five. We can not send in rescue due to weather. Contact again zero eight zero zero tomorrow. King Three Five out."

The antiseptic voice angered John. Let that sucker try it here for a night, he thought. He had not told them about Arata. Brown looked at John for the news. John shook his head and motioned toward the sky. All they could see was jungle canopy. Brown apparently understood and went back into his slump. John let him be.

He guessed they were fortunate. The top layer of branches was so dense that it stayed dark where they were, a small swamp, which was discouraging the NVA from a thorough search of that area. Brown looked at John and said, "You think they're gone?"

"Shut up," commanded John in a forceful whisper.

Brown lay back on his helmet, but John thought the exchange had been dangerous. He had to avoid Brown's eyes so that the man wouldn't talk to him and give them away. Silence in jungle escape and evasion (E & E) was one of the main points hammered into the men at jungle survival school.

They had been told that survival in the jungle was easier than in the sea or desert. Food and water were plentiful if you knew where to look. On the other hand, the animals were deadlier, and the diseases more dreadful. He must recall all that he had learned in survival school.

Everybody's favorite instructor at Ft. Rucker, Alabama, was Sergeant Walters, a short, craggy-faced World War II veteran. John lay back and concentrated on hearing Sergeant Walter's voice. "Almost anything short of death is better than gett'n' caught," Walters said, slapping the lectern for emphasis. "If yer out there alone and hungry and uncomfortable and you feel like givin' up, forget it. Charlie gets aholt of ya, it'll be a damn sight worse."

It was like replaying a record. John forgot about the dead man in his lap and instead of the terrible stink seemed to smell the chalky dust of the classroom. "No, you don't never want to get caught.

"POW treatment ain't changed much. The main reason for keepin' POWs is for gett'n intelligence data outta them and for prisoner exchange later on. The good interrogator knows if he uses extreme torture, the information he gets may be unreliable. Yer like as not to say anything."

The old sergeant had the full attention of his class now. "I don't know what consolation that is, though, when yer on yer back and some gook is jumpin' up and down on yer balls. I guess ya could point up at him and say, 'Uh huh, I know you. Yer poorly trained.' "

John found himself chuckling. The goddam sergeant and his jokes could get him caught right now. "Fact is," he could hear Sergeant Walters continuing, "the VC and NVA use plenty of torture. You probly heard stories of GIs found dead with their own genitals stuffed in their mouths. Well, it's a horrible thought, but it's happened, and ya got to know, cause you got to believe about not gett'n' caught."

Jesus Christ! That was enough of that. He sat up. Brown sat up, too. It was very warm, but Brown was shivering. He looked sick. "I got to shit," he whispered.

"Shit in your pants," John whispered back. There was not as much noise as earlier, but the NVA were still out there. Brown looked as if he was going to stand up. "Sit down and keep your mouth shut,'' hissed John. ''We're gonna die if you make noise.''

The young gunner raised up on his hands and relieved his guts. The water he had drunk was taking its revenge. He lay back on his helmet and sobbed silently.

Back at headquarters, the executive officer reported that the rain wouldn't clear for two days. Major Smith, the CO, knew that Vanvorden had been on the radio. He called in one of the officers to ask if the AC was hit.

''What's his name again?'' he asked the executive officer, who would later tell John about it.

''Arata, sir.''

''He might be hurt.''

''Wouldn't Vanvorden report it, sir?''

''Out there you don't go into your life's history on the radio!''

The exec said, ''Yes, sir. By the way, do you know the officers' club has steak tonight, sir?''

''No, I didn't. Good, Raymond. Do we still have a bottle of Mateus?''

''Yes, sir.''

The second night was worse. The rain never stopped, and neither did the NVA. They sounded like beaters in the bush on a tiger hunt. Occasionally, there was the sound of automatic weapons fire. Twice the North Vietnamese soldiers came so close that John thought he could reach out and grab an ankle. With the corpse smelling so bad and Brown in such an unstable state of mind, it was a miracle that they had not been caught yet.

Late that night, John thought he heard the NVA breaking camp. There were random clinking noises, an indistinct murmur of what sounded like casual talk mixed with orders. He understood nothing in the Vietnamese language, but there was a difference in the tones of the voices from the night before.

The only way to endure the physical discomfort was to shut down your mind. Brown had pulled himself into the fetal position. His helmet supported the crook of his neck on the right side, and he looked like an abused infant. John consciously tried to escape reality. After a while, he began to see things and hear music, and he dreamed that he was not sleeping.

Waking up suddenly in dim morning light, he heard a chirping noise. Opening his eyes, he saw a chameleon perched on his chest. The little lizards could swim but did not like water. The rain had diminished.

Arata's corpse, the clothes filled as if they were stuffed with balloons, had floated off John in the night. As John was released from the weight of the dead man's body, so was he released from a burden of guilt. Looking at the unrecognizable face, he knew he had done his best. His job now was to survive. He sat up and pulled the bloated body toward him with his foot to get the radio.

Something dropped from his ankle into his pants leg. He reached down and picked up a huge blood-filled leech. He began checking his arms and legs and found several more, one near his groin. He quietly pulled off as many of the nasty things as he could find.

Brown woke up and saw what John was doing. He bolted upright and began swatting the lumps under his own clothes.

"Stop it! Stop it!" hissed John, but it did no good. Brown had freaked out. He began stripping and was soon a blood-stained mess.

John stood up and tried to subdue him, but Brown was so enraged that John had to give up and let him go. As he scooped up water and rubbed the wounds inflicted by the leeches, he seemed to settle down.

Instead of arousing the NVA, there was only quiet. They must have moved out during the night. Still, John could not be sure. At 0800, John put in his call on the radio.

No answer. He shook the radio and tried again. "King

Three Five, King Three Five, this is Alpha Two on guard. How do you read?"

"Alpha Two, this is King Two Seven this time. We read you five by. You have to wait until tomorrow. The ceiling won't permit a flight."

"King Two Seven. There are only two of us now. Alpha One died from wounds. Alpha Two and Four are Okay."

"Roger, Alpha Two. Rescue will be coming tomorrow. King Two Seven out."

"Out . . . !" Those bastards, thought John.

One more night. One more. The only human sound was Brown, splashing around. John still would not let the gunner talk. He heard the same chirping he had heard that morning. Chameleons. He wondered what had happened to the one he saw on his chest.

The chirping took him back to Ft. Polk in Louisiana where he had gone through basic training seventeen months earlier. He had spent seven days in a reception center, bored stiff.

On the second day, a few trainees were fooling around and trying to catch chameleons. John had caught lizards in the Utah deserts when he was a kid and decided to have some fun. "I am the greatest lizard catcher ever to come out of Utah," he announced. "I've got this situation analyzed."

"Tell us all about it, Vanvorden!"

"No shit. I know what I'm talking about. You see, chameleons live in trees." Solemnly, he pointed upward. "They move from tree to tree by jumping from branch to branch when the wind blows them close together." He stuck two small branches in the band of his hat. "When I brush the limbs of the trees with these branches, a chameleon will think the wind is blowing and jump onto my branch. Then I'll pick it off and keep it under my hat while I catch some more."

"Vanvorden, you're full of shit."

"Right on, Tarzan. Lots a luck."

John walked out of sight and spent two hours chasing chameleons up and down tree trunks, across the ground, and in the bushes. They were fast like desert lizards and because of the trees even harder to catch. In Utah, he usually had help. Finally, he managed to catch eight of them and put them under his hat. Putting the branches back in his hat band, he strolled back to the group.

"Hey, Tarzan, you get any lizards?" one of them yelled.

"Sure did." John managed to look indignant. He gave them a peek.

The trainees could not believe it and immediately offered to buy the chameleons, a novelty because they changed color according to what they sat on, from fire engine red to Kelly green.

"No way," said John. "I showed you how. Catch your own."

The past silliness helped John to forget the night. He could still chuckle, remembering the gullible trainees walking around with branches sticking out of their hats.

Nobody else got any. Back in barracks, John put his haul in a butt can in his foot locker and decided to make some money by having a horse race with them. On the back of each lizard, he inked a number and made lists with the numbers opposite famous racehorse names like Man O'War and Sea Biscuit. He cut his bunk mate George in for twenty-five percent. Two-to-one odds on any winner in the first race, the odds to change if there was a consistent winner or two. John would run the races, and George would handle the bets. They made up several announcements and distributed them in the barracks. Race time was set for 2000 hours the next day.

By 1930 hours, their barracks was so crowded that John was afraid the floors of the old World War II structure would collapse. All the bunks, top and bottom, were filled, and so were the aisles. The racket sent vibrations through the place. John was trying to figure out how to draw a six-foot circle on the floor without permanently marking it, while George ran around taking bets. Somebody offered a foot-powder spray can, which worked. John centered a small circle inside the big one.

At post time, he put the chameleons under an empty butt can. When he lifted the can, the chameleons took off like a shot, and neither John nor George could figure which one got out of the big circle last, let alone first. The little lizards ran all over the place, and guys jumped out of the way, afraid of them, while John threatened loudly to charge five dollars for any that got stepped on. The first race was disqualified.

Rounding them up was tough, but when they took off again the second time, they were slower. John declared a winner and shouted down the various arguments.

Each consecutive race got slower and slower, and he had to resort to shaking the lizards up in the can to liven them. Everyone was yelling for a winner, and those who could reach the floor were stomping their feet. The building shook. The chameleons began turning brown, the color of the floor, and would no longer move. John declared the races over and sold the chameleons for a buck each. He ended up with $132 in profit.

Night changed to dawn and John peeked from their hiding place. There was nothing to see. Just jungle. Waiting for 0800 hours, John collected personal effects from Arata's corpse. Besides the survival vest, with the compass and first-aid kit, all he could find were the special four-digit dog tag and a pen knife. At 0800 hours, he called.

"This is Alpha Team Two transmitting on Guard to any Silver King radio. How do you read?"

"Loud and clear, Alpha Two. This is King Three Five."

"Hello, King Three Five. How does it look today?"

"Alpha Two, the closest LZ we can pick you up is five miles directly southeast of your location. It is a big one, and there should be no problem."

"Roger, King Three Five. We're on our way. Alpha Two out."

No problem, thought John. I'd like to see that bastard make straight course through five miles of jungle. "C'mon, Brown, let's go," he whispered.

They had scarcely moved for three days and nights. Each

time John took a step with his left foot, he felt a sharp pain in his hip, but he just kept walking and gradually worked out the stiffness. Brown was not talking. Instead of being careful to avoid whiplash from branches or sharp sticks, he just plowed right through, looking as if he were out on a Sunday stroll. He hardly looked at John, who would check the compass and point the way.

It took two and a half days to reach that clearing. Twice they backtracked, figuring they must have passed it. It was only through sheer luck that they finally stumbled into it. Even if it was not the right LZ, it was big enough, and John knew they could vector in on his signal. He also knew that the whole area was part of the Sihanouk Trail and extremely hazardous. He did not feel hungry, although they had not eaten for five and a half days.

"Silver King, this is Alpha Team Two. Do you read?"

"That's affirmative Alpha Team Two. This is King Two Four. You're coming in a bit broken."

"Roger, Two Four. We reached an LZ. Can you take a fix on us?"

"Alpha Two, come up beeper, and we'll give it a try."

The beeper on the survival radio gave out a high-pitched signal pulse and continued as long as the batteries held out. It took less power than using voice. If a disabled pilot put the switch on beeper, it signaled his location for a long time. Since it was a line-of-sight communication frequency, it took an aircraft to find the origin of the signal. That ruled out the enemy's tracing a pilot by the beeper—most of the time. The Americans had control of the skies in Vietnam.

"Alpha Two, this is King Two Four. Come up voice."

"Go ahead, Two Four. This is Alpha Two.

"Okay, A team. We have a fix. Rescue is on the way."

They were not out yet, so John controlled his excitement. No more communication was necessary.

They would have a rescue team waiting just inside the border of South Vietnam at one of the FOB staging points.

Blacky, probably. Four ships would be blasting out as soon as the ACs and gunners and peter pilots threw on their clothes. . . .

Brown was back in the trees, maybe taking a leak. John sat down at the tree line and looked around. The cleared area was on a fifteen-degree slope. Rocks were strewn about, and at the perimeter, trees lay broken and twisted. There must have been an outcropping of rock, he decided, expanded into an LZ by using high explosives. There was an old crater gouged out of the red earth with broken rotting wood nearby. He thought of Arata, broken and rotting where he had dragged him in from that LZ. What about all the other bomb craters and all the other broken and rotting bodies? Why were they doing this to each other . . . ? He would have to stick that word "why" away, or he would never make it through his tour. You just be a good pilot, Vanvorden, he told himself. Do what you're trained for. There's nothing else you can do.

Brown stumbled out of the trees with something in his hands. John stood up. Brown turned his back, but John could see that the door gunner was holding a baby monkey, no bigger than a softball. He knew the guy was on the ragged edge and thought maybe he needed a pet, like a kitten or something, to hang on with. Then he watched in disbelief as Brown bit off the little monkey's arm. The monkey cried out in a tiny voice. Brown silenced it by wringing its neck.

"Mine," growled Brown. "You try to take any, I'll kill you!"

John was so staggered by the madman eating a live monkey that he did not back away or turn around, but stood there and watched. Brown crunched the frail bones, making growling noises, and used both hands like someone devouring a watermelon. He crunched down the whole monkey, including the skull.

Then John heard it—faint at first—louder and louder—*whop, whop, whop, whop, whop*. The unmistakable sound of a Huey on direct approach. His emotions rose to the bursting point, and he felt the blood rush to his head.

As the Huey cleared the trees and touched the ground, John

and Brown were already running fast and waving. Blacky and the crew were waving back like crazy. The rescued men dove into the Huey like a couple of chicks diving for cover into the mother hen's feathers. Then Blacky took off.

When the crew cheered, John wept uncontrollably. In the air, when emotions had calmed, he noticed that the crew chief looked unhappy. "Everything okay?" he yelled in his ear.

The crew chief hesitated. John was the hero of the moment. Finally, he got it out. "You stink something terrible, sir."

John had forgotten the smell of the dead man. Perhaps he had become used to it. He began to strip and throw his clothes out of the helicopter. Brown did the same, but when they were both stripped naked, the smell of death was still on them. John noticed then all the cuts and bruises on his body, and his skin, white as flour, rolled off when he rubbed his arms.

The two came back to a hero's welcome from the company. Most of the men had turned out. Then they were taken off to the medics. The war was over for Private, First Class Brown. Within a week, he was sent home on a section eight. They would have sent John home, too, just because of what he had been through, but he fought to stay. The doctors in Ban Me Thuot did not know quite how to handle someone who appeared normal and refused a free pass back to the states, so they sent him on to Cam Ranh Bay to talk to the psychiatrists there.

John still smelled terrible. The nurse to whom he handed his papers recognized the smell but pretended not to notice. Instead of making John sit with the others in the waiting area, though, she hustled him into an examination room.

Two shrinks came in about twenty minutes later and introduced themselves as Doctor Greenburg and Doctor Thompson. One was a major, the other a captain. They looked very young. Most of the doctors in Vietnam looked very young.

"Glad to meet you," John lied.

"We understand you don't want to go home, Mister Vanvorden," said Major Thompson.

"Well, I just got here." said John.

"Yes, but you have been through quite an ordeal," said Greenburg. "Most people would want to go home after what you've been through. Why do you want to stay?"

"Look," said John. "I'm okay. I made it. If I can make it through that, I can make it through anything."

"Yes, but it's not normal to want to stay."

"Would you believe I'm patriotic?"

They were both looking at him suspiciously. "It wouldn't be drugs, would it?"

"Hell, no. It's not drugs. I want a career as a pilot. I volunteered as a pilot. I volunteered to fly in Nam. So I don't want to be sent home. If I get a bunch of hours under my belt here, I'll be worth more money as a pilot when I get out."

John was telling the truth, but not wholly. He wanted to become a great pilot, but there was more. Here in Vietnam, he felt powerful. He wanted one day to take his turn as AC, to command a ship and a crew, but he didn't think the doctors would understand any of that.

Greenburg seemed satisfied, but Thompson said, "You won't be worth anything if you get killed."

"Don't you want to stay here?" John asked the major directly.

"Well . . . ah. . . . I'm asking the questions, Mister Vanvorden."

John turned to Captain Greenburg. "Won't you be worth more money when you go back, doctor?"

"No way," said Greenburg. "I'm losing money every day I spend in the army."

"C'mon, Dan," Thompson said to Greenburg. "This isn't any bull session."

"Anyway, this man is obviously fit for service, so let's stop wasting his time and send him back to his unit."

"I guess you're right," said the major. "Well, Vanvorden, any questions?"

John sat silent for a minute and then, feeling secure about his flying job, asked the question he had deliberately avoided so far. "Can you tell me what it is we are trying to do in this country?"

Dr. Thompson looked as if he wished he had not offered an opening, and he walked out of the room.

Greenburg looked after him with frank disgust and turned to John. "Soldier, you're not the first to ask that question, and you won't be the last. For you, since you are here already, it's a question best left to God. Just go back to your unit and do a good job."

"Yes, sir," said John.

Greenburg walked back with him to the nurse's station. "We'll send the papers back by official mail. Don't worry."

"Good-by, doc. Thanks."

"Shalom, soldier."

5
GREEN MARKET

MAJOR SMITH GROUNDED JOHN FOR TWO WEEKS TO ALLOW him to recover from the shoot down. Until his flight status was restored, he was given extra duty as assistant mess officer. The chow was lousy, and having to watch over the chow hall instead of over his helicopter made John feel like an outcast.

He might be a "hero," but he looked freaky; his skin was fish-belly white, and he smelled of death. Everybody wanted to hear about the shoot down and evasion, and no one was bored no matter how many times they heard his story, but because of the smell, nobody wanted to stick around him after he told it. He was not welcome in the nightly poker game.

One afternoon the CO called John in. "Vanvorden, behind the paint shed there are six five gallon buckets of white paint. You round up some of the enlisted men and paint guidelines on the ground in the revetments. Paint them right down the middle and extend them out twelve feet in front and back so the pilots can see them. We've had too many guys tagging tail rotors when they turn into the revetments."

"The paint won't stay on that red clay, sir. Every time it rains it'll wash away."

"Well, get some sandbags, run them down the middle, and paint them."

John decided to quit talking his way out of it before it got worse. He had the glimmering of an idea. "Yes, sir. I'll need your jeep."

"Why do you need my jeep?" The CO hated for anybody to use his jeep.

"Well, I got to have something to carry all that paint in."

"Okay, damn it. You can take the jeep in the morning."

John planned to barter the paint for some decent chow. He knew of a mess sergeant in a Special Forces company attached to the base, out at Ban Me Thuot East, a few miles from the airforce base, who was supposed to be the wheelingest, dealingest character ever to hit Nam, and his main item of barter was beefsteak he kept in a huge walk-in freezer. He got the steaks by trading items like Chinese handguns and NVA flags to air-force mess sergeants. Air-force mess sergeants had more food than they knew what to do with, and since the air force never saw ground action they coveted war contraband.

If he got a stock of steaks for the CO's personal refrigerator as well as the chow hall, the CO might overlook the paint. After surviving that week on the ground in Cambodia, he figured he should make the rest of his tour as comfortable as possible when he was not in the air.

The next day, he went off post and found the air force mess sergeant without any trouble. He was known as Red and was in the chow hall.

"Sergeant!" said John in an official voice. His voice seemed to have developed authority since his trial in the jungle. "How many steaks will you give me for six buckets of white paint?"

"Five-gallon cans?"

John nodded.

"Well, now, let's see. Boy I could use that paint. Ten cases. A hundred twenty steaks a case."

"Make it fifteen."

"Twelve."

"Deal."

John and his driver unloaded the paint and loaded up the steaks.

I'll be talking to you again, sergeant," said John.

"Always happy to talk with the fly boys."

John felt a certain satisfaction driving back. Being assistant mess officer was a lousy deal for a pilot, but he could do something about the food, anyway. At the CO's hootch, John dismissed the driver. Opening up a box, he took out two dozen steaks and walked in. The major watched while John marched straight to his private refrigerator and filled the freezer with steaks.

"I couldn't find all that paint, sir," said John, "but I found a bunch of steaks."

Major Smith looked hard at him. He wanted to be furious about the paint, but he was too pleased with the steaks. He grumbled at John on principle and ran him out of the hootch.

After that, when he asked for the CO's jeep, Major Smith just said, "Take it and get outta here. Don't tell me anything."

War profiteering seemed wrong to John, but all he was doing was trading army equipment and supplies for army food. He called it his "green market." He took over food procurement and currency exchange as additional duties and kept them even after he was flying again. The chow hall, with its improved menu, began getting so much new business that John had to make two trips a week to the finance section in Cam Ranh Bay with the money. It was a nuisance, but it did give him a chance to go to the beach and soak in the ocean. As the dead smell faded and the quality of the food improved, John gained prestige.

Walking the nearly deserted beach one day at Cam Ranh, he saw an old man and a kid throwing a brick at something in a tidal pool. It turned out to be a large sea snake with yellow and black bands, thrashing in the shallow water. The old man and the boy were shouting in French, and John thought they must be from a nearby plantation. Neither could throw accurately, so John killed the snake and held it shoulder high by the tail. The body was thick and fluked, and the head just touched the ground. One thing about sea snakes—their mouths were so small they could not bite you anywhere except your fingers or toes or flaccid penis. John's sphincter muscles contracted at that thought.

A GI in a swim suit came over while the Frenchies were admiring the snake. "Whatjya kill it with, a brick?"

"Yup." John guessed the GI was an enlisted man. He looked to be in his late twenties.

"Horrible-looking thing, ain't it?"

"They're dangerous, all right," said John as he flung the snake on the sand and rinsed his hands in the pool. He walked away, but the GI caught up with him. "What's yer job in Nam?"

John did not really feel like talking, but the guy wanted to talk to somebody. He thought he had never seen a place with so many lonely people as he had in a war zone. "I fly slicks."

"Wow! Hueys!" The soldier's eyes were bright with admiration.

"What do you do here?" John asked. He liked people to admire him for being a pilot.

The GI looked down. "I ain't seen any action. I'm just a spec 5 clerk typist."

"Well, they need clerk typists to run a war, too," said John, wanting to spare the man some dignity. "What unit you with?"

"Ain't really a unit. I work in the inspector general's office."

John's mind began to click. When a general inspection was ordered, the supply officers of the company being inspected had a hell of a rush trying to get rid of equipment not on the property books. If John had advance knowledge of an inspection, more than the normal day or two, he could turn his green market into a big-time operation. "You mean the IG, the big one in Cam Ranh?"

"Yeah. It's no big deal, though. I just do all the paper work."

"It's an important job," said John, feeling like a con artist. "Hey, you want to go over to the officers' club and get something to eat?"

"Oh, I can't do that . . ."

"Sure you can. They don't ask for IDs at the one on the beach, and they can't tell who you are in a swim suit."

The beach club for officers was not any different from the one for enlisted men, nor was the food, but John knew the clerk typist felt honored. Both places were set up like burger joints in the states, with choc-van-stra milk shakes. They ordered, and John took the first bite out of a thick, juicy hamburger. "My name's John Vanvorden," he said with his mouth full.

"I'm Coy Jameson."

They relaxed that afternoon on the beach, and John enjoyed himself. Jameson really needed a friend. Finally, John gave him the pitch.

"Hey, Coy, I've been thinking. I could use some inside information from your office."

"Anything I can do," Jameson said happily.

"How long in advance do you know when the IG is going to inspect some unit?"

"Oh, a couple of weeks, anyway."

"Two weeks! Man, that's all right."

Jameson waited. He was not bright, but he was not born yesterday, either.

"Coy, I'll give you twenty bucks every time you tell me when the IG is going out on inspection and where. Will you do it?"

"Sure I will."

"Hey, you're all right, Coy. And don't worry about the money. I come here twice a week, and you can give me the unit number and date of the IG, and I'll get you the twenty right away."

"No sweat." Coy looked very happy. Moral or legal questions seemed to bother him not at all, and obviously the forty to sixty dollars a month he might make would come in handy.

The deal was so good that none of the commanders and property-books officers of the ten companies John contacted turned him down. He offered two weeks' notice of the inspection in exchange for their calling him to come and pick up any equipment they wanted to discard. They were happy to do it.

After it was set up, John went in to see the major. "Sir, I've got a deal for you."

Smith liked what John had already done for the company, although it made him nervous as hell. "I don't want to hear it. Just take what you need."

"No, sir. This is different. This is big."

"Shit. If it's big, just forget it."

"No, sir, listen. I found a way to really help the entire company this time."

"Let's hear it."

"If you'll give me those two slicks that are out of service, I'll use them for a supply train to keep the other ships running. We'll never be short of parts and equipment again."

The major's frown deepened as John began to fill in the details. "Wait! Don't tell me anymore. Besides, you'll never get those helicopters running."

"Let me try."

The two men faced each other silently. John knew that the CO wanted to have a first-rate company and to make colonel as well. Finally, Smith shrugged. "Give it a try."

Temporarily down for overhaul, the two disabled helicopters had been cannibalized for spare parts, some of which would not be available through IG discards. To get valuable parts such as engines, gear boxes, and rotor blades would require elaborate trading schemes.

Clerk typist Jameson never failed him. Convoys went out

each week to pick up unwanted equipment. They acquired so much that John got the motor pool's heavy-equipment operators to bury five huge steel connex boxes so that just the tops were visible. During an inspection there, all the contraband equipment, weapons, and whatever else that made the company run so smoothly could be stored underground in the connexs with a thin layer of dirt pushed over them.

Within three weeks, he had one helicopter in A-1 condition, and by the end of the month, both were in good shape. The CO took one away from him and said he would press the second into company service when he needed it, but John managed. In time, he had not only a chopper for his personal use but also two formerly disabled deuce-and-a-half trucks and a jeep that sported a 75-mm. recoilless rifle in the back.

When John thought about it, he could hardly believe his good luck at having such a cooperative commanding officer. Few COs he had seen were as capable as Major Smith, and therein lay the reason for his apparent leniency. Getting the company into top form in such a dangerous place was worth bending a few rules.

At the end of his first three months in Nam, John took stock. His green market was flourishing and making him a man apart in the company. In spite of the hiatus, he was seasoning fast as a combat pilot. A party was planned for that night, and thanks to his green market, they were having steak and beer. "Good going, supernewby," his platoon leader had said, slapping his shoulder on the way to set up a quarter-ton trailer as the bar.

6

FLYING DUTCHMAN

AT THE PARTY, SPLIT FIFTY-FIVE-GALLON DRUMS SERVED AS barbecue pits, and a vinyl-lined trailer, filled with canned beer, water, and ice, became the bar. Considerable amounts had been consumed when the platoon leader proposed a toast.

"Here's to our platoon's supernewby!" He waved at John.

"Let's throw him in the trailer," shouted Roger, the expert at escaping that sort of prank himself.

That was all it took. Four drunken ACs and Roger grabbed John. While they wrestled with him, two other newbys were tossed into the ice water. Before he was dunked, John yelled out, "Why don't you get Roger, too?" Roger immediately swung a full can of Budweiser and hit him behind the ear, damn near cold cocking him.

He was not unconscious, but he lay stunned under the ice water, unable to get out. All he could think about was killing Roger. By the time the ACs fished him out, Roger was long gone. The lump behind his left ear was enormous.

John took a plastic bagful of ice with him and went back to

his hootch with a splitting headache. Lying on his bunk, he held the ice to the knot behind his ear. He would pay that son of a bitch Roger back, but the system was really to blame. All that newby harassment.

Anyway, he wasn't really a newby anymore. He'd been there too long to still be called that. He decided to get a handle from Big Al the next day. Big Al was a crew chief who had been a magazine illustrator back home, famous in hot-rod and drag-strip circles. After that, he'd get that wimpy bastard Roger.

In the morning, John went to see Big Al, an enlisted man who painted logos on the pilots' helmets for $25. John had decided to call himself the Flying Dutchman.

He watched while Big Al worked on the helmet. With fast-drying enamel, he painted a clipper sailing ship emerging from some clouds. It was beautiful. Underneath the ship, he printed in Gothic letters, the "Flying Dutchman," and over by the clouds, in very small print, he wrote, "Big Al done it."

"That's fine work," John said. "I'll send all my buddies your way, if I get the chance."

"Thanks, Dutchman."

John felt lucky. The new handle caught on right away. From then on, he was called Dutchman.

His first FOB since the shoot down was to fly peter pilot for a hard-case AC he had heard about but never flown with. John threw his gear into the waiting jeep and climbed in. "Glad to meet you, Mr. Pratt," he said.

"Hey, boy, just call me Willy."

"I heard you called Hayseed in the Third Platoon, and I didn't think you'd like that."

Pratt's big hands with red hairs on the fingers tightened on the steering wheel. "Well, ya thunk right on that, boy. Them bunch of potheads—"

"Shit! Watch where you're going," John shouted.

Willy swerved, narrowly missing an old Vietnamese woman walking on the side of the dirt road that ran by John's hootch.

"What you worried about them fuckin' gooks for, boy? I wun't even close, anyways."

"That fucking gook is my hootch maid with my laundry."

"Y'ain't screwin' that old bitch, are ya?"

"No, I ain't—am not . . ."

"Sure, boy, sure."

"I wish you'd stop calling me boy," said John.

"Listen, I'm yer AC, boy, and if I want t'call ya boy, I'll call ya boy."

"Okay, boy," John said, keeping his eyes on the huge hands.

"Who you think yer calling 'boy', Dutchman?"

At least the hayseed knew John's nickname. "Doesn't it work both ways?"

Willy hit the brakes and turned toward John. "No, it don't, boy. Want to make somethin' of it?"

"Now, look, Willy, I don't want to make anything out of anything. I used to fly with the toughest AC in this whole company, and he didn't treat me the way you are."

"Oh, yeah? Who's that?"

"Frank Arata."

"Say, you ain't the one he used to call Utah, are ya? The one got shot down in Cambodia with him?" John nodded. "Frank and me EODeed together in this stink hole." Hayseed stared at the wheel. "Was it bad for that ol wop?"

"I don't think so. He was unconscious most of the time."

"Frank were a good man," said Willy, and started the jeep again. He was quiet until they got to operations. It would be all right now.

John saw Roger at the ops briefing. He was flying peter pilot with Blacky on B team. Willy had drawn the short straw and was flying A. John stared at Roger, but Roger did not seem nervous.

The briefing lasted the usual half hour. They were to insert a team of Special Forces body snatchers. John admired the body snatchers. Their teams consisted of five heavily armed Green Berets with no U.S. identification in their pockets or on their sleeves. Their sole mission was to kidnap NVA officers. Sergeant Weems was leading this one. He was an expert. John knew a bit about their operation because they sometimes talked with the AC on the intercom.

Their *modus operandi* rarely varied. The trail they planned to set up on was chosen ahead of time. Signs, like human feces or trampled twigs, had told the army outdoorsmen that the trail was being used. The body snatchers would set up a line of mechanicals—command-detonated Claymore mines—about three feet above the trail. Everything in the kill zone that stood three feet or higher got wiped out.

Once the mechanicals were in place, the team covered both ends of the zone and waited. Not only were they heavily armed; they carried water and dehydrated high-energy food packages as well. One of them, the marksman, had a long-barreled .22-caliber rifle with a silencer and a starlight scope.

When the NVA patrol centered on the trapped zone, the marksman shot the officer in the leg with the .22. There would be only a light "thut" when he pulled the trigger. If it was dark, it did not matter, since he could see through the starlight scope. If the officer went down, the patrol would stop, and the mechanicals would then be set off, killing everyone except the officer lying below the three-foot level.

The most dangerous part of the operation was the insertion. Frequently, an AC was rejected by a Special Forces team leader because he had performed badly during a previous insertion. When the body snatchers brought back a live one, they were all given three days, all expenses paid, at an in-country R & R center, usually at Vung Tau, Nha Trang, or China Beach, Da Nang. That was their motivation for staying with this type of work: beautiful beaches where you lounged day and night, ate good food, and worried about nothing.

On their way out of the briefing room, Roger passed by John. "How's your head, newby?"

"You son of a bitch," said John, but there would be

another time for Roger. Now John turned his mind to the FOB. It had to be perfect.

Once the four slicks were in the air, surrounded by four gunnies, he felt easy. The slicks flew in staggered right formation, while the gunnies flew loosely forward and aft.

The flight maintained altitude at 2200 feet as they passed over the green-covered hills and mountains. The AC talked to the Special Forces team leader on the intercom as they neared the target vicinity. ''We're on top a yer area now, boy. Ya jist tell us where.''

There was a choice of five hover holes. Sergeant Weems studied the ground, using his experience and sixth sense to pick one. ''The first.''

''Ya heard him, Dutchman. It's yers.''

John was not expecting to fly the team in, but it was his job to be ready. He took the Huey in a long, slow arc until he reached a point ninety degrees off their first course. Then he turned straight for the small LZ. The maneuver was intended to confuse the enemy. Over the LZ, he fell away from the formation and keyed the radio. ''Alpha team going in.''

Under his control, the Huey zeroed out its forward speed, turned on its side, and spiraled to the ground. The increased G force and sudden dive always took away everyone's breath no matter how many times they had done it. Even before the skids touched, the troops were clear of the ship and into the trees. John climbed out under max power and held the altitude at tree level, flying a zigzag course until he could take the ship to two thousand feet ten miles away.

''Gawd damn, boy. Arata couldn't uh dun better'n that,'' shouted Willy over the intercom. ''Few more hours, yer an AC for sure!''

John appeared not to hear Willy as he reported in, using his company call sign. The insertion had been letter-perfect.

Twenty minutes later, the helicopters were on the ground just over the border. They had provisions for a week. John had plans. He would go up and duke it out with Roger. Roger had it coming. But soon after the landing, three ACs grabbed

Roger. "C'mon and help," Torch yelled to Willy. "He's going to lose his cherry. We're going to thread this skatin' bastard."

Roger went wild, kicking and swinging his arms and yelling, "I'll kill you motherfuckers!"

Four ACs were sufficient, but John and a couple of gunnies joined in. Roger was had.

"How's it feel, skate? John asked as they lifted Roger up to the stinger. Roger kept kicking, so they banged his shin on the metal bar a couple of times. He stopped. They threaded the tail stinger up his pants leg while Roger cursed, and then all stood back and cheered while John popped a smoke grenade. Roger nearly freaked out. When he saw John grinning at him through the suffocating smoke from his upside-down position, he yelled, "I'll smash your brains in next time!"

That was too much. John walked up to the dangling man and hit him with his doubled fist on the side of the head. "You mean like that?" he yelled. Roger was out cold. They let him hang limp for a couple of more minutes while the smoke stained his skin and clothes; then John pulled him off the tail stinger. Roger lay there groaning while John went with the other pilots to find shade. Nobody said anything about the knockout punch. The skate had it coming.

The rest of that day, Roger sat by himself.

Once in a while, John looked over and saw Roger looking back. Finally, John got up and walked over to him. "You okay?" No answer. "Are you okay?"

"Yeah, I'm okay."

"Well, Christ, what did you expect? You hit me with a can of beer."

"I know."

"I just want to say, as far as I'm concerned, it's over." John turned to walk back.

"Okay by me, too, Dutchman. I guess," said Roger.

Without looking back, John gave Roger the thumbs-up sign.

* * *

A day and a half later, the call came from King One Six while John was asleep in a hammock inside the Huey. John unstrung his hammock and yelled to the others. Once in the air and over the border, the flight was in radio range of Green Briar. Willy still let John control the FOB. "Green Briar, this is Stagecoach Two One."

Sergeant Weims responded. "Stagecoach Two One, got our ticket to China Beach."

"Roger Green Briar. Copy. Five up front at Maryann's place," referring to a whorehouse.

The Flying Dutchman made another perfect single-ship approach. The Green Berets did not even look tired. They held up an unconscious NVA officer. His head was back, his mouth open, and a red spot stained his tan uniform at the hip. They loaded him on board, and John beat it out of there.

The body snatchers were dropped off with their prize at a MASH unit. The Hueys flew back to the company. Willy now treated John with respect, reversing his attitude toward the young copilot, though they had met such a short time before. Praise from someone like Willy had to be earned. John wondered if he would ever run into former classmates from flight school and how they were measuring up in combat. It might be interesting to see how that ass Captain Hayes was doing.

7

FLIGHT SURGEON

JOHN WOKE UP THE NEXT DAY STILL FEELING PRETTY GOOD. The early October weather was as nice as it got in Nam, sunny and not too hot. That day was his twenty-first birthday.

There would be letters and presents from his family—when the mail got through—making a fuss about his coming of age, a meaningless benchmark at the moment. Perhaps he should let himself think about home that day and maybe get homesick. But that was of no use. Just opening up that way a little bit made him wish for things. Like going skiing with his younger brother in Utah, a date with a pretty girl, driving around in an old car with his best friend. A game of chess with his father or a talk with his mother.

All kinds of small urges began to crawl around under his skin. The best thing was to be where you were, taking what came. If only he had a close friend he could talk with. Arata had been close, somewhat, in a war-time way. The enlisted men in the crew got close to each other and were fiercely loyal when they worked together a lot. Warrant officers were in a special limbo. Maybe it was better for lieutenants and captains, but he was not sure.

The 155th's flight surgeon was a loner but seemed friendly toward John.

His name was Ronald Thomas Swenson. Most of the men called him Bones, but John liked to call him Swede. To maintain flight status, which gave the flight surgeon extra money, meant he had to put in a minimum of four hours a month in the air. John found out Swenson was scared to death of flying and thus continually searched for the best pilots to fly with, and then only on ash and trash. His first choice had been to go with Arata and John. Then, after Arata died, he postponed flying again.

Swede's grave personality was a source of amusement during the Tuesday night safety briefings. He never missed lecturing about VD. There were about 150 whores in half a dozen houses just off base. The whorehouses had names like Angel Hut and Pink Banana, and the flight surgeon tried to keep a record of who got what type of VD from which whore at which whorehouse in order to warn the men. One week it could be the Pink Banana, the next Emma's. He spent more time giving VD shots than patching up the wounded, and for all his statistical efforts, nothing seemed to reduce the amount of VD in the company. Going to whorehouses meant about a 99.9 percent chance of infection. If a man checked Swede's weekly statistical indicator, he might reduce the risk to 99.2 percent. Maybe.

Now Swenson could no longer refuse to fly without losing his flight status, so he approached John in his hootch.

"So, they call you the Flying Dutchman now," he opened.

"Yeah. What can I do you out of, Swede?"

"Are you going on an ash and trash sometime soon?"

"Why don't you ask an AC?"

"I consider you a very safe pilot."

"Thanks, but I don't command a ship."

"I know that. It's okay."

"Well, sit down," invited John, motioning to the bed.

They got talking about where each other had come from. Swenson was descended from a long line of farmers, but his mother had told him to become a doctor, so he did. He sounded stoic. Cautiously, John asked him how it felt to patch up so many hurt guys.

Swede was silent for a minute. He was used to listening to others' complaints, not talking about his own. "It's bad," he finally said quietly, looking at his feet.

John felt that he understood. "I know," he said.

"You don't know," said Swede. "You can't know! It's not the wounded. It's being scared all the time. You're a pilot. You've gotten over fear. I'm just a doctor, and I'm afraid all the time."

"Hey, wait a minute," said John. "Who says I'm not afraid? I'm scared shitless half the time."

"It's not the same."

"Why not?"

"You face fear when you fly—every time.I just wait out the days. I'm sure I'll get hit by a mortar or a sniper bullet or something, and when I have to fly . . ." He looked away.

"Your job's different," said John. "You're a damn good doctor. You've saved a lot of men. That takes courage."

"No, it doesn't. I'm afraid for *myself* when I see torn bodies, so I get obsessed with making them whole again."

John decided to change the subject. "Say, I've been meaning to ask you. Do you play chess?"

Bones looked up surprised. "Yeah, I do."

"Are you any good?"

"Played in a few tournaments . . ."

"No shit? Well, I'm just an amateur, but I play. It's just poker here, so I haven't played in Nam."

"Tournaments are no big deal. Come over to my hootch any night. We'll play. I'd ask you right this minute, but I've got to look in on some patients."

"Hey, I forgot. I'll be flying to Cam Ranh tomorrow or maybe next day. Want to go along?"

"Sounds fine."

"Okay, Swede. I'll let you know."

"Thanks, Dutchman."

The trip to Cam Ranh was uneventful, and the following evening, John went over to play chess with the flight surgeon. The Swede lived with a dust off unit of Medivac pilots attached to the 155th. John could not believe the hootch. There was a clean rice mat on the floor and a small oriental rug alongside the bed. Under the bed was a large hole right through the floor. The sides and top were lined with perforated steel planking. Sandbags covered most of the planking. In a narrow slot between the wall and the bed, Swede had put a mattress. If the base was hit, he could simply roll out of bed and fall into his private little bunker.

"Goddam. Your own spider hole," said John.

"I told you," said Swede, looking as if he regretted it, "I'm scared."

"Hey, don't get me wrong. I think it's cool. It's a smart thing to have. How long did it take you to make it?" John leaned down and looked in.

"About a week. I built it after my first mortar attack."

"Man, you ought to be in the Seabees, doc."

"It wasn't hard to make. Let's play chess." They both knew the bunker provided only a margin of safety, and Swede seemed anxious to drop the subject.

John looked around while Swede undid several locks on a foot locker chained to the end of his bed. On two walls hung Vietnamese art work. One painting, of an ancient fisherman in his conical hat taking a drag on a cigarette, was done on black velvet. Another painting, in eggshell and lacquer on wood, was of two godlike statues carved in a rock cliff surrounded by forest. The room had class, especially with its spider hole.

Swede carefully placed a box of chessmen and a board on the table. John pulled up a chair. Concealing two pawns the Swede held his fists out to John, who chose the left. Swenson opened his hands to display a green jade pawn in his left and a white one in his right.

"Where did you get those?" asked John. "They're beautiful!"

"I bought them in Saigon. They were supposedly smuggled in from China."

"Wow. How much did they cost?"

"Two thousand U.S. The set is worth five or ten times that."

"How do you know?" asked John.

"I know," said Swede.

He opened the custom-made ebony box again and began extracting the matching pieces from the dark green velvet lining of the box. The set was carved in a traditional Staunton design. John picked up the two green rooks, polished smooth and obviously from the same piece of nephrite jade.

"Sure you want to play with these?" All the pieces were unflawed.

"Only ones I have."

"Aren't you worried they'll get stolen?"

"Nobody knows about them except you."

"Oh, no sweat about me."

"I know that," said Swede. "I start." The last piece in place, he opened with his queen pawn. "Aren't you being hard-assed for the first game?" asked John, but Swenson did not answer. He was concentrating on the board. It was a battle he could throw himself into.

John tried the Sicilian defense but soon had to admit that white was in control. John was planning three moves ahead, but his opponent was always set for six or seven.

During the first two games, it was as if a vice were slowly closed in on John's side of the board, ending in mate. It was remarkable; the Swede was confessing cowardice but making a vicious attack on the chessboard.

To avoid ignominious defeat in the third, John forced a draw by trading several important pieces. It was an uninteresting way to go, but he would have been defeated three in a row otherwise. It was late when he stood up.

The flight surgeon came out of his trance and suggested they play again.

"Sure. When my ego heals," said John. As he left, he saw the doctor looking at the slot in the floor as if undecided whether to sleep there instead of in his bed.

War needs surgeons, thought John, but this one surgeon doesn't need war. He liked Swede, though Swede's single-minded panic made him feel unsafe to be around. Now John knew how Arata felt about Vinny dressed for combat twenty-four hours a day before he left for the states.

8

ROGER

THE OCTOBER WEATHER SUDDENLY TURNED BAD. WORK HAD to stop on the new camp swimming pool, one of John's green-market projects, and the air force fighter bombers were so hampered that the base lost its protective air cover. Enemy infiltration was difficult to stop. Three times in one week there were sapper attacks followed by mortars and rockets. The pilots were ordered into the air to preserve their ships. They flew them in patterns nearby, waiting to evacuate wounded, or, if told, to beat it to Ban Me Thuot East. The gun ships went after the attackers, by firing at the mortar-tube flashes in the woods.

A rubber plantation to the north and east of Ban Me Thuot caused problems. The standard area for a base perimeter was 350 yards of cleared ground, but on one side and corner, Ban Me Thuot only had 150 feet because of standing rubber trees. The owner had been able to bring political pressure to bear.

On the third day of one attack, as numerous mortars exploded on the base, tube flashes were spotted within the stand of rubber trees. The gunships sprayed the area heavily. The next day no Vietcong or NVA were found, but twenty-eight dead ARVN troops were discovered along with their mortars. Vietnamese spokesmen claimed the ARVN troops were firing on the enemy and that the gun ships had made a gross error. The gunnies knew different. The mistake was on the other side. Vietnamese and American generals made the decision to avoid such errors in the future by refusing to allow the gunships' defensive fire during an attack on the camp. The group commander came from Nha Trang to deliver the order in person. John was on his way to see the CO but stopped outside when he heard shouting.

"What the hell do you mean, we can't shoot back with our gun ships?" Major Smith demanded.

"Now, Willard, settle down!"

"Settle down? I'll tell you what. I'll pull every ship out of here!"

"Willard. I'll work something out."

"If we go longer than a week without beefing up the perimeter, I'm pulling my boys out," Smith warned as the group commander started to leave. John backed out of sight. Good for the CO, thought John.

It had been less than a week when mechanized perimeter defense equipment came rolling onto the post. Two Quad-fifties and two Dusters arrived in single file. Each Quad-fifty had a turret armed with four .50-caliber machine guns, two on either side of the gunner sitting inside. The turret was mounted on the flatbed of a deuce-and-a-half-ton truck, which pulled a trailer full of ammunition. Two men on the trailer did nothing but feed the guns. Each turret turned so fast that there was no running or hiding from it. It could shoot through trees and tear away boulders to get at the enemy. The Dusters, armored vehicles with twin-forty-millimeter cannon, originally designed for antiaircraft use in World War II, also put out impressive firepower.

John stood duty officer soon after the Quad-fifties and armored Dusters had arrived. He had been awake for twenty-four hours and was ready for his relief when early in the morning he got a call from the MPs at the gate.

"We got a kind of problem out here. We don't know what's going on," the MP said.

"What do you mean, soldier?" asked John.

"Well, usually, this time there's local hires out here all lined up to come in. There's not anybody here."

"Maybe it's one of their holidays."

"No, sir. And there's not anybody. Nobody on the street. Nobody around anywhere."

"Listen, keep that gate locked. Keep your eyes open. I'll get back to you." John hung up and took off running to wake the CO. "Major Smith, I don't know what's going on, but there are no local hires waiting at the gate, and the streets are all deserted."

"No shit? Daytime? Boy, we got something bad coming. Go sound red alert. Get everybody up!"

John ran and started the red-alert warning siren. Smith immediately ordered all helicopters into the air. John found himself paired with Roger, who had just made AC. He didn't mind. After they declared a truce, they found themselves gravitating together somehow. Besides, John was the only one in the platoon tolerant of Roger's new love for a female interpreter.

All hell broke loose as mortars and rockets began exploding.

Roger lifted off in the confusion, narrowly missing two other ships coming from two different directions. Expertly, he avoided collisions and managed a max take-off at the same time.

"You must have eyes in the back of your head," said John after they had cleared the field.

Roger smiled without answering. John had known that Roger's sense of survival was powerful. Now John knew that it could be a very good thing.

The fighting went on all day. The Quads and Dusters were directed by the CO, using their heavy firepower to reinforce weakening points in the post's defense. It was late evening before the NVA broke off. As a result of quick action in the morning, the 155th lost only one Huey, still parked with no one in it.

Very little damage was done on the base, although a hundred mortar rounds and over seventy rockets had fallen on the post. The greatest loss was the PX, which had taken two 80-mm. mortar rounds. The NVA might have claimed a psychological victory because the troops were really pissed about that, but their suicidal rush into the Quads and Dusters and gunships had been a disaster. They had lost eighty-two men on the wire and an uncounted number in the trees. Most of their dead and wounded had been dragged off as darkness approached.

Roger was disturbed when he and John returned the chopper the next day. Because of their disappearance, before battle, the CO wouldn't allow any locals back on post, including Roger's girl friend, the Montagnard interpreter. She looked like an orangutan, but she was smart as a whip and had a fairly good body at thirty-five years old. She was Roger's first lay, and he had really fallen in love with her. Her camp nickname was Nooky, because she climbed in bed with anybody and everybody, except John. He found her aboriginal face so hard to look at, he stared to the side when he talked to her. She thought he was shy.

Roger refused to believe she was screwing anybody else. Roger figured her husband, an ARVN major, was supposed to be stationed in the south and would never make it back. Roger called her Carla, after a music teacher he had a crush on in the tenth grade, and he screwed her about five days out of seven. Either he got her to his room, or he sneaked off post at night to a place he had her rent so they could have privacy.

John was the only other officer who called her Carla. The rest of them not only insisted on calling her Nooky but razzed Roger about her.

John now appreciated Roger as a pilot and a friend, and Roger was willing to teach John all he knew, like deciding when and from what direction to approach a hot LZ. There were other factors most pilots never thought about—the direction from which the prebombardment had come, the angle of the sun and the wind, the most subtle features of the terrain. They flew a lot of missions together, and it now seemed strange to John that they had felt hatred for each other during the initiations.

Everybody needed comic relief after the stress of combat. As much as Roger had objected to tricks played on himself, he was ingenious when he played them on others. The Executive officer was an oversized, mean bastard nicknamed Bear. He looked like one, too. One day, Roger collected all the dogs he could round up on the base and filled the exec's hootch with them. When Bear opened the door, a dozen half-wild, growling and barking dogs rushed out past him. Everybody thought it was hilarious. Roger nearly died laughing, while Bear looked as if he were having a heart seizure.

That afternoon, Roger asked John to take part in some more fun. "Just a little ol' interrogation flight," Roger said. John had never been on one before.

The system was simple. Two special forces Green Berets and an interpreter would load a few bound and blindfolded enemy prisoners onto a Huey and take them up. The least likely to know anything was thrown out in order to make the higher-ranking gooks talk. In the early days of the war, the expendable gook was tossed out at high altitude. By this time, under pressure to be humane, the army had ordered the ships to descend slowly until they were about six feet off the ground before throwing a prisoner to the ground. That worked just as well, since the gooks were blindfolded and still thought they were up high.

The Green Berets flying with Roger and John were young but looked as if they had been through the process often. The three prisoners were VC, dirty, smudged with smoke and blood, and reeking with fear. One of them, John noticed, had his jaw set more firmly than the other two and kept his back more rigid. He would be the last to go. The Green Beanies shoved them roughly into the helicopter, and Roger took the ship up to 2,000 feet.

"Where's the interpreter?" John asked on intercom.

"These Berets speak gook."

The ship was flying over the trees. "How come we're not going back down?" John asked.

"They'll throw them out from here," said Roger.

John felt sick. "Goddamn, Roger, that's murder."

"Yeah? You ain't heard what those three did to that bunch of kids last night?"

"That's not the point. I say go down!"

The ranking Green Beret was listening on the intercom. John saw him make a face. As Roger told John later, the interrogators had known the kids. Living in the hamlet, they had administered to most of them during the last several months, tending cases of worms, toothache, and boils. The three VCs killed seven children after one had identified their position to the special forces unit. Anyway, Roger did not give a damn for any gook except Carla.

"I'm the AC here," Roger said, looking straight at John.

John felt a mixture of panic and misery. He was not afraid of combat, but he could not live with this. "*Please*, Roger."

Roger must have sensed his friend's anguish. "Well. Okay. Corporal, wait until we're at a hover in the LZ."

The interrogators looked disgusted, but they waited until the helicopter was only six feet above the ground at the LZ before they booted out the first VC. His scream was unforgettable. The other two immediately started to talk.

The experience haunted John. It was hard to believe how cheap life was held in war. Roger was not a bad sort, and he was sure an expert at preserving his own skin, but his attitude toward those helpless prisoners had been shocking. There were certain rules in war . . .

Perhaps John's problem was that he was looking for justice. If life was unjust, then it did not matter. All that mattered was who had power. He hated that thought. It went against his instincts.

There must be some better explanation for what Americans like Roger and John were doing in this war. Somebody around the place must have some answers. Maybe he could talk to a chaplain, if he could put away the uneasy feeling he always got in church.

It was a call from Sergeant Jameson at Cam Ranh that gave John a chance to ask some questions of an authority on morals. Jameson gave a date and unit designator, the Fifty-seventh AHC "Blue Star," where there was a load of unwanted material with a high proportion of weapons and ammo, including two .50-caliber machine guns the CO had asked John to mount on his Huey.

Usually, John would send enlisted men out, but this time he decided to go himself. The pickup, at Duc My near Ninh Hoa, was one hundred kilometers away from the post. After he had packed the .50s safely away, he left the men to load the rest of the contraband. He walked to a chapel he had seen about a quarter mile back. Looking at the cross above the door of the converted quonset hut, he almost decided not to enter.

Inside, a uniformed man with crosses on his lapels was setting up bingo tables. Since the hut was used for all services, he asked the chaplain what denomination he was.

"I am a Catholic, son."

"Oh, a priest. Well, I've been troubled with some questions lately, and I thought if I talked to somebody like a chaplain, it might help."

The priest put down the bingo cards and motioned to a chair. He was not old, but he tried to look sage.

"What are your questions?"

"You maybe haven't heard this from an officer. I've tried not to think about it too much, but does your church think we are doing the right thing here? Why are we Americans killing these people and dying?" John was startled by his own sudden outburst.

The priest hesitated but did not show surprise.

"Sometimes I don't know if it's right for us to be in this war," said John. "Can't you help me clear my mind?

"You are here," said the priest, "to stamp out the evil of communism, to stop the evil deeds the Viet Cong perpetrate against the people."

John hesitated. "Padre, I've seen evil on both sides."

"Now, son, you must not think that way. I can tell you that God is here with us. My name is Captain Vitello, and I do have a bingo night to work on for the boys. Maybe you could come back later. . . ."

"I kind of wonder if God is trying to get us to stay or go back home."

"I hope you are not mocking God, soldier," said the priest sternly. "You can get in trouble with the group commander for mocking God. Colonel Fitzpatrick is a good Catholic."

John was getting the old uncomfortable feeling. The padre was peering at him as if he suspected him of being a wise guy.

"I'm not mocking God."

"Well, then. I will explain to you why we are at war here. I do not want you to interrupt me." John nodded. His face froze. The padre gazed out the window. "Do you know that the South Vietnamese, the important ones, embrace the church as God's disciples have instructed all mankind to do? Do you know that the North Vietnamese refuse the people a chance to even hear about the grace of God? We are here to prevent the North from doing the same thing in the South. Saint Francis Xavier first brought the Holy Word to this country during the fourteenth century. Could lesser people, could we, allow the word to be driven from the Vietnamese?"

The priest waited for an answer to his rhetorical question.

"I don't know," said John. "I'm sorry, but I have to get back to my men."

"I hope I have helped you, son."

"Sure, padre. I gotta go."

Abruptly, John got up and walked out. As he left, he heard

the priest say quietly, "Bless him, Father. He does not understand."

John looked back once at the cross over the door. No, he thought, I do not understand.

His next flight was with Roger, flying lead ship on a CA, a combat assault. The objective was to drop ARVN troops just south of Ban Don to support a U.S. Army sweep down the Song Srepok river valley. When the formation set down, all hell broke loose. It became obvious the ARVN and U.S. strategists had miscalculated how long it would take the VC to move downriver. The VC were there, waiting for them. It was hot. Bullets and bits of shrapnel began hitting the ship. The ARVNs didn't want any part of this.

"If they won't go, kick the fuckers out," yelled Roger to his crew chief. The crew chief left his gun, climbed forward and began shoving the ARVNs out. It was dangerous because they were known to turn their weapons on Americans, but after he got the second one on the ground, the other five jumped out and ran for the trees. "Let's go," shouted the crew chief on intercom, above the gathering noise of the fire fight.

Roger checked the rest of the formation. Some of them had had the same problem, but all were now ready except the last ship. Its tail boom had been blown away by a rifle grenade, and the crew had abandoned it. As soon as they were safely inside the next helicopter, Roger took off, leading the formation.

He was a great lead pilot. Each ship provided covering fire for a certain segment of the formation. If the lead ship took off too soon or turned too sharply in flight, the integrity of the formation was ruined. This could cause shoot-downs.

Tracer bullets from something big blazed through Roger's intended flight path. Almost imperceptibly, he dipped and veered left, leading the rest of the ships out of danger.

Lead flying made him feel as if he were only the nose of one large flimsy helicopter that he was trying to keep in the air behind him, attached to his back and his arms by the thinnest of threads he must be careful not to break. He had never told anybody except John about this feeling. John tried hard, but he could never develop as keen a sense as Roger about where the other ships were. Roger swore he could tell if a ship was lagging because the thread pulled the hardest. John believed him.

The flight left the LZ with every door gun blazing. Ten miles away, Roger turned the ship over to John.

"Beautiful, Roger," someone in the flight blurted out on Platoon Frequency.

"Fuckin A," said Roger.

9

AC

IT WAS FUNNY ABOUT TIME. IF THERE WAS NO ACTION FOR more than a few days, life got dull and morale suffered, but too much action was even worse. Men stopped talking to each other. If they had a few spare minutes, they slept.

During the first three weeks in November, John flew fifty-nine combat missions. He got so tired events blurred into each other. What day was it when the captain went down, missing in action, and Blacky was made platoon leader? When had Shorty taken some shrapnel in his left side and been given a couple of weeks off?

Finally, a letup came. John decided to go find the flight surgeon, Swede. Maybe they could set up a chess game. He walked into the flight surgeon's hootch and found it empty. All the furniture, including the bed, was gone.

"Where the hell is the flight surgeon?" he asked the first man he saw when he went out.

"He moved down in the hospital. While ago."

"The hospital?"

"He thinks it's safer. The entrance is over there."

A long, steep ramp led into the ground, into the biggest bunker John had ever seen. It was three stories deep. No wonder he had never spotted it. They really had hidden it. He asked around and finally located the flight surgeon. The Swede was treating a man for shock. They were both shaking.

"Hi, Swede. How you doing?"

"I'm pretty busy," said the doctor with no welcoming smile. "Corpsman, you can take this man back with the ambulatories."

"Your face looks like you never go out."

"I don't."

"There's sun out there."

"I haven't seen the sun for a month."

"Is that healthy?"

"You're goddam right it's healthy. I'm not shot up, am I?"

"Aren't you ever going out?"

"Not until I'm shipped back or reassigned, I'm not."

"How about some chess?"

"I sent my stuff home. I'm too busy. I'm busy now."

"Well, look, Swede, you take care of yourself."

"I'll be okay. You take care of yourself out there."

John watched the doctor walk out of the room. All white, white clothes, white skin. Like a ghost. Though he had seen others with mental damage from the war, it was the first time John really felt pity. He began to grip the thought, to dwell on it. Then he cut it off and blocked it out. "Too much time left," he said to himself. "I got too much time."

Roger was looking for him when he got back to his hootch. John had no chance to tell him about the flight surgeon because Roger was full of news.

"We're deactivating," said Roger. "We really are."

Rumors of deactivation had been around for a month.

"What's wrong with that?" asked John. "Maybe we'll move someplace better than here."

''You can go straight to hell with the rest of the company!''

''Oh,'' said John. ''Carla?''

''That's right. Dutchman, what am I going to do with Carla?''

''Leave her.''

''Goddam you too.''

''Bring her?''

Roger was silent and then said, ''I was planning to. How'd you know?''

''Christ, Roger. You drive me crazy. When are we supposed to deactivate, anyway?''

''Maybe January.''

''Well, that's a month and a half from now.''

Roger started off and then said back over his shoulder, ''I also heard you're taking your AC check ride in a couple days.''

You knew when you were ready to be an AC because they made you one. It was no big deal. Three days later, John flew his first mission as an AC, transporting two scout dogs and their handlers to support an operation north of Ban Me Thuot. About halfway there, the two German shepherds started fighting. It sounded like a whole pack had broken loose, and the handlers were getting bitten as they attempted to pull the dogs off each other.

John tried to throw the animals off balance by slowing the ship's forward speed. At least that allowed the door gunners to slide the doors closed so the handlers would not fall out. Things just got worse. John changed course and headed for a MASH unit. The men, both badly mauled, had somehow managed to restrain the dogs by that time.

''What the hell happened, Vanvorden?'' asked one of the doctors. Both handlers had broken fingers and slashed flesh. One had a split thigh bone and the other a flap of cheek torn and hanging loose.

''They put two dogs on my helicopter that didn't like each other. Are the men hurt bad?''

"Bad enough so they'll be on their way to the States tomorrow."

"That bad?"

"It's that bad. The lucky bastards."

Before John left the MASH unit, he got new orders to pick up a MACV captain in Pleiku and bring him back to Ban Me Thuot. He asked his peter pilot, a newby called Fry, if he knew a Captain Harris. Fry was okay. He had stayed steady during the dog fight.

Fry was anxious to please the Dutchman. He knew flying with him was good experience. Even though John was a brand-new AC, he had a solid reputation among the peter pilots. "I know him," said Fry. "He's a real dodo."

"What's that mean?"

"You know, he thinks war is exciting, but all he does is shuffle papers."

"Oh. Did you finish the preflight on this helicopter?"

"Yes, sir."

They went through start procedure. "Battery."

"Check."

"Fuel."

"Check . . ."

While clearing the tower in Pleiku, John was surprised again at how his green-market reputation had preceded him. "That you, Dutchman?" the controller asked.

"Yeah, it's me."

"You want some chain-link fence?"

John needed something to reinforce the concrete in the swimming pool, now only a hole in the ground. "Yes, I do. What do you want for it?"

"Just get it out of here."

"How much is there?"

"Big roll."

"Fine. See you on the ground."

Captain Harris was waiting for him when he landed.

John got out, leaving Fry to finish shutting down the aircraft.

"Why did you turn off our helicopter?" asked Harris. "I'm here, ready to go."

"I got to refuel." Actually, the ship had enough fuel, but John needed time to pick up the fencing. "Let's go sit over there in the shade while they fill me up."

As the two men walked over to a makeshift shelter the mechanics had rigged with canvas, Harris said, "I heard you boys had a dogfight up there today. Heh, heh, get it? A dogfight. Like the jet fighters."

"I get it."

"Not funny, huh?"

"Not very. You should have seen the handlers."

"Got hurt, did they?"

"It's lucky one wasn't killed."

"I know what you mean. I saw a demonstration here on Armed Forces Day with the K-9 corps. Those dogs were mean. One was the biggest German shepherd I ever saw."

"That big, huh?"

"I'll say. They wrapped this guy up in mattresses and put a cage on his head and everybody was watching to see if this big dog would bite through the mattresses. Maybe two, three hundred of us were right up close. The gooks were watching, too, all on the other side of the fence. Some were sitting on top of the fence. Then they let that dog go." The captain paused for dramatic effect.

John was interested. "Well?"

"The goddam dog ran right past the mattress man and attacked the gooks on the fence. You should have heard the noise coming out of that animal. It even scared me."

"Did it get any of them?"

"I heard it tore off a gook thumb, but every one of the gooks fell off the fence and took off on the run and never looked back."

John laughed with the captain.

"So now you know you're safe around those animals as

long as you have a gook with you,'' said the captain with a straight face.''

A deuce-and-a-half pulled up to the pad, and John went over to take a look, excusing himself from the captain. The roll of fencing was so big it would take up the whole cargo area.

''You the Dutchman, sir?'' asked the driver.

''Yes. Put the fence in that helicopter when the fuel truck goes, will you? Where's the controller?''

''Who?''

''Who sent you with this?''

''The first-shirt just told us to bring it to pad number 12.''

As always, nobody knew anything, yet all the business was transacted. If the unit was deactivated, his operation would fall apart. Still, that would not be for six weeks; in the meantime, the roll of chain-link fence was a very good solution to the reinforcing problem. The company would still have time to enjoy the pool. Besides, maybe they would stay in Ban Me Thuot, after all. ''The fuel truck's going now, so you can load it up.''

Captain Harris appeared at his side. John had forgotten about him. ''Hey, Dutchman, you got a problem?''

''Not really, except you have to sit in the door-gunner well with the door gunner.''

''Really? Oh, boy. Can I shoot the gun?''

''Oh, sure, we'll let you shoot the gun.''

The fencing just fit, hanging out of both doors.

Three days later, the pool was finished. About a dozen men worked the whole time, using a cement mixer and spreading the cement by hand. No one there had ever built a swimming pool before, but they knew what they wanted it to look like, and within a week the pool was landscaped with palm trees. It had a deck and a diving board made out of a Charlie-model rotor blade with nonskid paint on it, but it took a long time to fill its thirty-by-twenty feet with water. Afterward, they had to leave a two-inch hose running into it from a nearby well because the concrete walls leaked like sieves. The water was murky green and never did clear up. The pool was crowded from the first day.

A week later, John was enjoying a cool dip with a bunch of others when two large snakes with black and tan bands swam up out of the murky water. Bathers scattered as the snakes slithered over the deck and out of sight into the grass. They were Southeast Asian kraits, capable of killing a man in seconds. From then on the pool was just used for sunbathing.

As an AC, John loved to execute the maneuver called the fly-by, performed after a return from combat assault. Flying in formation, the Hueys came in low and fast. When the formation neared the base, the gunners on each side of the ships popped smoke grenades and held them out on poles. It was beautiful. It gave John a real feeling of *esprit de corps,* and he only let his peter pilot fly it when he wanted to take pictures. Zooming over the base with all that smoke and then climbing as a group into hammerhead stalls, or maybe a peel-off sequence, seemed to him the most beautiful thing in the world.

If the assault involved the whole company, each platoon used its own color smoke. His platoon, the purple gang, trailed purple. Company fly-bys made a real air show, with each platoon trying to outdo the others.

Everyone was furious when the order came to stop the fly-bys. Some hot smoke grenades had caused fires in Ban Me Thuot city. That evening, some of the platoon sat around the card table grumbling about it.

"Now what are we gonna do after CAs?" asked Shorty.

"What do you care?" asked Torch. "You never got your timing right, anyway."

"You're the one who can't fly the fuckers," Shorty retorted.

"What are you talking about? You damn near took me out on that last fly-by. I had to break clean out of the formation. Ask any of these guys. They saw it."

"Well," said Shorty, looking around.

Nobody said anything because they did not feel like beating on Shorty about his lousy precision flying.

"Why don't you two lighten up," said Blacky. "We ain't going to be here much longer, anyway."

"You really believe that?" asked Shorty, relieved that the subject had been changed.

"Sure, I believe it. The dust off unit is leaving in five days," said Blacky.

"Man, the 268th at Qui Nhon! Nam heaven. Right on the beach and you never get hit by mortars." Torch shook his head ecstatically.

"Not for some of us. Some are going up to the DMZ," said Blacky.

"I hear the enlisted men up there are animals," said Shorty. "They frag their officers and all that shit."

"Don't sweat it, Shorty. You're too sh—I mean you don't have much time, anyway, do you? A couple months," put in John.

"Two months, two weeks, two days."

"How many hours and minutes?"

"Do you want to know?" asked Shorty belligerently.

"Screw you, Shorty," said Torch.

"You dumb fuckers make me sick," said Roger as he got up and walked out.

"What's eating him" asked Torch.

"You know," said Shorty. "Miss Vietnam. He don't want to leave her. Boy, is she ugly."

"You sayin' you didn't try to dip into that?" asked Blacky with a smirk.

"Well, she used to be better looking until she took up with him."

As usual, the group broke up laughing at Shorty.

John's mood was also one of growing depression as deactivation drew closer. He had won for himself a reputation at Ban Me Thuot not only as a pilot but as a negotiator, a sharp trader. His green market had paid off. Helicopter parts were much less of a problem now, and the chow was a whole lot better. The chances of making friends with anybody like Jameson in a new IG office were slim to none at all. His green market would disappear.

John spent part of a day installing .50-caliber guns on the CO's Huey. Because they replaced the smaller guns, he had had to get different mounts.

"They look kind of big on there." It was the XO, who had come up behind him and was peering over his shoulder.

"Oh, hi, Bear," said John. "They're big, all right."

"I'd like to take that ship sometime."

"Ask the CO."

"Sure. Hey, What I come over here for was to ask you a favor."

Had to be for that, thought John. The cave man. "Yeah?"

"We still got a hunnert an' fifty dollars in the kitty, and it's time to throw a party."

The officers' club collected five dollars from each officer on the first of the month to maintain a slush fund. It was usually wiped out by the end of the month.

The bear sidled up and brought his rough face close to John's. "What we'd like is for you to go downtown and get some gook to make a party at the club. Now, we got eighty officers, and we're gonna invite all them girls from across the street."

"I'll do what I can, I guess." It was bad news to say no to the Bear. "It's not much money."

"All we got." The Bear gave John a mean look.

John shrugged his shoulders as the XO walked away. As currency exchange officer for the company, he could exchange money anytime. The MPC/piaster rate had gone up from 118 pi per dollar to 275, which gave him a lot more bargaining power. The rate had been changed by the United States in a move to cut out the black-market sale of military payment certificates and greenbacks. Before the devaluation, he had been exchanging only a couple of hundred dollars a month. Now he was handling $25,000. Maybe he could get Bear his party for $150.

He went to the CO. "I need your jeep for the rest of the day."

Smith put his hands over his ears. "Just take it."

"It's not like that, sir."

"Take it!"

Damn, thought John, that's one squeamish CO. He found a driver, and they headed off base into the sluggish traffic. There was a large restaurant in Ban Me Thuot he had been meaning to visit.

The restaurant was a pleasant surprise. It had an upstairs, a dance floor, and a band platform. He figured it would take time to work out some kind of deal, so John asked the driver to sit in on negotiations. "You keep quiet unless I ask you something," he told him. It would not be easy to arrange food for eighty pilots and a bunch of whores on $150.

"Why you come so early? asked the manager, an ageless, cagey-looking Chinese. "*Va ton*," he ordered a skinny kid who peered in from what was probably the kitchen. His French sounded Chinese, and so did his English. Chinese voices went up and down in any language. "We no open yet, misters."

"We don't want to drink. We want to talk," said John.

"I want a drink," said the driver.

John ignored him. "I want to talk business."

"No open. No business."

John put a pile of crisp piasters on the table.

"Okay. What business you want talk?"

"We want you to bring food to the camp for the party."

"I no go out. I only have party here."

The place was nice and bigger than the O club. "I'll give you much money. We need food for eighty soldiers and fifty girl friend."

"I no go out. You come here, never mind, everything nice."

John shook his head.

"Why you no like?"

"I like it, but I don't have enough money."

"How much you got?"

"How much you want?"

The old man tugged on the few long gray wisps of hair growing out of his chin. "Eighty GI, fifty girl friend? How much food you want?"

"A bunch."

"You hungry now?"

"I'm hungry and thirsty," said the driver.

"Okay. You wait. I bring food and beer, then talk."

John glared at the driver. The food and beer sounded good, but why couldn't the pitiful guy keep quiet as he'd been told to? "I thought I told you I'd do the talking!"

"Yes, sir." The GI avoided John's eyes.

The manager returned with two bottles of Ba Mui Ba and a girl who carried two big plates of fried rice. The rice was good. John reached for more soy sauce.

"You like this food? I make ten more dishes for the party and give you one free drink. I also give dancing band and five girl for special show."

"What kind of show?" asked the driver.

"Do you want to sit in the jeep?" demanded John. "This is officer-club business." The driver went back to his chopsticks. "How much money?"

"Number one, five girls take off clothes," said the manager.

"Number one, pretty girls?"

"I no lie."

"How much?"

"Five hundred American dollars."

"Five hundred greenback? You're crazy. Nobody's going to give you five hundred in green!"

The old man went in back and got two more bottles of beer. Time passed, and the driver went out and sat in the jeep. This kind of negotiating could go on for hours. The old man acted as if he were being exploited by foreign devils. John behaved as if he were taking a terrible beating from the wily Chinese. Both of them loved every minute of it. There were many more beers and another plate of rice before they settled on eight different dishes of food, no free drinks, the band, and the strip show at the restaurant for twenty-six-thousand piasters. At the new rate, that left John with $1.42 change from what the XO offered. He felt like a fast-talking dude.

"You promise eighty GI and fifty girl friend so I sell many drink?" said the old man.

"That's it. I do. I'll give you half the money now and half the night of the party in two days."

"Okay, mister." The bony hand closed around the pile of new bills John handed him. He picked one up and straightened it out, then held it to the light. "You no have green?"

"No greenback, no MPC."

"Two day, night, big party." The old man smiled, showing his gold tooth and several gaps.

When John found the XO and told him about the arrangements, the Bear was delighted. "Man, that's some great dealin'. You done good, Dutchman. You told anybody yet?"

"Not yet."

"Well, don't. I want everybody to think this is my show." John looked annoyed. "Look, Dutchman, you get plenty of credit around here, and I need somethin' like this." The Bear always acted as if he wanted to pound someone. He buffaloed every subordinate with that manner of his, including John. No wonder he was hurting for friends.

"Why?" asked John.

"Because I'm a lifer, that's why. I'm up for promotion, that's why. And I can make things goddam rough on you if you don't do like I say, that's why."

"Sure, Bear. It's all yours. Here's the rest of the piasters. Just give them to the Chinaman the night of the party."

Even the CO was impressed with the great party the Bear had arranged, and Bear took all the credit. He told John he would invite the girls and take care of everything else, and he then assigned him to an FOB mission that would keep him out of Ban Me Thuot until the day after the party. "Sorry you'll miss it, Dutchman, but lemme tell you, I'll never forget what you done."

When John returned from the FOB, Blacky warned him that the XO was threatening to kill him. The party had been a disaster. Of more than 150 whores, only a dozen had agreed to come. No one gave a reason. Maybe they did not like the Bear, or maybe they would lose face, or maybe it was not safe. When the officers found out how few girls were coming, half of them decided to skip it and hit the whorehouses instead.

When Bear had made a big show of giving the manager the rest of the money, the old Chinaman had asked where the other mister and where all the men and girl friends were. Bear gave him the I'm-going-to-pound-you look and told him to get the food. Everybody stood around and waited. The girls, outnumbered, huddled together. Forty-five minutes later, Bear stomped to the kitchen, and food appeared. There were only five dishes and barely enough. Bear yelled for the manager.

"Where's the eight dishes. Where's the show? Where's the music?"

"No show tonight. You say 130 people. Drink many drinks. You got only fifty people. I no make money." The little old Chinese fellow was steamed. When the band did play, Blacky told John, it sounded like bad Guy Lombardo through a tin speaker. It was finally apparent the party was over.

Blacky had stopped by Bear's table on his way out. "You should a got the Dutchman's help for this, Bear." Then he retreated before Bear's pound-you look.

John stayed out of the man's way for a week, but the XO never tried anything. Someone said the major had given the Bear a warning.

John had been told to call Jameson in Cam Ranh. It probably was a miracle that the phone system in Nam worked at all. Every road had a mess of telephone lines, some on poles and some running along the ground. John figured that when a line got cut, they just ran a whole new one. After years of land lines being cut, wire was all over the place.

You had to go through several exchanges to reach Cam Ranh. Each one was manned by a GI who could cut you off without notice. There were no panels of lights at the exchanges to indicate whether a connection was still being used. A system of sorts evolved to let the GI operator know when a call was finished so he could disconnect. Tapping in to the different lines he controlled, the operator would shout, "Working." If there was no immediate response with "Working!" the GI unplugged the call. The system was so overburdened that if you tried to talk longer than five minutes, he pulled the plug, anyway. Getting through to Jameson and keeping him on the line was a hassle.

This call was typical. "Hello, Jameson, is that you?"

"Working."

"Working!"

"Hello . . ."

"Jameson, is that you?"

"Yes. Who's this?"

"Working."

"Working, working!"

"This is the Dutchman."

"Oh, Vanvorden, they—"

"Working."

"Working!"

"They are going to inspect—"

"Working."

"Working!"

"The IG is coming to your base on the eighth. In three days—"

"Working." Click.

"Work . . . son of a bitch."

So they planned to pull an IG before the unit deactivated. Those bastards are cute, thought John.

Before the inspectors arrived, John had all the extra equipment put down in the connex boxes he had ordered set into the ground earlier. There were thirty-two M-60 machine guns, eighteen M-79s, several door-mounted electric miniguns from the air force, small arms, starlight scopes, and tons of helicopter parts, tool kits, and other equipment that accounted for the company's fine flight record.

Major Smith sent John on a combat support mission to get his own helicopter with its .50 caliber machine guns out of the way. It had not flown in combat since the guns were installed. The CO didn't really take to combat flying.

As they neared the LZ, his peter pilot said, "Hey, Dutchman. See that smoke down there? Things don't look too friendly."

"Shut up, newby, and watch the instruments . . ."

The idea of men making a stand on some piece of real estate, getting mortared, watching them die for who knew what reason in the first place, and then moving away to do the same thing somewhere else was depressing him. Christ, what a waste. I just hope I get out of here alive, he thought.

"I thought the commander said this was a milk run."

"They need this ammo. We're going in. Take care of the goddam dials. Chief, you and the gunner can spray everything this side of that stream."

BAM BAM BAM BAM BAM BAM BAM

"What the hell is that? It's shakin' this chopper apart!"

BAM BAM BAM BAM BAM

"It's these fifty cals, sir. I can't stop it! We're takin' fire!"

BAM BAM BAM BAM BAM BAM BAM

John thought the fifties would jerk the light-skinned Huey to pieces. His nerves jerked with the BAMS. "Soon as we hit, throw the ammo and food off. They'll pick up on the right!"

"NVA on the left, sir. Request permission to—" BAM BAM BAM BAM BAM BAM BAM BAM BAM BAM

"Is the cargo off?" yelled John. "Let's GO . . ."

The tree line exploded in front of them. John had to spin around and beat it back across the stream. BAM BAM BAM BAM BAM BAM BAM . . . The ship shook as it flew. The enemy kept their asses covered as the coughing fifties shattered everybody's nerves.

Then John said firmly, "Chief, that ought to do it. We're clear."

"Just makin' sure, sir."

They were on smooth course now, and the helicopter seemed undamaged. "Right. Chief, I want you and the gunner to change those hogs tomorrow!"

"Yes, sir."

By the time they got back, the 155th had passed its last IG in Ban Me Thuot with flying colors. Major Smith had lost five pounds in sweat, he said, and would never let Vanvorden uncover the connexs. Official word had come through on deactivation. The 155th would stand down a week before Christmas, and everybody would be cleared out by the first of January. Anybody here ten months or more would rotate back to the states for discharge or reassignment. This was Vietnamization, and "our boys" were getting a break. The rest would either go to Qui Nhon, which was a good duty at the beach, or somewhere else not as good.

Shorty and Blacky were the luckiest ones in the purple gang. They were being rotated stateside. They chided the Dutchman for wanting to stay in Vietnam just to fly. John knew, as they all did, that the Vietnamese could not control the modern military machine the U.S. was handing over. But however wasteful and stupid the plan was, John had reached that stage of maturity a favorite instructor had once predicted: his senses and mind were keen to combat. He had achieved a special status attained only by the best of warriors. You knew when you had it, and the others knew you had it. It made an officer into a leader. It was a feeling, a look. It could stay with a man for years, or it could leave him in a day. John had it now.

10
STANDDOWN

THE STANDDOWN LEFT EVERYBODY FEELING DISORIENTED AND vulnerable. There were no more birds to escape in, and the supply officer was collecting all the equipment that belonged to the company, including their gas masks. But there was no way Roger was going to turn in his gas mask. Letting go of his survival vest and Smith & Wesson .38 special was already too much. With more ARVNs assigned daily to the camp, he worried about ground assault and slept with his arms wrapped around an M-16. The idea of insurgents made him paranoid. "No insurgents'll get me, nope, never," he declared. He knew where to get more weapons and ammo if he needed them. Over at the Dutchman's hootch.

John had virtually an arsenal cached in a wooden wardrobe in his room. The weapons came from his green market. He was especially fond of the M-79 grenade launcher and the sawed-off .30 caliber M-2 carbine. He also had two Colt .45 automatics, one S & W .38 caliber Targetmaster, an M-16, and a Russian-built AK-47. And stacks of ammunition for all of them. He even had two shells for the recoilless rifle on the jeep, though the jeep had long since been appropriated by the CO.

The money from his piaster exchange duties was supposed to be kept in the company safe, but John usually broke that regulation. It was more convenient to keep it in his hootch with the weapons. The risk was that if it were stolen, he would be liable. A final settlement was coming due, and since he had not turned any money in for a while, he had nearly twenty thousand dollars in MPCs and piasters in the locked wardrobe.

One night, a popping noise interrupted the usual card game. All the pilots instinctively stopped what they were doing and listened. Blacky came in. "Hey, I think somebody's popped tear gas out there," he said. At that instant, John got a whiff and quit breathing. He ran toward his hootch for his gas mask but then remembered he had turned it in the day before and headed back into the hall for the bunker. Everybody else was running the same way, which slowed him down. He looked over his shoulder just in time to inhale from a heavy white cloud of CS gas that caught up with him. He fell to the floor instantly with burning pain in his eyes, nose, throat, and lungs. It was like breathing fire.

Crawling outside, his mind fogged by pain, he bumped into a connex box that had been moved during the day. Like a dog trying to wipe off skunk smell, he rubbed his face in the grass and even tried eating it. He had to relieve his misery . . . water, water. Yeah, he needed water. There was a water tap behind the officers' club, fifty yards away. It was dark, and he could only open his eyes for a peek at a time. When he did, they burned like crazy. Doggedly, he crawled along the side of the club. When he found the water tap, he turned it on and lay under it for half an hour, flushing his eyes, nose, and mouth. Water never felt so good.

When he finally got rid of most of the pain and irritation and his head cleared, he wondered what was going on. Were they under attack? He went to the operations bunker. Everything seemed normal. He tried to look casual, although his face and eyes were red and his clothes a soaking mess.

"Hey. Somebody threw some gas over there. You know what it's about?"

"Yeah," said the duty officer. "Just some enlisted men trying to gas the NCO club. A little got into the officers' billet area. Blew into the barracks."

"Oh. That's all it was?"

"That was it," said the duty officer, unconcerned.

John got back to his room to find the door of his weapons closet ripped off its hinges. Guns were scattered all over the floor. "Gassed me and robbed me!" he thought in a panic. "How am I ever going to pay all that money back?" His brain was sure the money was gone, but then his eyes told him it was safe, sitting there on the top shelf. Sure enough, all twenty thousand dollars was intact. He couldn't figure out what had happened. Casually, he walked back into Torch's hootch where the card game had resumed.

"Somebody tore the doors off my closet," he said. "You guys know anything about it?"

"They get anything?" asked Blacky.

"Don't think so."

"Bet it was Roger. He was in there looking for bullets."

That figured. John went back to clean up the mess.

When he pieced together the story, it went as he thought it had. As soon as the gas was thrown, Roger had put on his mask and started to load his gun. When he couldn't find his clip, he thought of John's gun closet in the barracks next door. He was not about to go out unarmed, so he fixed his bayonet, threw on his flack vest and steel pot, and ran out.

Outside, a GI from a new MACV unit that had recently moved in was stumbling around in the cloud of CS gas. Roger, in his gas mask, was the only one that could see. The MACV guy, wearing a conical hat and Ho Chi Minh sandals, as did a lot of GIs off duty, looked to Roger just like a gook insurgent. As soon as he was close, Roger jumped at him and yelled, "*Kill!*"

The MACV soldier looked out of squinted eyes to see a monster coming at him. He let out a scream and fell straight backward. Roger didn't stop to stick him, but ran past him toward the Dutchman's hootch. The lock on the closet did not slow him down. He tore both doors off their hinges and raked through the guns until he found loaded M-16 clips. He ran back to his own room, bolted the door, and waited to shoot any gook who tried to get in. Everybody stayed away from Roger's hootch for a while because the crazy bastard was still in there, waiting.

During the standdown, orders came in slowly. Men moved out one by one instead of in groups. Those left behind had very little to take up the time. John, wandering over to the officers' club one empty afternoon, found the flight surgeon sitting at the bar.

"Hi, Swede. How's it going? How come you're up here out of the hospital?"

"Hi, Dutchman. I'll buy you a drink. I'm going to Qui Nhon in a couple of hours."

"Qui Nhon. That's great. Hope I'll see you up there. Hey, here comes Blacky. Black, look who."

"Swede," said Blacky, surprised. "Long time no see. I heard you made the hospital your permanent quarters."

"Not anymore. I'm going to Qui Nhon."

"Can't beat that. You remember Shorty?"

"No, I don't," said the Swede.

"Well, he's gone. The land of the big PX and round eyes."

"All *right*," said John.

"Shorty said something about you before he left, Dutchman."

"Did he? What did the little bastard say?" John was not much interested.

"He said you were one of the finest pilots the 155th ever did see, and he's glad he knew you."

John blinked, surprised. "Why would he say a thing like that?"

"You wasn't here long enough to really know Shorty, Dutchman," said Blacky. "He wasn't the greatest pilot or officer, but he tried, and he knew what good was."

"Well, hell, Blacky . . ."

"Listen, Dutchman. I'm leaving for the states today, too. You take care up north, you hear? Remember everything that big wop Arata taught ya. Just CYA for a few months and then FO." Cover your ass and then fuck off.

"Good advice, Blacky," said the Swede.

"Thanks, and good luck back in the world," said John. Every time someone D-ROSed, (date return overseas) the ones remaining felt as if they were being deserted.

"I gotta be going," said Blacky. "Good luck to you, too, Swede."

"I wish I were going back with you!"

John sat there for a minute with the flight surgeon.

"I got to go, too, Swede," he said, suddenly tired of the man who was so frightened, though he had it safer than anybody. "Probably see you at the 268th. Take it easy."

Most of the unit had been reassigned by Christmas time. Nobody gave a damn about the holiday, and John had to listen to the radio to make sure what day it was. He sat in his room eating a bowl of Lipton's chicken soup, the instant kind that came in a dry package. It tasted so good that it raised his spirits. That was worth a lot. His orders had not come yet, and he was depressed. A short letter would say thank you to the Lipton Company, so he wrote:

December 25, 1970

Dear Lipton Company:

I am a warrant officer flying helicopters in Vietnam. It is Christmas day, and I am all alone.

The only thing that reminds me of my home and my

mom's Christmas dinner is this bowl of Lipton chicken soup. And it's great.

That's all I wanted to do, write you and tell you Merry Christmas and thanks for your good soup.

John Vanvorden 155th AHC

A sergeant was sitting at the desk reading a Batman comic book when John went over to the orderly room to send the letter.

"Can you mail this? They took away the mailbox." The man nodded without looking up from his comic book. "Did any orders come in for me yet?"

The sergeant checked the name tag on John's fatigue shirt. "Vanvorden. No, sir, not yet."

John turned to walk out. "Oh, Mister Vanvorden?"

"Yeah?"

"I got a stack of mail and some packages, too, and there's nobody left to read them. You want a few?"

John took a look. There was a pile of Christmas letters and packages, all opened. "How come they're opened?"

"We have to read 'em in case there's a crank letter. Take all you want."

John took a handful of letters back to his hootch. They were Christmas mail for soldiers in Vietnam and pretty much alike—take care of yourself . . . have a Merry Christmas . . . hope you come home soon—except two. Those were special. One was kind of crazy, and the other one was a heartbreaker. Both were addressed to a GI in Vietnam. Any GI.

The crazy one was from a coed at the University of Southern California and was dated December 14.

Dear GI,

I have been meaning to write a letter for six months. Just got around to it, though. Hope your Christmas parties are not as embarrassing as the one I went to last night.

My girl friend Betty took me to a party last night because she hates to go places alone. I didn't want to go because I know Betty too well. Her and her parties you should see.

Well, I went anyway, because Betty really wanted me to go. When I got there, this one guy kept trying to grab me, so I kept trying to hide. He found me every time, so I went outside and climbed a tree.

It was a good hiding place, but when I was sitting there, a whole crowd of guys from the party came out. They all unzipped their pants and peed on the tree I was in. Can you believe that? I felt like laughing, but it smelled awful.

I have to go now.

Merry Christmas from California

Ellen Thomas.

That letter was funny and made John miss home, but it was the second letter that got to him.

December 10, 1970

Dear Mister Soldier,

I am in the sixth grade of Herndon Elementary School in Virginia. I am vice-president of the student body.

My big brother went to Vietnam, and I can't write to him anymore. He died trying to carry his hurt friend. My brother was a paramedic, and I loved him because he wouldn't hurt a flea. He always gave me rides when I was little.

I feel so bad because I can't talk to Robby anymore. I need someone to talk to.

Merry Christmas. I ask Heavenly Father to bless the soldiers every night.

Sincerely,

Patty L. Frazer

John read it over twice, tears streaming down his face. He was overwhelmingly reminded of his own little brother and of the rest of his family. He felt so bad for that little girl. There was a lot to feel bad for on this Christmas.

11
FIGMO

ROGER AND JOHN WERE AMONG THE FEW REMAINING AFTER Christmas who were not figmo, (fuck it, got my orders). They scarcely saw each other because Roger was spending his time shacked up with Carla. He planned to give her money so she could follow wherever his orders sent him.

No flying. No friends. In a dejected mood, John went to see Major Smith, still there, overseeing the deactivation.

"Sir, I came to ask you if you can find out why I haven't got orders yet."

"It's tough, Vanvorden, but there's nothing I can do."

"Can't you check with Cam Ranh?"

"Look, John, I'll be here four more days. If they haven't come by the time I'm ready to leave, I'll do something."

"Thanks." What do you know, thought John. He called me by my first name. Back at the barracks, he found the hootch maid waiting for him.

"Hi, Happy . . . you found all that underwear yet?" The hootch maids stole a lot of underwear.

"No, but Mista Roger, you friend, in BIG trouble!"

"What are you talking about?"

"Miss Carla. She gotta husband who got big money kill on Mista Roger. Very, very big. They kill him today right now. Right now. Mista Roger downtown with Miss Carla. Many bad man go now. Shoot Mista Roger."

"Goddam . . . how quick?"

"Right now! Right now! You late. . . ."

John ran out of the barracks and back to the CO's office.

"Sir, I have to use your jeep!"

"What for?"

"It's a matter of life and death."

"I don't want to hear about it. Take it . . ."

John grabbed the keys and ran out. There was no time to find a driver, so he drove off the base himself, trailing a swirl of red dust. He had only once been to the place Roger was renting, and he hoped he could find it again. It was getting dark. He made some lucky guesses and got to a shack of unpainted wood with a tin roof. Roger had fixed the hasp so he could close the door with the lock in place, making it look unoccupied. Since Roger was usually AWOL, he never answered the door if anybody knocked. John banged hard, but there was no response.

Cupping his hands, he yelled through the door, "Carla's ol man's got his whole army on the way down to do you in. We got to beat it!"

Roger did not bother with the door. He crashed straight out the window and jumped in the jeep with John, who floorboarded it.

"Let's get back on the post, pronto!" said Roger, mopping his face.

"If you go back on post, they're going to get you. Hell, half the ARVNs on base are probably looking for you right this minute. You're lucky my hootch maid came and told me."

"What'll I do?"

"There's no way you can hide in this area. You have to get the hell out of town. What about Carla?"

His love for Carla was a thing of the past. "To hell

with her. I got my own problems. You have any ideas, Dutchman?''

''Why don't you go down to headquarters in Dam Rahn and stay in those transient barracks? I can watch for your orders here. When they come, I'll send them and all your stuff to you.''

''Great idea,'' said Roger.

They drove from downtown straight to the air-force base at Ban Me Thuot East. A C-123 cargo plane was revving its engines. Roger ran into the operations building. ''I got to get on that airplane,'' he yelled. Nobody told him where it was headed, but they let him board the plane. John stayed until he saw the sturdy two-engine cargo ship lift off.

Covering for Roger back at the base was not difficult because of the stand down. He could intercept any messages for him. The next day, John called Cam Rahn. There was no sign of Roger. He was worried the gooks had got him. Three days later, he had still not located Roger. That evening, walking back from the latrine, he heard his name on the loudspeaker.

''Attention in the compound. Attention in the compound. Will Mister Vanvorden report to the orderly room.''

Maybe his orders had come in. John ran to the orderly room. ''Lima lima, sir,'' said the corporal there, referring to the land-line telephone.

John picked it up. ''Hello.''

''Hey, Dutchman, know who this is?''

''Where the hell are you? I been looking all over the place. You all right?''

''Working.''

''Working!''

''I'm all right—''

''Working.''

''Working, goddam it!''

''Where are you?'' John asked again hurriedly.

''Remember that place we used t'go down and shoot sharks?''

Roger did not want to disclose his identity or whereabouts to eavesdroppers. He was in Nha Trang.

"Yeah, I know where. How come you went there?"

"Lousy C-123 took me—"

"Working."

"Working! And I ain't been able to get a ride out. Besides, it's a lot better place than Cam Rahn."

"You going to stay there?"

"Working."

"Working!"

"How'll I call you?" John was sure the operators would cut off the call any second.

"I'll call you. Every day."

"Okay. Good deal—"

"Working. . . ." Click.

Roger's orders arrived. He was assigned to the 282nd AHC, the Blackcats, at Marble Mountain near Da Nang. It was the only army unit attached to the marine base there.

"You're figmo," John said when Roger called. "I'll send them to Cam Ranh."

"Where'm I going?"

"You know up where all the jar heads are?"

"Christ, not there!"

"Could be worse. I'll come see you when I get mine—"

"Working."

"Working!"

"Good luck, Dutchman."

"Good luck. . . ." Click.

Now everybody except John was figmo.

The CO checked as he had promised and called in to tell him the result. "John, your orders won't be coming in for two or three weeks. Some kind of a snafu. I straightened it out, but it will still take that long." He held up his hand as John started to protest, "In the meantime, I cut you some orders for R & R in Thailand. If you want to go somewhere else, I'll change them."

"Damn, major," said John, thinking about it. "Bangkok. That's just fine. I don't know what to say."

"You earned it."

"Thanks. Thanks a lot."

"Thank you," said the major, "for helping me make this unit run so smoothly, John. I could not have done as well these past months without you. If you ever need some help, you can call me. I'll be working at Cam Rahn."

"Promotion, sir?"

"That's right, son." The CO handed John his R & R orders. "I talked to Ban Me Thuot East, and there's a C-130 headed for Bangkok tomorrow morning. They're expecting you. Be at operations at 0800 hours."

"Thanks again, sir. And it's been a pleasure."

"For me, too, John. You're a fine officer."

John walked out, his load of depression lightened. Bangkok! Wow!

He decided to pack what few belongings he would take and go right over to the airforce base. There was supposed to be a traveling USO show that night at Ban Me Thuot East, and he could spend the night in one of the overstuffed chairs in the operations building. That way, he would be sure not to miss his ride in the morning.

He had sold off most of his guns during the past week. All he had left was the M-16 and the .45 automatic. These he could check with the rest of his gear. At the orderly room, they told him he could pick it all up at headquarters in Cam Rahn when he got back. After he had turned over his piaster exchange money, he went out to hitch a ride to the airforce base. It had begun raining, one of those rains that settled in and drizzled steadily. A deuce-and-a-half was headed his way. Its bed was covered and had side benches. He was the only one back there.

Rounding the runway at Ban Me Thuot East, the truck was halted by MPs. Wreckage of another truck was being cleared off the road. The red dust was turning to red mud, and the tree line, usually of various shades of green, was all one color, dark, like the rain-clouded sky. John could see that there had been an explosion. The medics were out in the rain wrapping the driver's chest with a wide roll of gauze. The gauze turned red through every wrapping. Rain and blood, thought John. Maybe that's what colors the dirt in Nam. The deuce-and-a-half was waved on, past the hole in the road. John shuddered at seeing wet soldiers cleaning up after just another small tragedy.

The USO show was held under a big tent with no walls. There were no girls, so only a small crowd came, a hundred or so, to hear an eight-piece band and an older male vocalist.

The singer's repertoire was of World War II vintage, songs from the late thirties and early forties. In fact, he wore a World War II uniform. The last song had the refrain "We'll meet again . . . don't know where . . . don't know when." The words gave John a feeling of melancholy longing, undefined.

While the rest of the audience strolled away, back to their tents and barracks, John went up to talk to the singer. He turned out to be a former colonel in World War II and thanked the young aviator from Utah for coming up after the show. They talked for a while across a gulf of time and wars, and when John excused himself to leave, the ex-colonel confessed that he wished this were his war. John told the older man he wished he could go back to World War II.

12

R & R

THE BIG HERCULES C-130 APPROACHED BANGKOK, SKIRTING magnificent anvil-topped cumulo-nimbus clouds. The force of vertical winds and lightning inside any one of them could tear the C-130 apart. The terrain below emerged as the plane began a slow, graceful descent. It was different from Nam. In Nam, coming down was a last-minute plunge to a runway to minimize the chance of being hit by small-arms fire.

The jungle was gone, as were the mountains. Tall trees rose individually from flat land. At altitude, it had been very cold in the plane. On the ground, the troops stepped into a blast of Southeast Asian heat and humidity. John's body adjusted rapidly to the extremes in temperature all flyers endure. Sweat, the natural body coolant, began to run down his chest between his pectoral muscles.

Vendors immediately trotted over to the Americans waiting for ground transportation. They pushed a trailer supported on an automobile axle and wheels with tires. Fruits, gum, soft drinks, and beer were for sale, the latter buried in ice. Gooks, thought John. Thai gooks.

"You buy drink, sir? Maybe eat?"

"I'll have a beer," said John.

The bottle the old Thai woman pulled from the ice was labeled Singha. John paid her in green and took a long swallow. "Doesn't taste a whole lot better than Ba Mui Ba," he said. "But it's cold. Better give me another."

"Maybe two, three?" she asked.

"One."

John's immediate impression of the Don Muang airport was a letdown. The United States had taken it over. There were civilian and military aircraft, ground-support equipment, motor vehicles; it was just another militarized airport that employed "indigenous Asian personnel," indistinguishable from the one he had left.

On the bus ride into Bangkok, he grew aware of differences. The calm atmosphere was that of a country at peace. He stopped exchanging small talk with his fellow Americans and listened to the quiet. No far-off muffled explosions, no aircraft clogging the sky around the city, no sign of refugees clamoring for handouts whenever soldiers passed by.

As they reached the outskirts of the city, a mixed odor of garlic, sizzling meat, and charcoal wafted through the open bus windows. Now and then, a rank smell would knife through to remind him of rudimentary sewer systems. Over it all was the fragrance of flowers. Thailand was a flower garden. Excitement rose in him, increasing as he watched the houses and neighborhoods go by until it was like the throbbing beat of a drum.

One of his crew chiefs had recommended a hotel, the Crown. When he was inside the city, he would take a taxi and try for a reservation there.

Like other large Asian cities, Bangkok streets were choked with cars, buses, motor scooters, bicycles, and pedestrians. His driver, seeing a hundred yards of open road, would floor the gas pedal for the first ninety, confident that he could stop in the next ten. John cursed under his breath until the taxi drove through a gate into a courtyard. The Crown Hotel had seven stories, and the rooms were approached via exterior balcony walkways. It felt strange to deal as a civilian after five and a half months in a combat zone. He had no trouble getting a room.

John threw the B-4 bag he had acquired in one of his trading deals with the airforce on the double bed. There were also two chairs, a desk, and a dresser. The bathroom was all tiled, floors and walls, and the tub looked like a sarcophagus. Here and there, chameleons clung to the walls and ceiling. He could not help the flash of memory carrying him back to the Cambodian jungle. The chameleon on his chest had taken the place of his dead comrade, who had floated off in the night.

The drum beat of excitement was still there. He took two sets of civies out of his bag, glad he had brought them to Nam. The casual slacks and dress slacks went with two nice-looking short-sleeved shirts. Military oxfords would do for dressing up. He had some leather sandals, made for him in Ban Me Thuot, which would be fine for casual wear.

After a bath, he dressed casually and went down to the lobby.

"Hey, buddy," he asked a GI, "where's a good place for lunch?"

"I only been here one night," the soldier replied. "Just don't eat the hotel food."

"Thanks for the tip."

John walked out onto Sukumvit Road. The sidewalks were wide and convenient, and he decided to walk until he saw a place to buy food. Then he remembered he had not changed any money. Military personnel were under orders to exchange at the official rate of twenty bäht to the dollar in Thailand, but military money exchanging offices were always hard to find. He went back into the lobby and spotted a small jewelry shop just inside the door. He asked the shopkeeper if he could change green for bäht.

"I will give you twenty-two bäht to the dollar," replied the slightly built Thai. He had a very proper British accent.

"How about twenty-four?" said John, fishing out ten twenty-dollar bills. "Say, where did you learn to speak English so well?"

"My father sent me to school in England," said the man. "I'll give you twenty-three to the dollar. Here is your money. I shall be glad to exchange any more when you wish."

"It's a deal," said John. He had never heard a gook speak better than this one. It made him slightly uncomfortable. Anyway, he had made four hundred bäht on the deal, and the man seemed very pleased, too. He stuffed a third of the bills into his wallet and a third in each front pocket.

His first taste of the local cuisine was a surprise. The rice dish he ordered through sign language was so hot he had to drink two bottles of beer to put out the fire. Mexicans had nothing on Thais when it came to hot food.

He spent the afternoon walking around. The Thais looked different from the gooks in Vietnam. The men were about the same size, but the women seemed bigger. Some of them were downright beautiful. And it had been a long time since he had had a woman.

That evening, after changing clothes, John found a 1954 Chevrolet in the hotel's circular drive. It was in mint condition, and the driver was giving its cream and aqua exterior a tender buffing.

"That's a beautiful car," said John.

"This my taxi. I stay at Crown Hotel. You want to go somewhere?"

"Do you know a good place to eat dinner? I mean a real good place?"

"You take R & R? You be here awhile?"

"Yeah. I take R & R. I stay awhile."

"I take you to Orchid Room for twenty bäht."

"Isn't that a lot of money?" John did not yet know one way or another about taxi fares in Thailand. Nor was he in the mood for bargaining, but he would not like to get taken on his first day."

"This expensive car."

"Okay, let's go. What's your name?"

"Johnny."

"Really? My name is John, too."

"Many GIs name John."

"No joke. Let's go."

There was tropical foliage outside and a pink neon sign: ORCHID ROOM. Inside, the tables were covered with double white linen cloths and set around a small teakwood parquet dance floor. Tropical plants were profuse inside, also, and John had the feeling of being in an old time movie.

The band was Philippine and very good. Filipinos were the best musicians in Asia and could make trumpets sound like trumpets instead of tin horns. John ordered steak and champagne.

At an adjacent table sat the most beautiful woman he had ever seen. When she stood up to dance with her escort, a wealthy-looking man who looked and sounded like a German, her figure was as stunning as her Eurasian face. Probably a mixture of Thai and French, he thought. When the band took a break, she sat gracefully down again at her table and looked over at John. Her gray almond eyes met his, and John felt his heart stop.

The man seemed unaware of John, and the beautiful woman was obviously enjoying his quick looks at her, but the whole scene was a downer. He felt lonely. The goddess at the next table was out of reach. His time was short, and he wanted more than the bar girls could provide. He tipped up the last of the wine and looked at the fragile glass in his hand. The band was now playing one of those familiar tunes from the forites he could never quite identify. He glanced at the exquisite woman again. She was looking back at him.

I got to get clear of this place, thought John. He stood up, paid, and walked out. Goddam German, he thought as he stepped out in the street. Why does he deserve her? The warrior from Vietnam felt like a second-class visitor in Southeast Asia. It was a new feeling, and he hated it. Bars, booze, and third-rate whores was all that R & R meant to most of the GIs. Maybe that was all there was.

"Taxi!" He hailed one of the many Japanese autos and got in without haggling over the fare. "Take me to the Crown Hotel."

In the morning John went down and had a breakfast of pineapple, papaya, mango, toast, and coffee, then decided to lie around the hotel pool for a while.

Several palm trees shaded one end of the deck. John stretched out in the shade. His eyes were closed, but he felt someone standing over him.

"Hey Mistah Vanvorden. You Mistah Vanvorden, the Dutchman?"

John looked up to see the young GI who had the heavy southern accent staring down at him.

"That's me. Who are you, soldier?" The return to officer status was automatic.

"I'm PFC Cumberland," said the young man. "You don't remember me?"

"I think I might," said John, because the boy looked so disappointed.

"You all fetched me outta the bush. 'Bout two months ago."

"You look different now," said John, who still could not place his face. "Oh! The LRRP."

"That's me. I don't do that kind of soldierin' no more. I'm just regular now."

John remembered picking up the lost soldier with the thick drawl. He had been missing in the jungle and had run from the VC and NVA for so long he had no idea where he was. For twenty-nine days, Private, First Class Cumberland had survived before John and Roger had picked him up at an old LZ ten miles west of the Duc Lap, just over the Cambodian border. The LRRPs, members of the long-range reconnaissance patrols, did some intelligence work, such as reporting on troop movements, but also they were snipers. They used the starlight and infrared scopes to kill and disrupt the enemy and were highly trained to survive on very little. With them, they carried high-energy dehydrated food packets. LRRPs were respected but had few friends outside their own specialty.

"You'll have to tell me about that experience over a couple of beers," said John cordially.

"I might. And I might not. Sir."

"Cut out the sir and the mister," said John. "This is a vacation for both of us. Call me John, like people in the real world. How long have you been here?"

"Jest a week, now . . . John," he said, tentative at using an officer's first name. "My name's Mike. How 'bout you?"

"I just got in yesterday, Mike. I don't know much about the place yet."

"Figured that. You stayin' in an EM's hotel and all. Most ever'body here is enlisted."

"That makes sense. My crew chief recommended it. *Machts nicht*."

"Huh?"

"German for I don't give a shit," John freely translated.

"Well, you picked a good place, boy . . . er, sorry . . . John. Every afternoon this pool is full of good-lookin' gook pussy. Hotel lets girls from Dino's Bar on the corner swim here during the day," Mike went on. "Hear tell it's good for business. Say, I got to go on now and see this girl, but how about we meet in Dino's this evening?"

"Sounds fine."

"'Bout nineteen hundred, then. Be seein' ya, hear?"

"Fine, Mike. See you then."

Probably a bunch of dogs in that bar, thought John as Mike ambled away.

After a swim, John went out to explore a little bit more of Bangkok. He had been told it was a lot like Saigon before that city had been overwhelmed by the war. Lining the streets, he saw dozens of store fronts with metal lattice work or metal roll doors to cover them at night. He bought two cigarette lighter housings into which you could slide a Zippo. They were made of silver, with oriental designs worked into the sides. He would send them to his two closest friends back in Utah. He also bought a star sapphire ring for himself. The way it reflected the sun intrigued him.

Meat markets and produce markets fronted every street. The size of everything was scaled down, the way it was in Vietnam. Cars, stores, stools, and tables were all made for small people. He got on a nearly empty bus that had scaled-down seats. If two Americans sat on one seat, the outside man would be half in the aisle. He had no idea where the bus was going, but if he got lost, he could catch a cab.

With all the empty seats to choose from, the next Thai who got on came back and sat next to John. What is this, thought John? Is this guy queer? There seemed to be a lot of queers in that part of the world—guys holding hands. Having the man so close made John sweat. The guy was probably just curious, but John realized that the bus was going out of the city, anyway, and got off. He found a taxi and had it let him off near the hotel. Sampling food and trying shops would pass the time until 1900 hours.

Then he would end up, as all soliders did in the evening, in a bar. Bars were the centers of bachelor life in foreign cities. It was the gathering place where you found a surrogate family.

For the most part, officers and enlisted men kept out of each other's gathering places. That might be difficult in an R & R city, but officers always tried to do things with a little more "class," even though their drives, motives, loneliness, and hangups were the same as the enlisted men's.

As a warrant officer, John was not supposed to be an "officer and gentlemen" in quite the full sense, and anyway, he worked so closely with enlisted men in the helicopter that he had no trouble feeling comfortable with them. However, he did have officer status, and the line could not be crossed completely. Enlisted men would never allow an officer to be one of them.

To hell with it. He would keep his date with Mike at Dino's Bar and stay on at the Crown.

13

OOD

DINO'S BAR WAS NOT VERY INVITING FROM THE OUTSIDE, AND inside was even less so. The front door led directly into a dining area with a bar and booths. The place was far from clean, and it was extremely noisy. An inside door opened into a larger room with live music.

"Hey, Mister Vanvorden! Over here," called PFC Cumberland. Mike and an unusually big Thai girl sat on one side of a booth. She was pretty enough, except for a pinched look that drew her eyebrows together.

Making his way over to them, John saw a girl, evidently intended for him, sitting across from them. She was a knockout. When she stood up to greet him, she smiled, displaying a perfect set of teeth. She was not very tall, and her tight-fitting dress revealed a flawless, sensual body.

"Meet my friends, Mister Vanvorden," Mike said. "This here is Senowin and this is Ood. Ood is strictly officer material."

Ignoring the crude remark, John took Ood's hand. "I'm glad to meet you," he said, adding absently, "Nice to meet you, too, Senowin. My name's John."

Ood took her hand away and put both palms together in front of her face with her eyes downcast, in a traditional Thai greeting expressing humility. "*Sawadi.*"

"*Shawadi,*" said Senowin, sounding drunk.

Mike beamed, pleased with himself.

"Ood only comes here to see her girl friends," said Mike. "She doesn't pick up GIs. Senowin tells me she's between boy friends."

"That man not nice," said Ood.

"Try to be nice, Mike," said John. "At least he introduced us," he said, turning to Ood.

Ood looked up at him as if he were a movie star. "Sometime he nice," she said, smiling.

The two sat down together on the red vinyl seats with red vinyl tape covering rips here and there. "Would anybody like something to eat or drink?" John asked.

"Senowin's always hungry," said Mike. "She ain't fat, but she's big."

"Senowin not hungry. Senowin thirsty." Her voice was surly.

"Why don't ya hold off for a while?" asked Mike.

Senowin raised her voice. "I want beer!"

A waitress walked over to take their order. "You better not pass out before midnight," Mike warned Senowin.

"This my friend Tuffy," said Ood, introducing the waitress.

"Hi, Tuffy," said John.

"Don't mess with Tuffy," said Mike. "She can fight."

"You give me money for juke box, huh?"

Ood pushed her outstretched hand away. "We play juke box. You bring two fry rice."

"And a Singha for me," said John. It wasn't great beer, but it grew on you.

Ood and John went over to the juke box, competing with the live music through the inner door. "Please play 'Et Dez a Wek,' " said Ood. The title sounded familiar somehow, but John could not place it. Ood took the coin and punched A9—the Beatles' "Eight Days a Week." Tuffy came over and tugged Ood into dancing with her. John went back to the booth and stared at Ood's body moving under the short, tight dress. The other men in the room eyed her, too, with envy.

"I like Beatles," Ood said when she came back.

"So do I," said John.

While they talked, John picked up a few Thai words from Ood. He tried to say a few words to Senowin, but she was not interested in conversation. Sex was on her mind, and she kept pawing Mike until he finally excused himself and the two of them left.

"Would you like to go in there and dance?" asked John, pointing to the next room.

"I don' like that room too much."

"Just one slow dance?"

"Okay." She put her hand on his cheek. "You are beautiful man." She was no goddess like the woman in the Orchid Room. Her face was pure Asian, with a flat nose and wide-set, large brown eyes. Her complexion was dark. But she was beautiful.

They danced. John could scarcely believe his luck. Two days earlier, he was in a hell hole. Now he was there, holding an incredible body in his arms. When he tightened his arms, Ood returned the embrace. "Will you stay with me?" he asked, holding her even tighter.

"I no like stay at Crown," she said. "You come my house."

There was always the possibility of ambush, but John dismissed that fleeting thought and accepted the offer as a compliment.

"I'll have to get some clothes."

"No need clothes."

"Wait just a minute while I go get a couple of things up in my room."

He ran up and back. A taxi took them to a newly built residential section of the town. The houses were all one or two stories and made of unpainted wood. Ood's was a one-story building with a small living room, a bigger bedroom, and a tiny kitchen.

In the moonless dark, they had negotiated a series of narrow boardwalks to the door, and John speculated that the whole section might be built over water.

"Now we wash," said Ood firmly when they were inside.

Unzipping her tight-fitting dress, she pulled it off over her head. Then she slipped out of her panties. Her breasts were firm and well shaped, her stomach flat, her buttocks round and smooth. He was amazed that at nineteen, the age she had given, she had almost no pubic hair. He stripped hastily and followed her to the back.

There was a washroom with screened walls protected by louvered slats. The floor was concrete and inclined to a metal drain. On one side was a single water spigot, on the other an Asian-style toilet made for squatting. Ood presented him with a washcloth, and they both began to wash themselves down in the cold water, which gave John goose bumps but did not affect Ood. She seemed fascinated by his fairness, the white skin of his rump, the blondness of his pubic hair. He could not keep his eyes off her smooth brown body. After the washing, they toweled each other.

In the bedroom, John got into the large, low, comfortable bed and pulled up the sheet, all that was needed in the tropical night air. Ood lit some incense near the head of the bed and switched on a fan near the foot to keep away the occasional mosquitoes that got into the screened house. She turned out the lights and slid in beside him. It was heaven on earth to feel the gentle breeze from the fan sweeping over the bed and the loving female beside him. He would never, as long as he lived, forget that first night with Ood.

For the next four days, John stayed in Ood's house. All the houses in that neighborhood were on stilts, built over a klong, one of those canals that crosshatched the city, a port built on an alluvial plain. The network of klongs had once been the main transportation system in Bangkok. All the garbage and sewage from the canals ended up in the Gulf of Siam. Rain run-off kept the water moving, and the smell was not bad.

Everyone in the neighborhood wore sarongs. Ood taught John to take the joined length of cloth, usually of bright patterned cotton and to hold the excess out to the side with one hand. With the other, he could form a crease, then fold it back and tuck it in, much as a bath towel might be held in place. The women wore their sarongs above the breasts, with the hem falling to the knee. Men formed their cloth tubes at the waist, the length falling to the ankle.

Ood looked different in the daytime at home, younger, with her face clean of makeup and her long, jet-black hair pulled back. She looked wholly Asian. But the word "gook" never occurred to him. He began to think of her and her people as equal to Westerners; in some ways, perhaps even superior.

Sometimes he felt ashamed that this recognition of human equality was so recent. He knew that Asians were also guilty of racism, but that did not lessen his shame, a feeling he carefully reserved for Thailand. If he thought of Vietnamese the same way, he would have more trouble. If you had to fight, killing an inferior was easier.

Ood announced that she must go to work that afternoon. It was not the money, which he offered to give her; it was her position as a hostess in a high-class bar. If she did not show up regularly, she would lose the job. Her love affairs, from which she gained presents of clothes and furniture and money, were separate from her work. She even refused to tell him the address of the bar. By drawing that line, Ood kept her sense of honor and independence.

"You come back tomorrow noon," she said.

Tuffy was in the bar at Dino's and immediately tackled John when he walked in. "*Ood bai nai?*"

"Huh?"

"Where my friend Ood?"

"She went to work," said John, his irritation showing.

"You mad now. Sorry 'bout that," said Tuffy, who was far from good-looking but bright. "Never mind. Ood really like you. Gimme money juke box."

"Take a handful," said John, pulling change out of his pocket.

"You and Mike good GIs. You gimme money for song."

Mike came in just as John ordered a Singha. Passing Tuffy, he slapped her rear. "Ya filchin' money for song again, Tuffy? Hey, where the hell ya been?" he asked John, joining him on the next bar stool. "I been lookin' in here every night for you, Mister Vanvorden."

"Call me Dutchman if you like it better than John, but don't call me Mister Vanvorden."

"Right, Dutchman. Where you been?"

"I stayed over at Ood's house for a few days."

"Hey," said Mike with strong disapproval, "you ain't turnin' gook on me, are ya?"

John answered stiffly. "What do you mean by that?"

Mike covered himself. "Hell, I was just joshin'."

"Well, don't," said John, his voice friendly again. "She's a fine girl, and I don't like her called gook."

Mike looked baffled but kept quiet. He could not think of Asians as human beings. Gooks were the enemy, and he himself had collected ears from their heads.

"I'd like to try one more before I go back to Nam, but I can't shake Senowin. She's in there." He jerked his thumb toward the dark room where people were dancing. "I promised to take her to Pattaya. That's how I got her in the first place. Now she checks on me all the time. I'm getting so I can't stand her, but one thing at least, she's sure a wild fuck."

"Pattaya's a beach resort, right?"

"Hey, man, would ya'll go to Pattaya with us? That way, I wouldn't have to spend the whole time talkin' to that Amazon wino!"

"If Ood would like to go . . ."

"You kiddin'? All them gook bitches talk about is going to Pattaya! Where you been?"

"Leave that gook talk in Vietnam!" said John between his teeth.

"Oh, goddam it. Sorry." Mike paused as if reconsidering his invitation. "Well, I'd still like ya'll to come with us."

Senowin came in from the dark room. She was drunk.

"How come you no dance with me?" she demanded of Mike, her words slurred. John said hi, but she ignored him. "How come?"

"I told you I had to get some cigarettes," said Mike.

"You lie."

"I don't." He held up a fresh pack.

"You come dance now."

"Wait a minute. We're all goin' to Pattaya tomorrow."

Her pinched eyebrows sprang apart. "We go to Pattaya?"

"That's right, girl. Ol' Mike comes through."

Tuffy, from behind the bar, asked if anybody wanted anything.

"He don' need you!" said Senowin. The two girls exchanged what sounded like impolite phrases in Thai.

"Come on, tiger," said Mike to Senowin. "Let's go dance."

"I guess I'll go get some sleep," said John to Tuffy. "You better be careful with that one, Tuffy. She's mean."

"*Mai ben lai*. Senowin no sweat," said Tuffy.

"Okay, Tuffy. Night."

"No sweat, GI," she repeated.

The next day, Ood was ready to go to Pattaya the moment John brought up the subject. She wanted a new swim suit first. While they shopped, Mike made travel arrangements. He took John's ration card and his own and bought all the cigarettes he could get at a small PX down the street inside a military service club. He also had some cartons he had brought from Nam for trading. Ten cartons, worth about 1,400 bäht on the black market, were enough for the cab driver, provided they bought his meals. His cab was a Datsun. He would spend the night in the rear seat and bring them back the following afternoon.

It was 120 kilometers to Pattaya, but there wasn't much traffic midweek. Mike sat in front with the driver for the trip, making it easier for him to ignore Senowin. The taxi moved along through the saturated heat, and John took off his shirt so air from the open window would keep him dry. After an hour, a roadside concession tempted them to stop for a drink. As they drew in, a double-decker bus loaded with high school students was about to leave. John got out of the cab bare to the waist. The teenagers leaned out of the windows to cheer and wave.

"What's all that about?" asked John.

"They yell at you," said Ood, beaming and taking his arm.

"Me? What for?"

"It's like you Miss America," said Ood. "You so handsome man. Strong. You know? Like movie star."

Ood looked proudly up at him and hugged his arm.

"Crazy," said John, turning to Mike, who was glaring at him enviously. Mike nodded, clicking his teeth.

After they finished their drinks and went back to the taxi, Senowin tried to crowd in front with Mike, but he would not let her.

The countryside was one rice paddy after another. There were curious single-prop windmills made of twisted boards that somehow spun in the wind, pumping water for irrigation. They were crude, but a big advance over the human treadmills in Vietnam.

Pattaya was a welcome relief from the densely populated city of Bangkok. The beach was wide and inviting, the water calm and warm. Vestiges of old Pattaya had survived the build up, accommodating the heavy influx of foreigners into Thailand in recent years. Mike and John rented two rundown but clean cabanas. It was a little like being on a honeymoon, thought John. Ood was obviously enjoying herself. They sent the driver to buy sea food and that night built a beach fire and made a huge platter of crab claws, butter, fried rice, and fruit.

Sitting at the dying fire on a star-lit beach, John felt somehow like a papa-san. The girls, Ood and even big, vulgar Senowin, were children. Into the silence, he said, "You ever hear of Goldilocks and the Seven Dwarfs?" Mike choked back a laugh, and the girls rolled their eyes suspiciously. "It's a true story," said John solemnly. "It's part of American history. You see, once upon a time there were seven dwarfs."

"What is doorvs?" asked Ood.

"Short people, real short, about so high," John held his hand near his navel.

"Oh, we have some, too," said Senowin.

"Right. Anyway, these dwarfs all lived in a little house, and their names were Sleepy, Happy, Grumpy, Dumpy, Sneezy, uh, Jumpy and, uh, Harpo."

"They all have reglar-sized balls?" asked Mike. The girls frowned at him. They wanted to hear the story.

"One day, when those dwarfs went to work in their star-sapphire mine, a little yellow-haired girl named Goldilocks came walking into their house."

"She have *gold* locks?" Senowin and Ood looked puzzled.

This is tough, thought John. "A curl of hair is called a lock," he explained. "Her hair was gold colored, see?"

"Oh."

"Well, she went in there because she was hungry, and I tell you, that tiny little girl made a big mess eating everything up. She dumped corn flakes all over, spilled milk, and all like that . . ."

"What is corn flakes?" asked Ood.

"It's like smashed rice that's turned brown." The girls grimaced. "Anyway, she broke a chair, too, and then she went upstairs and fell asleep on Harpo's bed."

"Why?"

"Ate too much, I guess."

"Maybe the dwarfs ate her," said Mike.

Both girls turned on him. "Shut up!" said Senowin. "She was sleeping?" Senowin asked John with rapt attention.

"Oh, yeah. And then, before long, the dwarfs came home. When they go to work, they are happy. They sing, 'Hi ho, Hi ho, Hi ho . . .' but when they come home, they are pissed. It's hard work in the mines. So they sing, 'Ug yuk, ug yuk, ug yuk . . .' "

Mike laughed, but the girls were silent. "When the dwarfs saw the mess the little girl made, they were really mad. None of their favorite food was left, like corn flakes with *nuoc mam*"—the girls grimaced again—"and as they were about to throw Goldilocks off the mountain, a handsome prince rode up on a big white horse. He grabbed her away from the dwarfs and clubbed a few of them. A prince is like a king's son. Afterward, he married Goldilocks, and they lived happily ever after."

"He save her," said Senowin with satisfaction.

"That's right. And this story shows how in America if you have gold hair, you will always get married and have a happy life."

"I glad I not live in America," said Ood, pulling a strand of her dark hair and looking at Senowin's.

The fire was nearly out. They kicked sand on it and said good night to each other. "Bedtime," said John to Ood, who smiled at him. He wondered what had possessed him to tell a story like that.

In the early morning, they hired a boat and driver and went water-skiing. The girls tried it once and gave up.

"You can say one thing for Senowin. She moves a hell of a lot of water," remarked Mike. After that, he and John did the skiing, while their dates applauded them.

On the sand, John was content to lie in the sun while Ood splashed about at the water's edge, running in and out of the gentle waves. Watching her in her new bikini, John kept shaking his head. Who would believe that? She had one beautiful body. Every so often, he called her over and touched her just to make sure she was real. Mike and Senowin came back with shells they had collected. Then the driver joined them, agitating for a return to Bangkok. Just before four o'clock, they loaded up and started back, with Mike in the front seat again and Senowin sulking in back with John and Ood. Ten minutes after they started along the road, the driver pulled into the parking lot of a restaurant.

"Best in Thailand," he said.

"You said you had to get back to Bangkok," said John.

"Best. This place close early."

"It's only four o'clock. . . . Oh, well, let's go on in and eat."

The proprietor greeted the driver like a long lost brother. Hell, thought John, he pulled us off the beach for this! He did not even feel very hungry, but when the platters began arriving, appetite followed. It was the best food he had eaten since he left the real world.

"Good's the Cag'ns back in N'Orleans," said Mike, gobbling the rest of his plateful. "Here, Dutchman, my share of the bill. Meet y'all in the car."

Mike was getting there ahead of Senowin so he could grab the front seat. When they walked outside and she saw him up front again, Senowin stopped in her tracks and squatted on the edge of the narrow sidewalk.

"Come on," said John.

Senowin just squatted, the way the Vietnamese did, as if she could stay there forever. Refusing to get up, she drew figures in the dirt with a stick. Obviously, she would not budge until she got the front seat.

Finally, Mike climbed out. "Goddam it. Okay, here you go," he said to Senowin as the driver took his place. Ood and John got into the back seat. Senowin grinned, stood up, and ran over to the left front side of the car. Mike grabbed her, threw her into the back, jumped in front, and yelled "Go!" to the driver, who took off at top speed.

"No gook whore's gonna tell me where to sit," said Mike. "No, sir."

They rode in silence until they came to the drink stand

where they had stopped the day before. The driver pulled in, and John walked across the road instead of going inside with the others. From the embankment, there appeared to be a ruin of some sort in the middle distance.

Ood joined him. "That old old Chinese city," she said. "See? Shaped like a boat."

The shape had puzzled John, but now he could see that the crumbling wall surrounding the ruined buildings rose to points like the bow and stern of a ship.

"China people come Thailand long ago. No can go home to China, so make city like boat going home to China."

"How about that! Why couldn't they go home?"

"China no let them in again."

John thought of refugees over the centuries. He thought of the streams of refugees in South Vietnam he had seen coming from the north, from the DMZ. Light from the setting sun gave the boat-shaped ruins a golden glow. He went closer to see better. He felt empathy for the banished Chinese, for he, too, was banished from his own home to this strange place.

"Bai home," said Ood, tugging his arm gently. "John, we go now, please, home."

It isn't home to me, he thought. But putting his arm protectively around her, he went with her back to the car.

14

BARS AND BUDDHA

On Mike's last night, John and Ood were to meet him and Senowin in Dino's for a small farewell party. John got there before Ood. Mike and Senowin were there, but not together. Senowin sat on a bar stool, swung around so that she could look at Mike, sitting alone in a booth. She held a bottle of beer loosely in her hand. Her legs and arms dangled; her mouth hung open. Christ, thought John, she's wiped out. Mike was staring straight ahead, refusing to look at her. John sat down opposite him.

"I ain't talkin' to Senowin," said Mike. "She's drunk. I think she's ready to kill me."

Senowin stood up, swayed, and gave Mike a stiff arm bump on the shoulder. "Hey." Mike ignored her. She bumped him again. "How come you don' dansh with me." Her scraggly hair was hanging in her eyes, and as she lifted the bottle to take another swig, Mike burst into belly laughter. "Drunk gook dame," he said, laughing harder.

Senowin attacked him, swinging and bouncing the bottle off his arm, which was raised to ward it off. Senowin began swinging wildly then, cursing in Thai. Mike backed up into the booth and held her off with his feet, laughing uproariously.

Tuffy came up and grabbed at Senowin to pull her away.

"I kill him!" yelled Senowin.

"You kill me first," said Tuffy, struggling with her.

The two women went down onto the floor, into the beer spilling from Senowin's bottle. No holds barred, they tore at each other. Tuffy's blouse was torn off her back, and her bra gave way, exposing her breasts. As the two big Thai girls wrestled, their skirts hiked up to their waists, a crowd gathered. John had never seen so many people in Dino's. The bartender moved in to break up the fight and was booed by the audience. When he fell down, slipping in the beer, a loud cheer went up. Someone helped pull him free of the melee as the girls got death locks on each other's hair.

A huge master sergeant waded in to help, pulling Senowin off the floor and holding her in a bear hug from behind. The bartender grabbed Tuffy, his hands cupping her breasts. Senowin went crazy, kicking, screaming, and swinging her arms, but the sergeant held her a foot from the floor as she flailed and kicked at him harmlessly. Then she suddenly went limp and passed out cold.

Mike had prudently split. It was only a matter of time before some MPs would show up. John spotted Ood coming in through the door and made his way to her.

"Let's go," he said.

"What happen?"

"Senowin and Tuffy had a fight."

"Oh," she said, unconcerned. Bar girl fights were common. "Let's go play pinball machine."

The place to which Ood led John was down on the waterfront. Sailors and marines hung out there. It was called Anchor and had two floors. Upstairs there were old wooden tables and chairs on a dirty wooden floor, but no bar. The one pinball machine had a line of girls waiting to play. Waiters came up to serve drinks. It was not as crowded or dirty as the ground floor, but just as noisy. John wished they could be on the beach again or could just go back to Ood's place.

One drunken bar girl started wailing and tipping over chairs until two marines talked her into having another drink and settling down. These Thais can't handle booze any better than the Indians in southern Utah, thought John. Ood, who drank little, looked like a kid while she waited intently for her turn at pinball. When she got to it, her eyes lit up, just like the machine.

He sat on a tall stool at the side. A short marine came over and leaned his forehead on John's shoulder. "Line for the pinball machine forms behind those girls," John said coolly.

"You got to hide me," said the marine. "The MPs are comin'."

A taller man joined them, less drunk, and said, "Hey, 'scuse my friend, but we're past curfew, and we got to be back on the ship before twelve."

It was after midnight. Two military police tramped up the stairs. One was navy shore patrol, the other a marine. They headed for the men with John. "You two, come with us."

John was in civvies, but he summoned his best officer manner. "What's the problem?"

"We're taking these two back to the ship, sir," said the navy man. "They've been AWOL two days."

"How about I see they get back to the ship," offered John, feeling somehow responsible for the little fellow.

The MPs looked at each other. "Well, I guess that would be all right."

"Let's go," said John. "Ood, come on. We have to take these two back to their ship."

John left the MPs looking blank and walked down the stairs with Ood and the marines. He was glad to leave the place. Once outside, he turned to the strangers. "I'm turning you loose on your own recognizance," he said with a wink. "You better get moving."

The tall marine gave John the black man's fancy handshake,

motioned his friend to follow him, and disappeared down the street.

"We go home," said Ood with just a faint trace of reluctance. She seemed to sense John's sour mood. He felt grimy and beat from the crummy bar.

At four that morning, they were awakened by a sharp knock at the door. Ood ran out, tucking her sarong around her, and when John, after pulling his pants on, reached the front room, he saw a man in a white shirt at the front door with a wide leer on his face. Ood looked upset, so John charged at the man.

"Oh, *no*," shouted Ood, stepping in his way. "It's police."

The man still smiled. Behind him, in the shadows, were two uniformed Thais holding automatic rifles. The man in the white shirt said something to Ood in Thai.

"He say you no can stay here," Ood told John. "Law say no."

Through the doorway, John saw other GIs being turned out of the housing project. As one sailor, towed in handcuffs, went past the door, he looked in. Blood was running from his nose and mouth, but he seemed to be feeling no pain.

Could have been me, thought John. "Now what do we do?" he asked Ood.

"I no want live here if I can't have friend stay."

"My room, then, until you find another place?"

The man in the white shirt would not let them close the front door. He waited until Ood and John were fully dressed and ready to leave.

"Sorry 'bout that," she said as they moved along the dark back street.

"Me, too."

There was little traffic at that hour, but finally a cab came along. For a big tip, he agreed to drive them to the Crown Hotel. It was not right to break the standard Ood had set for them, but there was no choice. John was uncomfortable as he led her to his room, but Ood was completely at home. She seemed to forget the incident at once. It was just one of those things she could not change. John did not like being rousted, but after Vietnam, it seemed a minor aggravation.

Lying down on the bed, Ood held out her arms for John to come to her.

For the rest of John's R & R, they stayed out of bars most of the time. Ood seemed content to show him around Bangkok or occasionally to slip back to her house with him and just relax.

One morning, he woke up very early, after they had taken the chance of spending the night at her place. Ood was in a corner of the bedroom on her knees. He had never noticed the small altar before which she knelt. It was recessed into a low closet and had a small curtain in front of it. The curtain was drawn now, and in front of the altar was a dish of fruit between two sticks of incense.

Ood shook her hands, palms together, and bowed, emphasizing what she was asking for in her silent prayers. He had seen people doing that in Vietnam. He did not know much about Buddhism except that it was the main religion in all of Indo-China. You came back to earth in another life. If you screwed up, you got to be a grasshopper or a frog or something bad. The words reincarnation and karma baffled him. Karma, he had gathered vaguely, was the record of your good and bad deeds in both your past lives and in this one. An individual took on new lives through being reincarnated until his bad debts were worked out—sort of sentences you served until you paid up and went on to another level. Nirvana or something, a distant Buddhist heaven where you were part of God.

Ood was embarrassed that John had caught her at prayers. She stood up and closed the curtain.

"You're a Buddhist," he said. She nodded. "Then why do you wear a cross?"

"So if some GI want to do something I don't like, I can show it to him."

"Did I ever do anything you didn't like?"

"No. Not you."

"Do you believe you come back here after you die?"

"Oh, yes. Man, woman. Come back many times."

"S'pose a man kills another man. Will he come back as a—snake?"

"Maybe not snake," she said seriously. "But he have problems."

"How do you know?"

"My teacher tell me. I believe."

There it was again. Unsupported belief. John did not like to think life ended at death, but he had not yet heard a good argument otherwise.

"Yeah, but you don't *know*."

Ood looked at him with pity. He was kind and friendly, her look said, but he was just a foreign GI, and there was no use trying to talk about such things.

"You hungry?" she asked brightly, and went toward the familiar kitchen to fix his breakfast.

It was the eighteenth day of his two-week R & R. He had long since decided to make it three weeks. Maybe he should make it four, but if he did, he might stay longer than that. He had better go back. On day twenty-one, he would go. What did he mean to Ood? He was just a "GI," a pilot. He felt the pull of combat as he thought about Nam. He needed to be back in the air again soon, flying Hueys. Buddy, that's it.

Sunday in Bangkok was special, the day of the Sunday market. It was held on a very large, hard-dirt field. On Saturday night, up went a maze of canopies, each connected to its neighbor, with walkways to protect the shoppers from sun or rain. Under most of the canopies were carpets and mats. Bangkok's answer to the American shopping mall, it brought together native handicrafts, food, light manufactured products, and foreign goods. There were also fortunetellers and entertainers.

A food peddler held up a round wicker tray of crisp, deep-fried three-inch-long roaches as John and Ood entered. "You like?" he asked. The roaches were laid side by side in a spiral, starting in the center and going round and round to the outside of the tray.

"Nice design," said John, "but no thanks."

Ood pulled him along to a food stall. "Buy us them, please," she said, pointing to some awful-looking things on sticks.

Foot-long squid had been stuck onto big lollipop sticks and pressed flat. They were candied. "Well, I'll be dipped!" said John, letting out his breath.

Ood held up two fingers.

"You go ahead. They're not my favorite."

Her pretty white teeth gnawed through the squid. She looked as happy as a kid going after an all-day sucker. John felt a cultural separation more powerful than this small difference between them. He could just imagine somebody in Utah trying to push squid lollipops at a state fair. He bet these people would go ape over cotton candy. . . .

For two hours they wandered through the market, emerging on the other side of the field. Just outside, a snake charmer was attracting a small crowd. He stood among his half-dozen large covered baskets, inside of which were deadly Indian cobras, or so Ood told him. A black velvet cloth was on the ground to collect bäht so the snake charmer would put on his show. A few GIs in the crowd had tossed in green.

The snake man looked very old, with many wrinkles in his skin, although his brown shoulders and arms were well muscled. His hair was as white as the undershirt he wore. As John and Ood worked their way to the front, the old man held out his hand, looking disgruntled. "Nee more monee." John added a few bäht to the collection on the cloth.

"Okay, now let's see something, you muthafuckah," said a black GI in the front row.

''Nee more monee,'' repeated the old man.

A few more coins were tossed down. The pile was not large, but it seemed a respectable amount, and no more was going to be given. Slowly, the old man bent over, picked up the cloth, folded it around the money, and popped it into one of the baskets. He got under the shoulder pole to which the baskets were attached and stood up with his load. The writhing snakes made the baskets bounce as he walked away.

''Well, you sorry muthafucka,'' shouted the black. ''What about the show? What about our bread?''

The old man did not look back. A few Thais in the crowd jabbered, sounding discontented. Several GIs cursed, and one flipped the snake charmer the finger, but no one tried to stop him, and no one followed.

John hailed a taxi and got in with Ood. ''Why did the snake man take the money and not give the show?''

''I think that nigger GI make him mad.''

''Hey, where'd you learn to say nigger?''

''White GI call black man nigger.''

''What do black GIs call the whites?''

''Monkey, I think.''

''You mean honky?''

''Honky. Yes.''

''You known many black soldiers?''

''I see niggers. In bar. Many niggers come Bangkok.''

''Nigger isn't a nice name, Ood, and honky isn't, either.''

''Why many GIs say not nice names?''

''Because GIs are not nice.''

''You nice. You beautiful.''

Warmth flooded John's heart. He felt like a good man. He was flattered. It was not allowable to fall in love with this girl.

''You know in Nam I have to kill people.''

''No. You pilot. Pilot no kill.'' She was very positive.

''Some pilots kill.''

"You no kill. You good."

"You kill me," he said. They laughed, and she hugged him tight.

John decided he would like to visit one of Bangkok's famous Buddhist temples before he went back to Nam. For some reason, the idea of a man or woman coming back many times, as Ood believed, intrigued him. It was reasonable to give people another chance. The poor or the crippled, for instance. But it had to be crap. You're born. You die. That's it. And you better settle for it.

Ood chose the temple they would visit. It was Wat Phra Keo, on the grounds of the royal palace, and its Buddha was called the "Emerald Buddha."

Inside the temple courtyard, it was clean, cool, and quiet. High walls kept out the street noises, and the ground was paved with stone. Within the square, mosaics of porcelain tile adorned the lesser temples. He picked up an English-language description of the Emerald Buddha and learned that it had been carved from a particularly fine piece of pale green jasper. Originally discovered in the early 1400s, it was removed from Thailand in 1552 and taken to the Lao kingdom. In 1778, it was recaptured by a general who became Rama I. Thais believed that so long as the Emerald Buddha remained in Thailand, it would be an independent country.

He had seen pictures of towering Buddhas made of stone or wood, but entering the main temple, John was startled to see how small the Emerald Buddha was, sitting high on top of a throne, out of reach. The diminutive statue and the crowded room aroused no feelings of reverence. Ood wanted to stay, but he decided to walk around in the courtyard.

On one side of a lesser temple, John sat down on a marble step in the shade. It was cool, and there were few people about. A light breeze moved a line of bronze leaves hung under the eaves of the Emerald Buddha's temple. The tinking sound was to frighten the evil spirits away, according to the brochure. Indo-China had a long, turbulent history, thought

John. It had a religion deeply believed in by millions. These were things the Americans did not seem to care about. It was not easy to care about somebody's history or beliefs when they were lobbing mortar rounds at you or shooting at you with Russian-made bullets.

He leaned back against a mosaic and closed his eyes.

"We go now, okay?" Ood was standing in front of him.

"How did you find me?"

"Easy. No Thai sit there."

John jumped up. "Something wrong with sitting here?"

"No. Nothing wrong. Only bad luck."

"*Mai ben lai,*" he said.

"No sweat, GI!"

On the way back, he told her what she had already known. "I have to go back. Tomorrow. Back to Vietnam."

"Yeah?" said Ood, as if indifferent. "Good. I go back to work. But maybe I don't have job. Maybe fire me."

"No way," said John. "Your body is too great."

"My father call me pig when I was little. Ood is sound pig make."

"Pig go oink oink," said John.

"Thai pig go ood ood."

They laughed, and John realized how little he wanted to leave her. "Let's go to my room," he said.

They made love the rest of the afternoon. That night, John held her in his arms. It was like holding sand. Tomorrow would come. The sand was trickling from his hands. He knew and she knew that they would never see each other again. Ood's eyes were brightly glazed with tears she refused to shed.

✪ 15 ✪

REASSIGNMENT

WHAT DID SHE LOOK LIKE? JOHN COULD REMEMBER OOD, her form and the way she felt, but her face was losing clarity. His senses held the memories of the past three weeks more clearly. He could still smell the garlands of jasmine and hear the bronze leaves at the temple of the Emerald Buddha. Outside the C-130 that was carrying him back to Vietnam, he could see wispy cirrus clouds above and indistinct jungle far below. It was too short a trip from Bangkok to Cam Ranh for the adjustment he would have to make. If he continued thinking about Bangkok, he would drive himself crazy.

On the ground, his reversion was instantaneous. There were the sounds of war, distant, muffled explosions, screaming jet fighters, so many planes on the ground, wreckage. The smell. The garden that was Thailand had vanished, the way a dream does.

His orders and his personal belongings were waiting at battalion headquarters. He was reassigned to the sixty-first Assault Helicopter Company, 268th Combat Aviation Battalion, in An Son, close to Qui Nhon. His company was at Lane Army Heliport.

Mountains surrounded the heliport to the west and north. Perched on top of a hill in the middle of the camp was the officers' club, which served the half-dozen units spread around it. His unit, the Sixty-first, was on the north side of the hill. The billets were built in a terraced area. On the flat below were the ramp and revetments. It looked like a more comfortable setup than the 155th.

His first bit of business was to check into the orderly room to be introduced to the executive officer.

"Sir, a new officer in the company," reported the clerk.

"Send him in, Holmes." The XO—executive officer—was a balding captain sporting a mustache.

"Sir, Mister Vanvorden reporting for duty," John said, saluting. Then, before the man could reply, "Hey, cunt, is it you?"

The XO had spent some time in the 155th, minus the mustache. His unfortunate nickname derived from his real name, Robert H. Kant. He frowned at his despised nickname, then smiled at John.

"Yeah, it's me. How the hell you doing, anyway?"

"Great, sir. I just got back from R & R in Bangkok."

"Lucky you. I probably never will get mine. Too busy."

"You lifers love it over here!"

"The hell we do."

"When did you start the fuzz?"

Kant fingered his mustache. "My hair got thinner, so I had to do something."

"Might grow one myself," said John. "How long've you been XO?"

"About a month. The promotion came with it."

"Hell, you'll probably be a general before the war's over."

"Let's hope it doesn't last that long."

"Amen," said John.

"Come on, I'll show you around. You've been assigned to

the Second Platoon, under a guy we call Gorebag,'' said Kant.

''Gorebag?'' John started toward the outer room where he had left his weapons and personal stuff. ''What kind of name is that?''

''It's after some bad guy in the books he's always reading.''

John paused. ''What's he like?''

''Judge for yourself. Do you still go by ''the Dutchman'?''

''That's me. The Flying Dutchman. How did you know? They were still calling me newby when you left.''

''We heard a bit about the 155th and Ban Me Thuot before deactivation. Somebody over there had one hell of a trading operation going on.''

''Yeah. I heard about it.''

The XO shook his head. ''Things are too good here. No need for that sort of thing.''

''It wasn't that big a deal,'' said John, and the captain dropped the subject.

Kant showed John his quarters and introduced him to a few of the men in his platoon. He also pointed out the only bunker available to the Sixty-First. Not many even knew where it was, since An Son had never been hit. The XO let John know that he had a lot of respect for him as a combat-seasoned AC. The 155th had been a well-known outfit, with two presidential citations. Ban Me Thuot was known as pretty rough duty because it had been shelled so much over the years.

Back in the orderly room, Kant said the CO was on sick call. ''He has a cough,'' he told John.

''What's his name?''

''Major Parlow. He's not a bad sort. But Dutchman, I have to tell you, you won't be an AC in this unit right away. You have to learn the AO first, fly with the other ACs.''

It made sense to acquaint himself with the area of operations before flying AC, but John did not like feeling like a newby again.

''Guess I better get to my room and unpack.''

''Nice having you aboard, Vanvorden.''

"Thanks," said John, who almost felt like saluting. Roles changed in the military.

He felt less like a newby after he had flown with a half-dozen ACs at the Sixty-first. Nor was he treated as one. The company had been VIP and had done very little combat flying, so when the Sixty-First flew in its first combat assault in a joint operation with another company, John found out how really bad the ACs in his unit were. They knew only how to fly one formation, and that was trail, the easiest but the least effective for covering yourself. They had never flown the echelons, staggers, or vee formations, which kept the slicks in tight so the gunships could cover them. Furthermore, the trail formation they flew was ragged, strung out all over the place. Lead usually flew as if he were alone, and hardly anybody else could stay with him.

Once into the landing zone, the first ship to unload took off. It did not seem to matter whether it was lead, trail, or in the middle. The integrity of the flight was ruined immediately, and the gunships did not know who to cover. John made a private resolve that there would be some changes made. It was his life, too, at stake.

One day, when John was flying peter pilot for an AC called Buck, a colonel, flying with them, wanted to do a visual recon of a road on which he planned to move a convoy. The road wound through high trees that sometimes obscured it from view.

John was handling the controls and had the ship at 2,000 feet when the colonel asked if they could go lower so he could see better.

"Sure," said John. He spiraled down to fifty feet above the trees, rolled out, and zoomed along the road at high speed, dodging back and forth—normal flight procedure in a combat zone.

"No, no," said the colonel. "A little higher. I can't see this close."

"Okay," said John as he pulled the nose back and shot up to two thousand feet as if nothing could hold the ship down.

The colonel did not like it that high, either. Buck took over. "No," he said, "like this," and flew down to three hundred feet and sixty knots.

It was the best altitude and air speed for looking at the road, but at that range, any helicopter could easily be shot down. One bullet in the wrong place was all it would take.

"What the hell are you doing?" John looked over at Buck.

"This is what he wanted to see," said Buck smugly.

"You're crazy. We'll get shot out of the sky!"

"They can't hit us."

"The hell they can't. You're supposed to be above two thousand or below fifty."

"I don't have to."

"You by God better."

"I'm not gonna."

"Get up or down or I'm taking over this aircraft," said John.

"You wouldn't dare!"

"Get up or down!"

"You mess with me, you're in a lot of trouble."

John lurched over and smacked the AC hard on the helmet. Then he took control, dove for the treetops to build up air speed, and shot up to two thousand feet.

"What the hell's going on?" asked the colonel, who had not listened in on the intercom.

"Sir, this aircraft commander doesn't know what the hell he is doing," said John. "If we continued to fly at three hundred feet, we'd probably die. It's within effective small-arms fire range, and we were sitting ducks, and I'm not flying at that altitude."

"I've seen enough. Let's go home," said the colonel.

All the way back, Buck had a sly sort of smile on his face. He figured he had the Dutchman's ass. It was a cardinal rule that the peter pilot never, under any circumstances, took the controls unless the AC was wounded.

"You're in big trouble," he told John after they had let the colonel off and returned to the post.

In a very few minutes, John was called in to see the CO. Major Parlow was on his third tour as a combat pilot. He knew about flying in Nam. John planned to stand on his AC orders from the 155th and the fact that he had more hours and experience than Buck.

"What the hell is the story, Mister Vanvorden?" the major asked him.

At the end of John's careful explanation, the CO commented, "Buck is an idiot. But you're pretty new to this outfit, Vanvorden, and this is a lousy way to start. You won't make many friends around here."

"I don't care," said John. "I want to live. I got a mission to do. I want to complete my mission and get through it alive."

"I can correct some of the problem. We'll just cut you AC orders tomorrow. You can keep out of that other pilot's way—and out of the way of his friends."

"Yes, sir. Thank you. Good deal."

Several of the ACs were less than friendly after that. They resented the way he had treated Buck, but John didn't care. He was gaining influence over other pilots and doing what he could to pass on all that he knew about the importance of procedures in combat. Big missions were coming up. He already knew some of the areas better than anybody else since the Sixty-First's AO had expanded to include much of what had once been covered by the 155th. There were arguments, of course, but the CO usually backed John. It was important to improve the ability of his company now that they were flying serious missions. John's reputation had preceded him to some extent, and now word was getting around that the Flying Dutchman was the best combat AC they had. As a result, the unit began to shape up.

Before a combat assault, the landing area was routinely "prepped" with a B-52 bombing run, followed by artillery. During the aerial bombardment, while perhaps a half-dozen B-52s dropped sixty five-hundred-pound bombs each, the flight of helicopters would be closing from ten miles away. The flashes and shock waves, clearly visible at that distance, were what gave these bombing runs the name Arc Light.

Timetables guided everything. Radio communications confirmed each action. Artillery opened up following the B-52s. As many as three batteries were aimed at the landing zone and surrounding area. Shooting was continuous until the flight was ten seconds to landing. The fire knocked out any mechanical mines and, it was hoped, killed or drove away the enemy from the LZ.

Ten seconds after the final blast, the lead pilot should hear from the artillery batteries, "Last round on the ground tubes clear," and then go in. If no such word came, he would break out of approach until it did.

The next move was for the gunners to open up with their M-60s. Sixteen helicopters meant thirty-two machine guns blasting at the trees and LZ perimeter. Gunships fore and aft shot rockets and miniguns simultaneously. Good radio procedure was paramount. UHF radio was used for company frequencies, VHF for interplatoon communication, and other frequencies kept the air force tuned in. The lead had to monitor several signals at the same time, so extra chatter was confusing and dangerous. The rule was to stay off the air unless you had business. Air to ground communication on FM radio kept the artillery batteries and the troop commander in touch once the troops were inserted.

Ground troops began unloading instantly upon landing. It took less than a minute if done right because all the helicopters landed at the same time. As soon as a chopper was unloaded, it picked up and hovered a few feet off the ground. Trail watched for the moment they were all hovering and said, "Lead, your flight is up." The flight then went out at low level, with the gunnies flying front and rear, while the ground troops provided cover fire for the LZ.

Lead ship was the most critical position in the flight. Lead had to fly at proper speeds and make turns the rest of the flight could keep up with. The lead pilot was the only one who knew at each moment where the flight was going. If he got lost, everybody got lost, because each AC flew position maintaining a six-foot rotor distance, or less, from the ship in front of him. An AC could not take a split-second look at instruments, let alone a map. Instruments were the peter pilot's job.

Flight integrity allowed the gunships to cover the helicopters, a formation at a time. The pilots had to trust each other. There were only two reasons for breaking out of formation: aircraft trouble or human injuries.

John flew lead ship during the Sixty-first's first really hot CA. No sooner had the formation got off the ground than it began taking fire. All the ships were getting hit. Bullets penetrated lead ship's cockpit. Shrapnel and other pieces of metal ricocheted as John and his peter pilot ducked their heads and blasted out of the LZ.

He tried to maintain flight integrity, and according to standard operating procedure, as soon as his Huey was out of range of ground fire, he checked his flight. In the meantime, all the ACs were checking their crews.

''Everybody okay in here?'' asked John on the intercom.

''Instruments fine,'' said the peter pilot. ''The panel took a hit, but it doesn't look like anything is screwed up too bad.''

''Okay, it's yours. . . .''

The peter pilot took the controls, then looked over at John and started to scream. He froze on the controls and would not let go, so John smacked him to shock him loose.

John thought the peter pilot must be hit, but when the newby let go, he started yelling over the air, ''The Dutchman's hit! The Dutchman's hit!''

John looked down and saw blood smeared over his clothes, on his shirt, his legs, the floor. Wind coming into the cockpit was spattering the blood. Using his right hand to fly, he checked his body for wounds with his left.

He tried to concentrate. Where was he hit? A little blood

could cover a big area. Where was it coming from? He tried to feel pain. There was no pain. That frightened him. Not to feel pain meant that you were hit really bad. . . . He even felt lightheaded. Keying the mike, he said, "I'm hit. Lead is hit. . . ."

"Where?" asked someone in the flight.

"I don't know, but I'm bleeding like a stuck pig. I'm breaking formation and heading for a MASH unit. Chalk two, take over."

The peter pilot tried to grab control of the ship, but John did not like the wild look in his eyes. "Goddam it! Stop it. Chief, come help me with this crazy bastard. He won't let the controls alone."

His crew chief came forward, pulled the emergency release on the peter pilot's seat, and took him out of it. He seemed to settle down then. He was a good pilot normally, but he had not seen much action before. The crew chief stayed with him. John, worried he might pass out, cranked the ship around and headed for the mobile hospital. Diving into the landing area, he flared out, planted the Huey on the pad, shut everything down, and jumped out. As he ran into the medics, he started tearing off his clothes. When he pulled the left glove off, he tore his already-injured finger, yelled with pain, then sighed with relief. His finger was pumping out blood from a severed artery.

"Well, shit," he said. "Is that all it was?"

The doctor cauterized the wound with an electric needle to stop the bleeding, stitched up the finger, put on a bandage, gave John a tetanus shot, and that was it.

The other helicopters in his flight had followed him to the MASH unit to see how bad the Dutchman was hurt. Some of the ACs had looked into his ship and thought he really must have gotten it bad because of the blood splattered around the side of the cockpit. They all looked surprised when John walked out, holding up his bandaged finger and looking sheepish.

"That it?" asked Mac, an AC. "Just a finger?"

"You fucking gold brick," said Buck, who was in the flight. "We thought you were hurt!"

"What the hell's the matter with you guys?" asked John. "Would you be happier if I got my guts shot out?"

John, weary of heavy combat casualties, thought of his former unit. They would have been overjoyed that it was just a finger. Perhaps there would have been some mild joking, but they would have been happy because they knew all the ways you could get hurt. The reaction of these men reflected their inexperience rather than any dislike of John. The Sixty-First had a lot to learn.

16
SENIOR AC

AFTER GETTING SHOT IN THE FINGER, JOHN TOOK TO WEARING his sidearm in front of his groin when he flew. The Colt .45 automatic was one more piece of metal between him and a bullet that might have his name on it. He thought about seeing Oód again after this tour, but he shoved the memory out of his mind. Bangkok was peace and sanity. This was no place to think of peace. It weakened the survival instinct.

That instinct was vital, but there they took no incoming, and incoming shells were a continual reminder of war when you weren't flying. John did not miss crowding into the bunker with his platoon while rockets and mortars pounded everything topside, but he missed the resultant camaraderie, the *esprits de corps* that developed in that atmosphere. Platoons did not really hang together here and the spirit in this unit was low. In a lot of ways, it had been better at the 155th, and he missed his old friends.

One man could make a difference, though. He thought of his green market and what that had done for the 155th. What this unit needed was to learn to fly right for combat. He was gaining a following among the peter pilots, especially the newbys, who appreciated having the benefits of his experience. Teaching seemed to come naturally to John.

A new guy came in that evening while he was reading. "Mister Vanvorden?"

"Hi. Your name's Bates, isn't it?"

"William Bates."

"You go by Bill?" He hadn't asked earlier when the newby was flying peter pilot with him.

"No. William."

"Well, have a seat, William. What can I do for you?"

"Can we talk for a minute?"

"Sure. Let's talk."

"Well, I kinda haven't been here too long, and I don't know everything yet, but since I flew with you, I decided I would like to do a lot more flying with you."

"Thanks. You're in the first platoon now, aren't you? I'm due to go into that platoon pretty soon. Maybe we can do more flying then."

"I sure hope so," said Bates. "Those other ACs. I don't think they know what they are doing. Not after the way you showed me to fly."

"Anybody in particular?" asked John.

"Yeah. Captain Barnes is my platoon leader, and he scares hell out of me."

John knew the officer. He was a straight-arrow nerd who did everything by the book. His uniform was always pressed, his hair cut and brushed, his boots spit shined. And he was always clean-shaven. He did what John called "helicopter driving." His climb outs and descents were five hundred feet at sixty knots, and at altitude he accelerated to eighty knots. Barnes had taught his friend Buck to fly the same way. Now, after going out with John, the peter pilots were all scared to fly with Barnes. When John had first come, the captain's nickname, probably self-chosen, was the Red Baron. Now they called him the Red Barn.

"By the way," said John, changing the subject. "I usually ask my peter pilots—do you play chess?"

"Yeah, I do. Would you like to play?"

"I would. How about a game now?"

"Great," said Bates eagerly.

John had a chess set bequeathed to him by a rotating AC from the First Platoon, now short of pilots because of rotations back to the real world. The newby turned out to be better than Swede. John was drubbed in three straight games.

"Where did you learn to play that well?" he asked, putting away the set. "My ego is bruised."

"Well, I'm a grand master," said Bates.

"How many tournaments does it take to get to be one of those?"

"I've been in hundreds. . . ."

From then on, John called William "Master Bates" and so did the rest of the company. It was just three days after Master Bates had come to see him that John was assigned to the First Platoon.

At first, he had no reason to talk to Barnes, who was platoon leader, so for a while things went fine. Then, one morning in the shower room, John was admiring the mustache he had been recently nurturing when Captain Barnes arrived to shave at the adjacent sink.

"Mister Vanvorden," said Captain Barnes, "it's a good thing you're not in my platoon or I'd make you cut that thing off!"

"Yup, it's a good thing," said John, who had been in the platoon for two weeks now. According to the book, mustaches were not to extend beyond the corners of the mouth or hang over the top of the lip. John's was doing a little of both.

When the captain found out that John actually was in his platoon, he made him trim his mustache and tried to assign him extra duty, but the XO canceled the orders, exasperating Barnes.

There was a pilot named Samson assigned to the Sixty-First who had been in flight school with John. Samson, the most brilliant student in their graduating class, didn't look like much. He was medium-sized and quiet, so nobody guessed his special ability. Barnes despised him because he had refused to fly since his first month in Vietnam—six months earlier. While still new to the Sixty-First, Samson had been flying peter pilot on a point to point mission and was at the controls when the ship took heavy fire from the ground. He panicked. The AC, who had been catching some sleep, woke up in time, and they got out of it, but Samson was scared so badly that he went to the CO as soon as they were on the ground and announced he would not fly anymore.

With the CO's permission, Barnes gave Samson the most unpleasant assignments he could think of to get him to fly. He made him motor-pool officer and put him in charge of building new latrines and shit burning. After six months, Samson was so sick of shit details he decided that risking his life flying was better. He and John soon became friends because both were good pilots and both were disliked by the Red Barn.

Samson would be made AC the following week if he passed his check ride. He often flew peter pilot with John. On one routine combat support mission, having gotten off a little late, they clipped along at one hundred ten knots. Coming up on another helicopter, John keyed the mike and said, "Beep, beep," as he flew past. Two minutes later, he gave Samson the controls. Samson spiraled down into the LZ at one thousand feet per minute, the minimum descent rate for a good single-ship approach. Just before he touched down, John told him to go around again to make it down faster and more accurately. Samson made his second approach, still not good enough by the Dutchman's standards, but better.

The ship they passed followed them in at a plodding five hundred feet per minute. "Lucky One One, this is Lucky One Six," they heard over the air. That had to be the Red Barn. Six at the end meant commander, and One meant First Platoon.

"Go ahead, One Six, this is One One," said John.

"Just what in the hell do you think you're doing. What kind of a goddam landing do you call that?"

"Where are you, One Six?"

"On the other side of the fuel depot!"

"Give me time to shut down and we'll get off the air and talk about this."

Stupid of Barnes, thought John, to chew out an AC in front of his peter pilot and his crew, and doing it over the air was not only asinine but a violation of radio traffic rules.

When John got to Barnes, the platoon leader was fit to be tied. His jaws were tight, and the veins in his neck corded. The crew had followed John over and stood nearby.

"How fast was you goin' down?" yelled Barnes.

"Not too fast," said John, who thought the descent had been too slow.

"You were descending at least a thousand feet per minute. That's the worst flying I ever saw. Don't you know how to fly, boy?"

"What are you talking about?" asked John. "Come on; let's go over there and talk so we don't have to yell in front of these men!"

Red Barn stalked off, and John followed him. The crew started to come, too, but John stopped them. "Hey, guys. Hold up. This is between me and him."

"Ah, c'mon, Mister Vanvorden," pleaded the crew chief. "We never get any fun." None of the enlisted men gave a damn about rank, officers, gentlemen, or any of it. What could the brass do to them? Send them to Vietnam?

"You heard me," said John. He joined Barnes. "Now, what's this all about?"

"I'd better never see you fly in like that again or I'll pull your AC orders!"

"Pull them right now, then," said John, "because this is a nonsecure airfield. As far as I'm concerned, there aren't any secure landing zones in Vietnam, and I'll make a combat approach into all of them. A thousand feet a minute is too damn slow, if you want to know. There's no red line on the vertical speed indicator. The aircraft is capable of descents up to four thousand feet per minute if you do it right, and there's no reason in the world not to."

"You know what?" said Barnes. "I'm going to hang your balls from the flag pole. You are finished in this company!"

John stayed cool, stifling his anger. He did not want the commander to have him up for insubordination. With careful courtesy, he replied, "I won't lie to you. I'm going to fly as safely as possible, and that's the way I just landed."

"You won't for long!" yelled the captain, and stamped away.

There was a note on John's door when he returned from the mission. "Mister Vanvorden, report to the CO immediately."

John went right over. "Sir, Mister Vanvorden reporting as ordered."

"Sit down, John,"said the CO after returning his salute. John was surprised at the invitation and the CO's casual manner. "Now tell me about your problem with Captain Barnes."

At the end of his story, John said, "I was as polite as I could be."

"That fucking Red Barn!" said the CO as if John were not there. He had only a short time left on his tour of duty and was beyond caring about many things, but he looked at John as if he were a younger version of himself as a good combat pilot. "I'll fix him."

"I appreciate that," said John, "but he's going to be screwing me over, giving me bad efficiency reports and all that kind of stuff. I still work for the guy."

"How would you like to be company senior aircraft commander?"

Would I! John thought. "Yes, sir. But I don't know if I can handle it."

"You can handle it. There's no AC here that knows more than you do. I'll have the orders cut tomorrow morning. That way, Captain Barnes will have to fly the way you tell him to.

But John, back on the ground, he'll still be your boss. Don't forget it.''

''No, sir. I won't.''

''So stay under cover.''

''Yes, sir. Thank you, sir.''

''Dismissed,'' said the CO briskly.

17

ROKs

THE SIXTY-FIRST WAS SITUATED JUST NORTH OF A LARGE Republic of Korea, ROK, Army division, one of the military contingents sent by other countries to show support from the free world. The difference between the South Koreans and other nationalities such as the Australians or the Nationalist Chinese, for instance, was that they seemed to enjoy the violence. They were ruthless.

The Republic of Korea's division next to the Sixty-First had put out word as soon as they got there that if they took any incoming, any at all, they would burn down a strip of land around their base of operations measuring twenty kilometers by fifty. They listed the towns within the strip that would go up in smoke. That was why the VC set up no mortars.

Half the missions flown by the Sixty-First were in support of the Koreans. The ROKs had look out posts positioned strategically around a place the Americans had named ''Miami Beach.'' In addition to ROK combat support, the Sixty-First flew ash and trash missions three times a week to keep their outposts supplied.

The ferocious devotion to orders displayed by the Koreans could be amusing. If the ROKs were in an area they had not worked in for a while, they would pop smoke grenades as a helicopter approached, enabling the pilot to see exactly where they were. If it had been Americans, the GIs would pop one canister, but the ROKs always threw a half-dozen or so.

As a trick, John enjoyed sneaking up on them. After he had worked the area for two months, he knew the position of every LZ, and he always had a Korean interpreter on board for communication. One day, during a supply mission, the interpreter said, "AC, sir, they want to know if they should pop smoke."

"Yes, but tell them not to throw 'em until they see me."

The message was relayed, and John dropped the helicopter to a few feet off the trees and made a beeline for the LZ where the ROKs were waiting. They could hear him coming, so they pulled the pins, but they could not see the ship. Suddenly, the Huey roared into sight and landed just as ROK soldiers threw smoke grenades all around it. Master Bates nearly split a gut laughing. The smoke was so thick that John took off again to wait for it to clear, and that worried the Koreans, who thought they had done something wrong.

It was a while before John learned how violent this race from the north of China could be. Resupply missions, on the whole, were routine. Usually, there was a lot of equipment to move, and it took a full day of flying. With the exception of combat assaults, the American pilots were under orders to stop what they were doing and return to base at seventeen hundred hours. The mechanics needed time to service the helicopters, and besides, unsupported by gunships, it was dangerous out after sundown.

Occasionally, in the morning, the ROK officer in charge kept the pilot waiting several hours before he got underway. If five o'clock in the afternoon came around before the job was finished, the pilot had to leave, and that fact worried the ROK in charge of resupply. If an ROK screwed up, he was beaten up. Every ROK officer could kick the shit out of every one below him.

John had been kept waiting that particular morning, so at seventeen hundred hours, there was still a lot left to do. The officer in charge spoke some English and kept saying, "One more, one more!"

"One more," said John at five-thirty. "And that's IT."

John flew in one last load of ammo and Korean C rations and when he returned to dump some trash, the ROK officer yelled, "ONE MORE!"

"No way. I'm going home. I'm late already."

"We go now. We go. Just one more!" The ROK patted his sidearm.

"Hell,no. Get off my helicopter."

The ROK patted his forty-five again. "Go NOW."

"Chief, watch this guy. He's going to pull a gun," said John to the gunner over intercom. "Get off NOW!" he yelled at the Korean.

The officer, with a catlike movement, drew his forty-five and turned sideways so he could keep an eye on the crew. He pointed the gun at John's head and said, "We go NOW!"

Enlisted Koreans began throwing on more food and ammo. John just sat there. So did the ROK officer. When the ship was loaded, the ROK slammed the barrel of his gun under John's helmet into the right side of his throat. The pain was sudden. "NOW we GO."

John took off.

"Bates, take it," he said to his peter pilot. Using the floor-mike button so the ROK could not see what he was doing, John called out on Guard Channel and put the code for hijacking on the transponder: "Attention all aircraft in the area of Lima November. This is Lucky One One on guard. I am being hijacked by a South Korean and am headed for the ROK fire base two klicks west of Song Can."

The reply was immediate: "Lucky One One, this is Skip Jack Three Seven. I have a Phantom fire team here. We can be on your location in four minutes. Can you use us?"

John could tell the voice came from an F-4 because they had such great microphones. When the carrier wave clicked on, it sounded like the speaker was in his head.

"Sure," answered John. "Come on."

Another call came in: "Dutchman, we got a heavy-fire team of snakes here. Meet you ten minutes out of fire base and escort you in."

"I appreciate it," said John. Every time the Korean felt John talk, he jabbed the gun into his swollen neck. Despite the pain, John kept calm.

In less than ten minutes, three Cobra gunships flew up to the Huey in tight formation, one on each side and one in trail. It was a warning, and the ROK began to sweat. John prayed he wouldn't get too nervous. If the guy jerked his trigger finger, John's head would be in his lap. The fighters showed up next, making dry gunnery passes at the diamond formation of four helicopters. They could not fly slow enough for escort.

It did not look friendly to the South Koreans on the ground, especially after the F-4s made passes at them. As soon as Master Bates set the ship down, John got on the intercom to the door gunners. "Keep your guns trained on those ROKs out there. Don't help them unload."

The ground troops came to help. The ROK officer inside tried to push cargo out and still keep his pistol trained on John. The boxes were too heavy, so finally he stuck his automatic in his belt and bent to unload C rations. The crew chief took the barrel out of his machine gun and when the ROK was looking out the door, clubbed him in the back of the head. The officer fell in a heap in front of his subordinates, and Master Bates pulled a max take-off. As they flew away, the gunners kicked out the remaining boxes. For good measure, the Cobras made several low passes as the F-4s circled overhead.

A full report to headquarters took two days, during which the hijacker's CO was informed of his officer's behavior.

"What'll happen to the guy?" John asked his CO, Major Parlow.

"Chances are they'll execute him."

"What?"

"He'll die," said the major.

He and John looked at each other. That kind of harsh discipline by the South Korean forces was to become legendary with the American units who worked with them.

There was a report to make to the CO and then to the battalion commander before John allowed himself to think much about what had happened. He lay in his bunk and stared at the ceiling. The furnishings in his hootch at the Sixty-First were all GI, unembellished with locally made furniture, floor coverings, or wall hangings. He did not feel as he had about Ban Me Thuot.

That Korean soldier would be executed. Would John ever run into his own executioner? He had had a number of close calls. As he thought about it, his neck began to feel sore again. How did one maximize one's own security in this godforsaken place? Of course, after eight months in the war zone, he was becoming a bit more careful. But in too much caution there was danger, too. He must not get old before his time. He still had a job to do and men whose safety might depend on him. . . .

His thoughts unexpectedly turned to Bangkok, but he pushed them away. Instead, he concentrated on a combat assault he knew was coming up. It involved an island thirty-one kilometers south of Qui Nhon and about halfway to Miami Beach. A large Vietnamese village had been established where a spit of land attached to the island. The island itself was reachable during low tide by a three hundred yards long and twenty yards wide sand bar. It had been learned that the villagers were Viet Cong sympathizers, which merely meant that the VC were there. If the VC wanted to play in your back yard, you "sympathized." The Koreans had just discovered, after interrogating a captured VC, that there were VC and NVA in the village. Some NVA were also on the eastern part of the island, where they could enjoy the sun and surf.

If it had not been for the villagers, the operation would have been simple. The air force would have been sent in to bomb everything back to the Stone Age. Turning the Koreans loose on a village and island was scarcely more humane, but the American adviser had no choice, or so John had heard.

The CA on Miami Beach was big. An American adviser with the Koreans was to coordinate with command and control in the air. The Sixty-First was to provide air support. The operation began when the Koreans rolled up tanks and armored personnel carriers with twin fifties. They took up a position on the beach, where the spit of sand joined the mainland, to wait until low tide.

As soon as firm sand emerged, the Koreans drove toward the village. They met with stiff resistance, which surprised the adviser and the ROKs, who didn't know that the island held five combat-experienced companies. The only way anybody could get off the island was over the tanks or to swim for it.

When the ROKs started taking heavy fire from the village houses, the adviser called command and control. "I'm popping smoke. Have your gunnies shoot up everything immediately around us."

The white phosphorus marker went up in a straight plume on that calm day. Two cobras worked the surrounding houses with fleshette rockets. The nails did the job. Enemy fire around the tanks and APCs subsided. The Vietnamese translator then got on the bullhorn and told the VC to let the villagers go. No one came out. The villagers must have been too afraid to move.

"You got minigun up there?" asked the adviser, calling the gunnies.

"Affirmative on the minigun," came the reply from above.

"Listen, I want you guys to shoot up some minigun down the main street. Right down the center. Do a real hard run."

The snakes came in one after the other and shot up the main street at four thousand rounds a minute.

"Okay. That's working real good. They're coming out now. Don't shoot them."

Women and children began moving out of the houses toward the tanks in the main street. There were fifty or sixty of them, some carried, some dragged, none walking very fast. John, who had been circling out of range, was called in with two other slicks to begin evacuating the villagers. The chopper landed on the sand spit and waited for them.

"You gunners get out and help the people," John ordered. They all looked as if they had some kind of injury. Ten or twelve kids and mothers were packed in easily, they were so small and frail. The wailing was constant. John felt heavy, heavier than he had felt ever before in Nam, and the rest of the crew was on edge. Harvey, the peter pilot, turned pale, and John hauled him up sharply. "What's the matter, newby? This is what war's all about! Hurting and killing." When he had taken off and peeled back toward the mainland, he said, "you take it. Over to the Vietnamese medics."

Two trips evacuated all the freed villagers to the Vietnamese hospital at Qui Nhon. As soon as the village was cleared, the adviser called in all the gunships. "Now, you gunnies, go in hard. Level everything in this town."

Flying over, John looked down at the island. It was divided by two tree-covered hills with a saddle between them. To the east were beautiful, golden white beaches around a jade peninsula nestled in a blue sea. Death and destruction had come there that day. The gunships made pass after pass at the village on the west. When they ran out of ammo, they would go reload and come back at the village again. They did that all day long. It was like shooting fish in a barrel. . . .

Command and control got on guard and called out, "We got a barrel shoot here. Any armed helicopters or fighters in this vicinity that want to come and shoot up the enemy a little bit, we can use you."

So any plane that happened by would drop its ordnance on

the village. At the same time, John's company flew several hundred ROKs up into the saddle that cut the island. Those forces blocked the mass of VC and NVA on the island from escaping the village onto higher ground. The enemy soldiers who tried to swim for it were picked off from the air and turned into shark bait. At dark, the operation was halted until the next day.

When John and the rest of the First Platoon got to the island in the morning, the Koreans had already gone into the town in a pincer movement and cleaned out the VC and NVA. The other end of the island was wiped up, too.

"Flight this is Lucky One One," radioed John. "I'm going down to see if the adviser needs anybody lifted out of there. Two, you take lead."

Dropping out of formation, John landed on the beach near the village. From there, he could see eight large piles of bodies, each maybe twenty-five layers high, stacked on the beach. It was like a scene from a World War II documentary when the U.S. Marines were island hopping in the South Pacific. The Koreans were soaking the piles in fuel. Then they burned them. The smell of burning flesh from the human bonfires was overpowering. As soon as the adviser let him go, John thankfully took off.

The Korean commanders knew that some VC and NVA were still hiding out in the hills, and they did not intend to lose them. There was no way off the island. Within a week, the ROKs ended the operation. All enemy troops taking R and R on that green jewel in the South China Sea had been annihilated.

18

THE NEW CO

MAJOR PARLOW CALLED JOHN IN NOT LONG BEFORE HE WAS due to leave. He asked him to sit down, and it was obvious that he had something on his mind.

"I am about to break with military etiquette, son, because I want to talk to you about my replacement. I'm worried about his experience level, to be frank, and I'm worried about this company. Will you hear me out, Dutchman?"

"Yes, sir," said John.

"I haven't been the best CO I could have been," Parlow said. "We were a VIP unit, and then things changed too fast. You've helped a lot, John, and I have appreciated it. Now I'm asking you to keep a watch over my boys here. I know they have a CO and an XO and a platoon leader, but you are senior AC. You can keep them out of trouble. If you were regular army I could give you more authority, but W-2 is the best I can do. I'll speak to Captain Kant about listening to you on flight operational matters. He already does, I know, but strictly between us, I don't like turning things over to this Hayes."

"What's his name?" asked John. His breath stopped short.

"Captain Cortland B. Hayes, from some old military family in Virginia. He had an infantry command here in Nam in 1967, then went into helicopters. Now he's back in Vietnam with less than three hundred hours flight time, none of it combat."

John couldn't believe what he was hearing. How could it happen? He absent-mindedly rubbed the spot on his breastbone.

"Why can't Captain Kant take over for you, sir?"

"I have nothing to do with that decision," said Major Parlow. "All I can suggest is that you treat Hayes with respect. But if he starts fucking things up, you make sure between you and Kant things get done your way. You know the more we depend on the dinks to fly CAs, the more you have to cover yourselves."

The CO had no more to say. Of course, John would do what he could to protect against incompetence no matter what Major Parlow advised.

"I will speak to Captain Kant," said Parlow, and shook hands with John.

The news of Hayes nagged at John's insides. Luckily, he was busy, and he could push it to the back of his thoughts at times. However, Hayes would be on post, in charge, in four days. That couldn't be pushed back.

Giving prospective ACs their final check ride, a main duty of the senior AC, was one thing keeping John busy at present. An aircraft commander had to have three months in country and three hundred hours of flight time as a minimum. Normally, the ones chosen had five months and five hundred hours. It depended on whether the company was short of ACs, as it was now. A peter pilot named Greeny was next in line. Greeny had been in Nam four months and had flown with every AC in the company except John. He was very popular. He told a funny story for every occasion, and was the life of the party. He also took the newby hazing well.

During preflight on the day of his check ride, Greeny tried to get John in a good mood by being jocular.

"I ever tell you about the gook that liked it in the ear?" he asked.

"Nope," said John.

"Every time I tried to put it in her mouth she turned her head."

John did not laugh. "Let's get this over with, okay, Greeny?"

"Sure, Dutchman. Whatever you say. I heard you're good . . ."

Twenty minutes out, John pulled the circuit breaker on the six-pack instrument package. It was part of the test. From the beginning, new pilots were told and told again to be aware of changes in the gauges. The needles give you time to react to a potential hazard, such as falling transmission oil pressure. With no oil, the transmission seizes up in sixty to ninety seconds, which, from five thousand feet, is not enough time to descend at anything under several hundred miles per hour straight down.

Greeny went fifteen minutes without noticing the six-pack. With no gauges, John got nervous himself and periodically punched the breakers back in. The needle jumped each time he did it, but Greeny paid no attention.

Finally John put his hand over the gauges. "What are your instruments reading?"

Greeny took a look. "They're reading zero because you pulled the circuit breaker out."

"How long have they been reading zero?"

"Couldn't be more than two minutes."

"They've been off for over fifteen. Right now, you, me, the gunners, and seven troops could all be dead."

"Well, you win some, you lose some," said Greeny.

John felt like choking him. "You lost this one, newby."

He took the aircraft away from him and flew it back to the post. He did not say another word. Back at An Son, John refused the motion to make Greeny an AC. His decision did not sit well with several of the ACs, especially those unfriendly to the Dutchman. Red Barn was the most annoyed. The blackball could be overruled, but John knew Major Parlow would not do that.

Major Parlow had already been gone for two days when Captain Hayes arrived to assume his role as company commander. Most of the pilots were present at a meeting called to introduce the new CO. He made a good first impression. He was tall and aristocratic and gave commands in such a manner that men automatically obeyed. He had probably made a first-rate infantry commander, thought John as he stood back in the crowd of pilots. It had been a long time since flight school. Maybe the man would work out despite his shallow flight record.

"This is your senior aircraft commander, Warrant Officer John Vanvorden," said Kant, motioning to John.

John stepped forward out of the crowd and saluted. "How do you do, sir?"

Captain Hayes didn't salute back. He didn't say a word. He just nodded slightly and stared. It was an uncomfortable moment. John stepped back into the crowd, his fears confirmed. Difficulties lie ahead, he thought.

Hayes soon found out that the senior AC, now called the Flying Dutchman, was much respected when it came to combat flight decisions. In flight briefings, his opinion was solicited rather than the CO's. In no time, the CO was opposing John on operational decisions, and no matter how diplomatically John behaved, his advice was ignored by Captain Hayes.

Just a week after Hayes took command, the Red Barn appealed to him to make Greeny an AC. His tactic was to claim that Mister Vanvorden had blackballed Lieutenant Green because of a personality clash.

Captain Hayes, seizing a chance to gain popularity, overruled what he called "a hasty decision on the senior AC's part" and said his decision was "for the good of the company." Greeny's orders were cut, and Barnes gloated.

One week later, Greeny broke a cardinal rule of combat and overflew a known enemy position. He was shot down and crashed in a great ball of flame as fuel and ammunition ignited. Everyone on the helicopter, two pilots, two gunners, and seven U.S. infantrymen, were killed.

John knew each crew member who had gone down with Greeny. The deaths were senseless. He was senior AC, virtually in charge of training all the pilots. He was the one who could tell when they were ready to be responsible for the lives of the crewmen. The business of making war from the air was serious, but the system had permitted an incompetent like Captain Hayes to give a fool's command.

John was so enraged he went to the CO for a showdown. It was a risk. He could be court-martialed, which was not likely, or the CO could just make it rough for him. But what could be rougher than losing men unnecessarily? He had to take a stand whatever the consequences. Under the circumstances, an "accident" like Greeny's would make the CO look bad, which he must have known, and Hayes could not afford to get rid of John because too many of the older ACs had either DEROSed or were close to leaving.

Walking into the CO's office, John did not report properly but said, "Captain Hayes, we have to talk."

"Well, what is it, Mister Vanvorden?"

"With all due respect, eleven men are dead because that man Greeny was incompetent to command a helicopter and you gave him that authority. Overflying a known enemy position is something an AC never does if there is a way around. Those men died needlessly. What the hell business did you have making him an AC?"

"Who do you think you are, coming—" Hayes looked flabbergasted, as if no subordinate had ever spoken to him like this before. "Of course you lost men in wartime. It could have happened to anybody. . . ."

"Cut the crap, captain. It happened because of you. Now I want to know one thing. Are you going to listen to me, your senior aircraft commander, when it comes to flight operations, or are you going to get some more boys killed without reason?"

The captain pulled himself together and stood on his dignity. "I'll listen to you, Mister Vanvorden," he said in his deepest voice with a flavor of Virginia in his accent, "but you will show me the respect this command deserves."

"You will get the respect you deserve—sir." said John.

"Is that all, Mister Vanvorden?"

John was afraid he would really lose his temper and go for the captain's nose. He turned and walked out.

"Dismissed," said the CO.

The peter pilots came to visit John's hootch with increasing frequency. He was their teacher, and they were learning from him how to survive. The Sixty-First was no longer safe duty. They flew increasingly dangerous missions. Being with the Dutchman, even if only to play cards, made them feel better.

John tried not to be too friendly with the newbys. Since Arata had died in his lap, he had been aware that caring too much about any individual was dangerous. To a degree, he couldn't help himself, even though he only had three and a half months left. He should be withdrawing, but somehow he felt more responsible than ever. It was not right that tours in Vietnam were so short. Experience and expertise were continually drained away, and the result was needless casualties, ever increasing in number. The grunts and newbys knew it.

Already the peter pilots had somehow found out about John's showdown with the CO, although he had not said a word. The guys had all liked Greeny, and now almost everybody admitted they had been wrong about him. They were also wondering about Captain Hayes. John kept telling them to reserve judgment, but he himself was worried. He was in a constant struggle to prevent the captain from planning some sort of super screw up.

There were diversions to take John's mind off his problems,

like the day a big package arrived for him that had been forwarded from the now-defunct 155th. He carried it into his hootch where the card players had already gathered.

"You gonna call or what, Samson?" he heard as he came in the door.

"I fold . . . hey, seventh man's got to move out and let the Dutchman in, remember? What ya got there, Dutchman?"

"I don't know," said John. "I'm just going to open it."

"Good. A CARE package," said Holihan, licking his lips. Boxes of goodies were shared with whomever happened to be around. That was the unwritten rule.

"Stand in line!" John unsheathed his bayonet and slit three edges of the box top while everyone watched. Inside were Lipton chicken soup packets by the dozens.

"Well, I'll be damned! What do you think of that?" The Lipton Company had responded to John's letter sent at Christmas time. "Hey, here's a letter. . . ."

It was from the president. John read it and then passed it around.

January 15, 1971

Dear Mr. Vanvorden:

We received your letter dated December 25, 1970, with warm feelings. We are happy that our soup provided some degree of comfort to you in your present duty so far from home. Please accept this case of soup as a small token of our appreciation for the job you and your fellow servicemen are doing in Vietnam.

I am a veteran of World War II, and I know how you feel away from home. I spent eighteen months in the South Pacific driving the Japs out. I know you have not been supported very well back in the United States. We are having a lot of problems here, but I want you to know our company supports you men.

Sincerely,

A. Robin Phillips
President, Lipton Company

The pilots thought it was pretty cool that John had written on Christmas day about the soup and were delighted to get the packets he gave out. Only one man spoiled John's pleasure.

"Couldn't you ask for another flavor?" asked Tex.

"I didn't ask for anything," said John. "What are you complaining about?"

"I'm just not too wild about Jewish penicillin."

John visited operations regularly to check on what the CO was planning and to ask Captain Kant to hold Major Hayes down if he could. "You got to help me keep a handle on how these operations are being planned. You're the XO, Cunt, and you got the most influence."

"He's learning," said Kant. "What are you getting so upset about?"

"I want to know when he has something big up his sleeve.

Hayes wanted every operation to be big, which scared John because large operations were nearly impossible to keep secret. This was guerrilla warfare, and you rarely caught a large unit of North Vietnamese. They knew when something big was coming and could slip back into the jungle. If they stayed to fight, their ambushes could be devastating.

For large-scale operations, it was best to call in the B-52s and saturate bomb the suspected enemy area.

John had seen at first hand what heavy bombing could do. The First Armored Cavalry Division Air Mobile had developed an effective means of clearing LZs by strapping a ten thousand pound bomb to the underside of a Sky Crane and dropping it where they wanted the LZ. When the air force found out what the army was doing, they protested. They claimed dropping bombs was the job of the air force. The problem was that the air force did not have planes configured to drop ten thousand-pound bombs as the Sky Cranes could.

Some bright commander in the First Cavalry got around the air-force protest by putting delayed fuses on the ten thousand pounders and calling the operation "mine laying."

The air force then stuck two fifteen thousand-pound bombs into a C-130 cargo bay on rollers. When the plane was over the target, a parachute attached to one of the bombs was thrown out the back, catching the wind stream and ejecting the blockbuster. The open bay and the violent lurch upward when the bomb cleared the plane made this process somewhat hazardous for the "blue collar" bombadeers in back. Still, the kill zone was one-half mile in radius, and you did not need a bomb sight. The bombs were rigged with a six-foot pole on the nose to make sure they went off at ground zero to avoid blasting a moon crater. When one of those behemoths exploded, it looked like a nuke detonation. The mushroom cloud rose, and the blast pulverized everything it touched, while the shock wave killed every animal or human within a one-mile circle.

John flew lead into an LZ cleared by one of these "daisy cutters" north of Kontum. None of the men in the flight could forget what they saw. Dropped into dense jungle with a two-hundred-foot canopy, the blast had completely cleared a circle one hundred meters in diameter. The ground was baked hard. When the slicks landed their troops, there was not even dust. Stumps and trunks of trees ringed the hardpan circle. Running at a thirty-degree angle from the stumps were torn and burning trees as far as you could see. Sixteen slicks could land in the clearing at one time.

When the U.S. troops fanned out through the kill radius, there were no live enemy, only bodies. They spotted one camp where things looked normal, with NVA soldiers sitting up and lying down. They charged in shooting, but nothing moved. Everyone had been killed by concussion. Blood ran from their eyes, ears, noses, and anuses. No skin was broken, but their bones were shattered.

Outside the mile circle, they found several hundred NVA just wandering around. Some were blinded; others were seriously injured or in shock from concussion. Many strange stories had come out of the jungle about the effects of heavy bombing when it happened to catch a troop concentration. Now John believed them.

19
IN THE FOOT

"ALL THIS ACTION UP NORTH, WE MIGHT AS WELL MOVE UP there,'' said Holihan, John's peter pilot for the day.

He and John were in the operations building waiting for flight briefing on the scheduled combat assault. It was the fourth in a week. Headquarters was taking advantage of the good weather in the middle of the annual ARVN push to interdict men and supplies to the south. ''Don't blink your eyes,'' said John absently. ''We might take you boys off this cool beach and move up where it's hot.''

I ought to worry about my own safety, thought John. I'm too interested in these CAs and too proud of what we can do. I'm not getting paid enough for it. It was the training he had been giving the men for weeks that was paying off. The company could even fly echelon formations now. . . . Holihan was saying something. . . .

'' . . . so do you think I'm yellow?''

''No, ah, but could you run that by one more time? I was thinking about the CA.''

''I said sometimes I can't think about the next mission. I

shut the whole thing out of my mind. Does that make me a coward?''

I'm no chaplain, thought John. Why did guys talk like this to him? It got under his skin. ''Hell, I do that myself sometimes, Holihan. What kind of name is that, anyway? Don't anybody call you anything else?''

''Well, my father calls me Skipper on account of my way with sailboats.''

''That's better than Holihan.''

''Or Holy Land,'' said Holihan, making a face. ''That's what some stupid ass called me last night.''

''Tell you what to do. Paint 'Skipper' on your helmet, and that'll fix it. Here's the XO. Let's go.''

After the operations briefing, the pilots walked the half mile to the helipad. They carried all their equipment, guns, survival vest, helmet bag, plus the chicken plate, which weighed forty pounds. The half mile was a workout. Just as they reached the helicopter, John's plate slid out of the harness and landed edgewise on his left big toe.

John swore vigorously, hopping up and down on his uninjured foot. His left toe hurt like hell. He had seen a man with a broken toe, in a cast up to his knee. They would never let him fly with a cast. John did not want to be taken off flight status.

''Come on, Holihan, get in!'' he yelled.

''What about your foot?''

''It's fine. Get in!''

The CA this time turned out to be a milk run. His toe throbbed for a while, but then the pain eased up, and he forgot about it. After the first insertion, they got a call on UHF.

''Lucky One One this is White Horse Three.''

''Go ahead Three.''

''I got a call from a couple bird dogs who need assistance. Can you help them out?''

''Roger White Horse. What channel?''

"Go up channel eight. Call sign Red Bird Two One. Follow their instructions."

John informed his flight. "Lead, this is trail. I'm breaking to go with the bird dogs. Lucky One Two is now your trail."

"Roger One One. See you back home."

John fell back and dialed in the observation plane's frequency. Two of them were up, an air force Skymaster and an army bird dog.

"Red Bird, this is the Flying Dutchman. Can I assist?"

"Where are you, Flying Dutchman?"

"On the north side of the Phu Cat Mountains."

"We got a guy out here in the open on the south side. We want you to pick him up. We're about fifteen kilometers southeast of Phu Cat City."

"There in ten minutes," said John, heading for the location.

Cruising the treetops at one hundred twenty knots, John felt for an updraft to lift him over the jungle-covered mountains. When he caught one, the Huey rose like a rocket. John flew so close it felt like he could reach out and touch the trees on the steep mountain slope.

"I think I could do that next time," said Holihan as they popped over the green ridge.

"Catching on to this mountain stuff, are you?" said John.

"Aye ya."

"That's good. Next time you get to try it. But be sure you keep her close so Charlie won't get a good shot."

Rather than fly above two thousand feet once they were atop the ridge, John accelerated down the other side at treetop level.

"Yahoo," shouted the crew chief as they dropped down the cliffs like a falcon. Being that close to the trees and experiencing near zero Gs gave you a sudden rush no matter how many hours you had in the air.

The hills gave way to flat land and neglected rice paddies. For miles ahead, all they could see was tall grass. The spotter planes stayed high and vectored John in.

"Is this a Uniform Sierra or a Victor November?" he asked, using the code for a U.S. troop or a Vietnamese.

"Victor November, Flying Dutchman, Victor November."

Must be a wounded ARVN. With no cover, John flew just ten feet off the deck. The message came in. "A little left . . . more right . . . closing five hundred meters . . . three hundred meters . . . good . . . one hundred . . . okay, right now . . ."

John, from five feet overhead, saw the man kneeling in the tall grass, trying to hide. John banked hard around to the left, swung back, and landed right next to the man. "Get in," yelled John, with a roundhouse arm motion.

Instead, the Vietnamese jumped up and took off running.

Oh, no, thought John, this guy is an enemy. "Chief, keep your gun trained on him. Gunner, cover us from the other side."

The crew chief was a young kid from California, and as they herded the man with the helicopter, cutting off his escape, they could all see his shocked face. If John ordered the crew chief to shoot, he wasn't sure the youngster would be able to pull the trigger. Just then, the Vietnamese fell into a bomb crater filled with water. John could not see him now, so he drew the ship away, afraid the man would come out shooting. Instead, he burst out of the water like a missile and started running again.

"Enough of that," said John. "He isn't going to shoot." Flying forward, he knocked the Vietnamese over with the skid and landed. The crew chief jumped out and grabbed his captive, expecting a fight, but the Vietnamese just froze to the ground. The crew chief looked back at the Dutchman. "Get him in! Get him in!" yelled John.

They were sitting ducks for gunfire or mortars. The other gunner jumped out and helped to drag the man into the helicopter. John flew out of the paddies for Qui Nhon and radioed, "Qui Nhon tower, this is Lucky One One. We got a flight of three about two miles north for landing." Usually, nothing flew in formation with a helicopter except more helicopters, but the two slow-flying FACs, forward air controllers, could stay with the Huey. "We got one UH-1, one Oscar one, and one Oscar deuce for landing."

"Roger, Lucky One One. This I got to see. Cleared to land." It was a rare sight, two airplanes and a helicopter flying in formation.

John radioed the information about the prisoner before landing, and as soon as he set the Huey down, an American major and a half-dozen ARVNs ran up. The ARVNs took the prisoner off and began beating him.

The two FAC pilots came over as soon as they were out of their planes. The air-force captain grabbed John's hand. "Man, that was something to watch. That's the best thing I've seen since I've been here. The lieutenant and I are going to write you up for a commendation."

The army lieutenant held up a Pentax camera with a big telescopic lens. "We got it all on film, too!"

John jumped down from the Huey. A sharp pain from his left big toe shot up his leg and he winced.

"You all right, Dutchman?" asked the captain.

"Fine. It looked good from up there, huh?"

"Great. Top drawer. Come on, Mister Vanvorden, we'll buy you a beer."

The prisoner turned out to be a prize—a doctor and an NVA captain. The peasant clothes he wore had allowed him to slip into town to buy supplies for an NVA hospital in the Phu Cat Mountains. The ARVNs had been hunting for the hospital and staging area for five years without success. Now they knew where both hospital and an NVA sapper battalion were, and would get them the next day.

That night, when John got back to base, his foot was so swollen he could not get his boot off. He stayed in his hootch and took anything he could lay his hands on, aspirin, APC, to kill the pain. If he slept with his boot on, he figured the toe would be immobilized and might get better, just as if it had a cast on it. No way would he get taken off flight status if he could help it.

But by the second day, the pain was so intense he gave up and went to see the flight surgeon. When the doctor cut the boot off John's foot and pulled the sock off, the smell was enough to knock them out. The toenail came off with the sock, and the toe was swollen twice its normal size and had turned black around the edges. It reminded John of a peeled avocado cut and left out too long.

"Gangrene," said the doctor. "We'll have to amputate."

"No," said John. "No. I can't fly if I don't have a big toe." He did not know why, but he remembered that during his first flight physical, they had made sure everybody had all their toes and fingers. "You're not going to cut my toe off."

"It's fucked up bad. You'll have to go to Qui Nhon and get it x-rayed and have them look at it."

"We've got an x-ray here. The dentist has one," said John desperately.

"That's for teeth. It has only little slides."

"It's only a toe. It'll fit on the slides."

"Well, I guess we could try. I'll clean it up a bit first, but that's one fucked-up toe." He shot the foot full of anesthetic and cortisone, then took a scalpel and began cutting away the bad flesh. He sliced off the rest of the toenail, the pieces on the side, and all the spots that had turned black. Once in a while, he stopped to rub in iodine, then cut some more, spending about an hour picking at the toe to make sure he had cut away the infected parts. Then he soaked it and bandaged it and after that took John into the dentist's room for an x-ray, returning when the plate was developed.

"See?" The doctor held up the slide.

All John saw was a mass of lines. "I don't know what it means. Is that where the break is, there?"

"No. That's the knuckle. All those other lines mean you smashed that bone. You're going to have a hard time with it from now on. I really think you had better get that toe cut off."

"No way."

"You could lose your foot."

"How about giving me a lot of antibiotics and pump me full of drugs, doc, and see if we can fix it."

John spent the next week constantly soaking his toe in hydrogen peroxide and swallowing antibiotics. During the day, he read, and at night he played cards. Tex, Bates, and Samson were regulars in the games.

All the pilots were edgy, with the Dutchman temporarily out of action. It was the same feeling that had grown up in the 155th when Arata was gone. But being grounded was harder on John than on anyone else.

The games were acrimonious. Tex said he thought the shit the Dutchman was soaking his toe in gave him bad luck.

"Hell, Tex," said Samson. "Everything gives you bad luck. Why don't you just admit that Texans aren't smart enough to play cards?"

"Don't see you rollin' in chips, boy," said Tex nastily.

"Who you calling boy?"

"Oh, shut the hell up and let me think," said Master Bates.

Luckily, within a week and a half, John was flying again. For three days, the platoon was flying so hard in and out of the bush that he had no time to soak his toe much or change his socks very often. The first day off, he tried to make up for his neglect and was admiring his new toenail when he noticed a red patch on the new skin. He ignored it until the next day when he saw that the redness had spread over the whole foot. That night, his foot swelled up and hurt so much he could not sleep. In the morning, the medics sent him to Qui Nhon to the hospital. By the time a doctor came to look at his foot, it was huge. Blisters had formed, broken, and were weeping clear fluid.

"Hell, son," said the doctor when John had removed his wet sock, "I never saw anything like that, ever. I'll get you to a dermatologist."

John didn't mention the accident to his toe and the gangrene. The doctor ordered him to the hospital in Dan Nang immediately. He left on crutches, and by the time he hobbled into the Da Nang Airport Terminal, both feet, and both hands had it, and his right foot was swelling so fast he had to chuck his right boot, too. Both feet were turning black now, and he could hardly handle his crutches, his hands were so tender. Blisters popped as he gripped the handles, and fluid was running on to the crutches. A hole had developed in the bottom of his left foot about the size of a quarter and poured fluid.

The terminal was jammed with soldiers. John hobbled up to an information counter manned by a private. "I've got to go to the hospital. Can you get me some transportation?"

"Which hospital? There's three."

"I don't know. I got a bad skin thing. Do you know which one I ought to go to?"

"No idea . . ."

"Well, how can . . ."

A major pushed past John. "Look, I need to know how to get to Monkey Mountain."

John could have made a fuss, but the PFC obviously did not know anything, anyway. Then he found he could not walk anymore, so in total frustration he threw his crutches at the wall. They hit a hard-looking marine, who walked over to John with his fists doubled, yelling, "You throw them crutches at me, you da—"

John held out his hands. The marine made a face and faded back into the crowd as if John were a leper. John sat down on the floor.

A short, gray-haired WAC colonel came over. She had seen the whole thing. "Can I help you, mister"—she looked at his name tag—"Vanvorden? I'm a nurse. I'm going to the Ninety-Fifth Evacuation Hospital."

The little old lady with the silver leaves on her shoulders looked to John like an angel of mercy. "I could sure use your help, ma'am," he said. He felt feverish, and he hurt. She helped him stand up and held his elbow as he hopped with her out the door. A jeep was waiting, but it was piled over with bags and boxes. Before she left, she sent the driver to order an ambulance. He never saw her again, but he would think of her many times.

In about twenty minutes, the ambulance arrived and took John to the Ninety-Fifth Evac, where he sat in the emergency room until two doctors came to look at him.

"Well, what's the matter with you?" asked the short bald one.

John pulled off one sock and showed them his blackening foot. They both recoiled. "Well, we can't get you in here tonight. Come back tomorrow . . ."

John, at the end of his rope, blew up. "I'm not moving! I can't walk! And where the hell do I go? I'm sick. You doctors do something about it. There's supposed to be a dermatologist someplace, so go find him."

"Just a minute," said the first one, and disappeared.

At long last, an orderly came with a wheelchair and took John to a bed in the ambulatory ward. As soon as his head hit the pillow, he fell asleep, physically and mentally beat.

"Mister Vanvorden, Mister Vanvorden! The doctor is here!" A medical orderly stood by the side of the bed.

John struggled out of a dark sleep.

"I'm Colonel Ashton, the dermatologist," said a tall, gray-haired man at the foot of the bed.

"Colonel Ashton is the hospital commander," added the orderly.

"How do you do, sir," said John, trying to raise himself on his elbows.

"Take it easy," said the colonel. He took John's filthy socks off. "Why did you keep these on?"

"I was worried I better keep something on them . . ."

The doctor took the left foot in his hands, looked it over, spread the toes, and squeezed. It did not seem to bother him. "You've got a bit of a skin disease here," he said. "You'll be all right. We'll have you fixed up pretty soon." He started to walk away.

"It hurts a lot," said John. "Can you give me something

for it?" He wanted to be sure he could sleep.

"Sure." The doctor patted John on one foot. "Don't put your socks on."

"If I need to walk—"

"Doesn't matter. You aren't contagious."

The treatment consisted of massive shots of cortisone and some antibiotic pills. Whenever he was awake, he was told to soak his feet in an antiseptic solution. Although he was usually too tired to eat, they woke him each morning at 0600 hours. The nurse on the morning shift was Second Lieutenant Bradshaw. Since the ward was ambulatory, she expected John to get out of bed before breakfast and to walk to the nurses' station fifteen beds away to take his pills.

He stuck a note on the end of his bed with chewing gum that read, "DON'T FUCKING WAKE ME UP!" and lay there with a pillow over his head. Nurse Bradshaw just yelled down the ward, "Vanvorden! Vanvorden!" He had no trouble hating her, although she was a good-looking blond. After the second time he had struggled to the nurses' station on his sore feet to get his medicine, he said to her, "Next time you put the pills on the table by my bed, and I'll take them when I wake up."

She just smirked. She knew how to run her ward, and no malingerer was going to railroad her. John walked slowly back to his bed on the sides of his sore feet and figured he had a month's sleep to catch up on. Next time, he was not going to get up.

The ward was barely awake the next morning when Bradshaw started in on John from down at the nurse's station. "Vanvorden!" He held the pillow tight over his ears. "Vanvorden!" She came out from around the counter, and her heels clicked down the center of the rows of beds. She leaned down close to the pillow, shouted, "Vanvorden!" and poked him in the ribs.

John reacted in rage. His right arm shot out, and he grabbed Nurse Bradshaw by the scruff of the neck, jerking her down to him. He held his doubled fist in her face. "Listen here, you bitch, you wake me up again, I'll knock your head off!" He almost let her have one with his left. "My name's *Mister* Vanvorden, and I do not want to hear you yell Vanvorden across this doggone ward again!"

With her eyes so wide, she looked like a little frightened animal. To keep from hitting her, he shoved her away hard. She fell onto the patient in the next bed, who yelled out in pain, "Damn, girl, you trying to break my back?"

Second Lientenant Bradshaw recovered and ran out of the ward. Twenty minutes later, she was back with two MPs and a major, a doctor John had not seen before.

"Here he is," she said, standing well clear.

The MPs looked relaxed and made no moves. The doctor picked up John's chart and stood by the side of the bed.

John sat up, and the major saw his feet. They looked awful, dark brown to black, and puffed up. "Boy!" he said, shaking his head. "You're a helicopter pilot?"

"Yes, sir."

"You're just out of some tough action, eh?"

"We had it pretty rough," said John.

"Well, now, what's the problem?"

"I'm tired. I've been flying hard for weeks, and I'm sick. I don't want to be here, and I wouldn't be if I didn't have to. I'll take those pills if she just leaves them by the bed. That's all I want. Some peace and quiet!"

The major looked at the nurse, at John, then back at the nurse again. "Lieutenant," he said, "I expect you had better do what he asks, or he just might knock your head off." He turned and walked away while the MPs stood there grinning. Lieutenant Bradshaw whipped around, and the grins disappeared. She stalked back to the nurses' station, and the MPs walked out, elbowing each other.

"Welcome to tent city," said the man in the next bed.

John smiled. "Thanks. What are you in for?"

"Herniated disc. Got it riding too many tanks. Master Sergeant Paul Gebler, pleased to meet you."

"I'm John Vanvorden. Hope I didn't disturb you."

"Hell, boy," the old sergeant replied, "you been sleeping for three days, and when you wake up, you throw the nurse at me. Now normally I wouldn't mind, but not now, and not *that* nurse!"

"I damn near hit her," said John. "She drives me crazy."

"I been wanting to do something like that myself. Now if you want anything, food or anything, let me know. I gotta go take a leak." The sergeant rolled his big belly out of bed and took careful steps down the aisle. De facto leader of the ward, partly by reason of seniority, he waved, tapped beds, and spoke to every patient as he passed. Exchanges about Vanvorden and the battle with Nurse Bradshaw rippled down the ward, making John a celebrity.

That afternoon, he was sent to take a blood test. A corpsman tied a tube on his upper arm and started poking with a needle. Instead of taking the needle out when it didn't hit a vein, he kept working it around in the same hole. It did not hurt too much but was unpleasant to watch.

"How about pulling it out and trying again?" asked John.

The orderly pulled out the needle. To John's surprise, he looked over and saw some guy who looked exactly like him slumped in a chair with his eyes closed. The same corpsman was in front of the unconscious figure. John thought he must be back in bed, dreaming.

He watched the corpsman leave the room. Very soon, he came back with something he held under the double's nose. John realized that the double was himself and that the corpsman was trying to revive him. He watched with interest. Then the corpsman panicked as if he had killed John. That scared hell out of John, too, so he closed his eyes tight. When he took a peek, he saw himself again, still slumped in the chair. He tried to make a noise. Nnnnngh. Nnnnngh. If he could make a noise, he could return to his body and wake up. Nnngh nnnnnnnnngh—he wished somebody would shake him. Every time he peeked, he tried harder. Finally, he succeeded in producing a sound, got out a real *nnnnngh*—it felt good. A doctor came in and held John's body's head down between his legs.

"What's the matter? What's the matter?" the doctor yelled at him as he pushed hard on his neck.

His neck hurt. For a moment, that was all he could think about. "My neck," he said. "My neck hurts."

The doctor let him up.

John rubbed his neck. He was embarrassed. Obviously, he had passed out, but he decided he would act as if he had not. He held out his arm again and said to the corpsman, "You going to take my blood today or what?"

The corpsman was white as a sheet and shaking. He would take nobody's blood for the rest of that day. "You go back to your ward and have the nurse take it," ordered the doctor. "Sit down immediately if you think you might faint."

"Hate to come all the way over here for nothing," said John, acting nonchalant. "I never passed out before in my life. Don't worry about it."

"Sit down, anyway, just in case." The doctor saw him on his way.

Back in bed, John tried to figure what it all had meant. He had been outside himself. He had seen his body as plain as day. He held one hand in the other and stared.

After five days, John knew he was getting well. The swelling was almost gone, blisters and everything. There was hard brown skin, on both hands and feet, that began peeling off. It came off the toes in one piece, along with the nails. He lined his ten toes up on his table to freak people out. Underneath, the old skin was tender, new pink skin, including brand-new paper-thin pink toenails. They looked perfect, like a baby's.

The gunnery sergeant saw the toes on the table. "Goddam, boy, what are you doin' there?"

"Hanging ten. The hard way," said John.

Old Gebler was properly grossed out.

20
MARBLE MOUNTAIN

RUMOR WAS THAT COLONEL ASHTON WROTE ORDERS FOR men to go home on very flimsy medical excuses. His liberal policies were getting him some heat, but he was careful. The hospital was always at near capacity, and when he needed more room, he just medivacked men out, as if he had a mission to turn the Da Nang hospital into a safe haven from which as few men as possible went back into the war.

He argued with John, for whom he had already written orders for the states, but in the end, he relented. "I guess I'll have to let you stay. You're fit enough. But I insist you have rest first."

"I'm all right. I want to go back to my company," said John.

"Well, I'll report to your CO that I recommend another two weeks of rehabilitation. If he insists, you can go back in a few days."

John knew Hayes would not insist. On the contrary.

"Think about it," said Ashton. "If you change your mind, let me know."

He would not change his mind, but there did not seem to be much he could do about the next couple of weeks. Try to get strong. Try to find Roger. Ever since he got to Da Nang, it had been in the back of John's mind to visit him. As far as he knew, there was only one army Assault helicopter unit in the area, Roger's unit, the 282nd Assault Helicopter Company at Da Nang Marble Mountain.

The small mountain rising straight out of the coastal plain could not be bombed because it was considered a sacred shrine by the Vietnamese. Honeycombs of caves in the mountain, with their ancient religious carvings on the marble walls, hid unknown numbers of Viet Cong, but since it was surrounded by friendlies, the VC couldn't make too much use of it. It was just another thorn in the side of the American military.

John managed to commandeer a jeep and driver to take him to Marble Mountain.

The private did not know that the mountain was off limits. John had heard that the 282nd was within sight of the mountain and figured he'd find it when he got to the area.

At the gate were U.S. and ARVN guards. Outside, the road was paved but was covered with fine red dust. Along the main street were the usual shacks and black-market peddlers selling stolen BX goods.

The bridge over the Da Nang River had been sabotaged and repaired time after time. Over its cancerous rust-colored superstructure, a mass of black telephone wires connected the various military camps on both sides of the river. He saw sampans crossing with one oar astern. Small oceangoing ships were disgorging the material that kept the war running in its peculiar style. John also saw a powerboat with a waterskier and military patrol boats, all competing for space on the river.

On the other side of the bridge, an ancient Vietnamese woman squatted in the dust, eliminating her bowels out of one leg of her loose black pajama pants. As the traffic and people thinned out, the driver shifted into high gear. The tree-lined road had a look of order. Da Nang had probably been a very pleasant, perhaps beautiful port city under the French, an area popular with tourists. Now the city, overburdened by refugees from the north, was run-down and poverty-stricken.

They drove on past a large marine base on the left and toward the coast. Marble Mountain loomed straight up in the distance. It got larger and larger as the countryside grew quieter and quieter.

"You sure you want to go to that mountain?" the driver asked nervously.

"Stop the jeep," said John. He felt that something was wrong. He had made a mistake. Nevertheless, he sat there a few minutes, listening to the quiet in the green countryside. The sun beat down. It was unusually pleasant, without much humidity.

John's unease grew. He felt exposed. No military personnel, no planes overhead, no military vehicles on this section of the road except their jeep. It felt like ambush country—not the big sort of ambush, with heavy artillery, but the little plinking kind where a jeep could be discovered a day later, with flies buzzing around the dead occupants.

"Turn around and go back to that marine base," said John.

"Yes, *sir*." The private wheeled the jeep around and drove back as if someone held a broomstick to his tail bone. Both men unconsciously crouched in their seats.

Back at the marine base, John spent an hour and a half asking around about Roger's unit. He had let the driver go. The base was so spread out, his feet got sore from all the walking. Sitting down on a big wooden spool, the kind that held transmission wire, he took off his boots and socks to air his feet. When two marines passed, he called to them. They came over, looking at him curiously.

"Can you tell me where the 282nd Assault Helicopter Company is around here?" asked John. Seeing helicopters in the air didn't mean anything. The marines had plenty of their own.

"You mean the grunts?" The marine scratched his ear.

"I mean the army."

"Oh. Yes, sir. If you cut through that field for about fifteen hundred yards, you'll run into them. That is, they're the only grunts we know about."

John thanked the marines, who went back to the road. He got to his sore feet. If soldiers are grunts, what do they think they are? he wondered to himself. Soon after that he reached the orderly room of the 282nd and inquired about Roger.

The news was bad. Roger had been hurt. The orderly clerk knew all about it. His platoon was coming in from a CA in the mountains far west of Da Nang. Lead ship was being flown by Roger in a staggered left formation. Men from the other helicopters said something streaked up from the ground and exploded. The door gunner was killed and everybody else wounded. The peter pilot, hurt least because of his door shield, coaxed the crippled ship back to Da Nang. Roger was hit in the right side under the arm by a dozen pieces of shrapnel. All the wounded were at the Ninety-fifth Evaucation Hospital, where John was staying.

The best guess was that the ship had been struck by a Russian-built SAM-7, a hand-held missile capable of hitting an aircraft at five-thousand feet. On his way back to the hospital, John worried about the VC armed with SAM-7s. No helicopter pilot liked to think about it. It changed all the rules. They lost enough ships to conventional arms. Jesus! thought John. Good thing the war is winding down for the Americans.

As soon as he found out where Roger was, John went in to see him. His wounds were dirty, and infection raged in his body. He was in very poor shape, drifting in and out. He came into consciousness and saw John by his bed. "Dutchman! Is that you?"

"Yeh, buddy, I heard you got hit, and I had to come see if it was true or if you were just goldbricking."

"I been dreaming about you and some of them other guys. Dutchman, did you really come?"

"It's me, Roger. Don't sit up." He leaned over so Roger

could see him better. "See? Same old good-looking son of a bitch as before."

"You got a mustache."

"Yeah." John fingered it. "After we got away from Carla's old man, I went incognito."

Roger didn't laugh. "You seen Carla?"

"Think I'm crazy?" John changed the subject. "Aren't you going to ask me about my new unit or how I got here?"

"Sure, Dutchman." Roger was slow and looked more gaunt than ever. His breath smelled sick.

"The unit I went to didn't know diddly about combat flying, and they made me senior AC a couple weeks after I got there," said John.

"Big . . . fuckin' . . . deal," said Roger, closing and opening his eyes. The whites were yellow.

"I know it's no big deal. It just shows how lousy the unit was. It's the Sixty-first near Qui Nhon."

"I know you're the best they got, Dutchman."

"Hey," said John, changing the subject again, "you know they say a SAM-seven hit you guys?"

"Wha's a SAM-seven?"

"One of the Russian hand-helds, you know?"

Roger nodded.

"I heard you got hit in the right side."

"A lot of it is still in there."

John knew that shrapnel was often left in.

"Dutchman, what did they tell you about me? I mean, they won't tell me how sick I am. I get weaker every day. They're taking me out of here tonight or tomorrow morning. I think I'm dying . . ."

"Roger! Get a hold of yourself. You aren't that sick, buddy."

"You ask the doctor and tell me, will ya?"

"Okay, Roger. Cool down, now. You're going to be fine. They're going to make me get out of your room pretty soon. . . ."

"Don't go, Dutchman." Roger held John's wrist in a weak grasp, digging his fingernails in.

"Don't worry. I'll stay until they throw me out."

There was silence for a minute as Roger let go of his wrist. Then he said, "Dutchman . . ."

"Yeah."

"Tell me something."

"What, buddy?"

"What happens after you die?"

"Roger, you aren't going to die!"

Roger had his wrist again. "Just tell me. Tell me what happens."

John doubted whether Roger had ever been concerned about existence after death before. It was his overpowering need to survive asking now. "I don't know what happens, Roger. Probably nothing."

"Dutchman, I've done some things over here . . ."

"You don't need to . . ."

"No, I ain't gonna say what I did." Roger's voice was very low. "They're some things I ain't proud of. I'm scared of dying because of those things. I can't die, Dutchman!" His fingers dug into John's wrist. John felt as if he did not know this man. He wanted to get away.

Sweat glistened on Roger's forehead, and his palm was wet. His chest heaved as he fell back on the pillow, and then he slipped out of consciousness.

John went out and found a doctor. "Could you come see my buddy in here, doc?" he asked. "I don't know about him."

After one look, the doctor went out and returned with a nurse who had a tray of syringes. He asked John to wait in the hall.

"How is he?" John asked when they came out.

"Stable."

"What does stable mean?" What's wrong with him?"

"He's not responding well to antibiotics. We haven't been able to get the infection under control."

"He said you were taking him out. Does that mean medivac?"

"Yes, it does. He'll be gone in two hours. We want to get him to a specialist in the states while he still has the strength."

"Can I tell him good-by?"

"He won't wake up for hours."

"Oh. Well then. Thanks, doc."

John walked slowly back to his ward. He was tired, troubled by his sick friend, and his tender feet hurt.

21

HUEY

IN THE MORNING JOHN WOKE OUT OF RESTLESS DREAMS. HE HAD seen many dead and dying over the past nine months, but then there was Roger, the closest friend he had made over here. Before this, he had written the dead off, erasing from a mental blackboard the names of friends and acquaintances who no longer existed. But Roger was different. He was so much a survivor, it was impossible to think of him as ever being nowhere, gone.

Since he had passed out that time in the hospital, John had a strong sense that there must be a hereafter. He had seen his own body slumped in that chair. He knew if he had not gotten back into that body of his, he would still exist somewhere. But where? What came after here?

He tried to read but could not concentrate. The morning went slowly. For lunch, they served C rats, and he thought about the time Roger had filled several cases of C rations with nothing but ham and lima beans and sent them with Blacky and some of the men on an FOB. Wow, were those guys pissed when they came back. Nothing to eat but ham and motherfuckers. Sometimes Roger had a certain genius.

John's thoughts about death were too disturbing after a while. He would try the library that day to see what he could find about Buddhism, about what Ood and her people believed in.

It wasn't much of a library, two small rooms built of wood with slatted and screened walls. Thousands of GIs were stationed on and around the base, but most of them had no reason to enter the central compound. Few of them found out that a library existed at all. It had become mostly officer territory.

Outside the building, there was a bench press, made of two-by-fours, and barbells, ordinary cast-iron weights, not olympic. John made a mental note to come back and work out. Several men were lifting, sweating in the late afternoon heat. A dozen or so bicycles were parked outside, too. They could be checked out by the day.

The desk was in the front room, and behind it sat a staff sergeant reading a fresh copy of the *Pacific Stars and Stripes*.

John said, "Hi," as he closed the screen door. "Is this the base library I haven't heard that much about?"

"This is it," said the sergeant pleasantly. "Take what you want, but bring it back in two weeks. If you take a bike, I hold your ID card."

Most of the books were paperbacks. John glanced around and then said, "I'm looking for something on Buddhism."

The sergeant looked closely at John. He had a calm manner that put John at ease. "Nobody ever asked me for that before. I do have some material, but I'm the only one who reads it."

"I just want one book. . . ."

"On Buddhism?"

"That's right."

"Do you mind my asking why you want it?"

John might have been embarrassed or annoyed. It was an impertinent question in a sensitive area, but somehow he did not mind. "I'm—kind of—looking for some answers."

"You're a helicopter pilot. Am I right?"

John nodded.

"I get mostly jet jockies in here. Where are you stationed?"

"Qui Nhon. Ban Me Thout before that. I'm here in Da Nang getting my feet taken care of. I'll get back pretty soon."

"You're going back, and you need some answers," said the sergeant quietly. "Tell me about it out there."

The way he listened, occasionally smiling or laughing or adding a word of commiseration, somehow drew John out. John talked as he had not before. He told the man about his time on the ground in Cambodia with the spaced-out gunner and about the war and his opinions, including his nagging doubt that anything was being accomplished. He talked with only occasional interruptions when someone came in to borrow a book or check out a bicycle. His listener did not seem like a noncom but more like a superior officer to whom you could say what you felt.

"What about you?" asked John, realizing that he had done all the talking. "How did you end up in a library in Vietnam?"

"Not much to tell. I was drafted after graduate school, and when I got over here, I wouldn't order my men out into the bush. I was OCS, top of my class, but they busted me to buck sergeant. I have just been promoted to staff."

"You wouldn't order your men?" John thought about the kind of commitment it must have taken to make him give up his commission. John shook his head. "I couldn't do that," he said.

"No matter. Will you let me advise you on what to read about Buddhism?"

"Sure," said John. He felt at ease now.

"I've been concentrating on this field of study since they put me in the library two months after I got to Nam."

"What's so interesting about Buddhism?" asked John.

"It isn't only Buddhism. It's the teaching that all the great cultures have had in one form or another. Call it divine wisdom or ancient wisdom. It is a religion and an ethic. It is a way to live. It's been analyzed by many who were trying to identify a unifying thread running through all religions. The motto of one group, probably from the Sanskrit, is that there is no religion higher than truth.''

''I guess I can't disagree with that,'' said John slowly. He watched the sergeant's eyes for the pious look he had seen in the eyes of other religious men, in the eyes of the chaplain back at Ban Me Thuot East. . . . It wasn't there.

''Of course, it's not for everybody. Some of the principles are hard to accept at first. Reincarnation, for instance.''

''Yeah. I can understand that's hard to believe.''

''Actually, the principle of reincarnation is easier to take than the mechanics of it. . . .''

An enlisted man came in. ''Hey, man, sorry I'm late. I was fighting a mama-san about some shit she was trying to pull on me.''

''No problem.''

He was the librarian's relief. John and the sergeant walked out together and headed for the chow hall to eat supper. Several night-patrol men with green and black faces and camouflaged fatigues vacated a table as they walked from the chow line with their metal trays.

''I know your name is Vanvorden, but what do they call you?'' asked the sergeant.

''Dutchman, the Flying Dutchman. My real name's John.''

''I'm glad to meet you, Dutchman. My name is Hughes L. Parker. My friends call me Huey.''

John smiled at the coincidence. They shook hands.

''You were saying about reincarnation?'' said John.

''Yes. I said the principle was easier to take than the mechanics. How a spirit moves in or out of its body is hard for me to conceive. I pinch myself, and I know this is me.''

''It's no problem for me. Not now.''

Huey was fascinated as John told him about the blood-giving incident.

''That is very interesting,'' said Huey after John had finished. ''I've read things like that, too, but I've never heard about it firsthand.''

Huey had brought with him a small tan-colored book, which he handed John across the table.

"Where do you get these books?" asked John, thumbing through the pages.

"Oh, I have an almost unlimited budget, and I order anything I want to read. It takes a month through the APO. That book was published in India."

"Is it a good one?"

"It gives the fundamentals. There are a lot of books on the subject, but you must work hard to learn from words that sound simple.

"Is it so complicated you can't talk about it?"

"No. Basically, reincarnation is central to the whole wisdom. It's the process of advancing as a person or a spirit. But that's too direct. I have to give you some background."

"I'd appreciate that," said John.

The two men put their trays away and went outside. In order to talk undisturbed, they found a comfortable spot on top of a bunker close to the back door of the chow hall. As teacher to student, Huey explained about karma. The debt of every deed, good or bad, lofty or degrading, was carried from one life to another. The individual's karma, his fate, was formed through those deeds. The law of retribution was the immutable natural law—that each action had its equal and opposite reaction, thus demanding full repayment in this life or in subsequent lives. The time between earthly births was spent assimilating the lessons of the former life. The quality of life on the nonphysical planes was directly proportionate to the quality of life led on the physical plane, so a morally debased life would be met with a full measure of tough lessons upon its termination.

"We create our own hell, so to speak," said Huey, "with the fears and evils of our lifetime."

Good living also returned in equal measure on future spiritual and physical planes. Though a man had just one charitable thought in the past life, it was repaid in full before he returned for another life and another chance to help himself and his race progress. If a man's spiritual advancement reached a certain high point, no more lives on earth, no more testing, was needed. Then a state the Buddhists called nirvana is reached. Beyond that point, it was given to man to understand only that progression continued.

"I don't know," said John. "I appreciate a lot of what you say, but some of it sounds like bullshit. Why should a murderer be given a second chance, or as you think, all the chances he needs?"

"We never fully know the circumstances under which someone commits a base act. We are not to judge. The act will receive full justice. It is the law."

"Then what's the use? I've got things coming to me, and there's nothing I can do about it, so . . . ?"

"By some faiths, perhaps. An unlucky incident may seem like a bolt from the blue, but when these happen, you pick yourself up because you know that negative karma is worked off and that if you adhere to a good life and decency, you can avoid those bolts in the future."

"That's hard to swallow, Huey. I don't think we can avoid hard times in the future. It's the law of averages."

"But if we're all just part of some cosmic crap game, what justice is there in man's world? How can nature be so well ordered with evolution of form if there is no progression of the spirit? To me, reincarnation is a fundamental necessity if life is to be intelligible and just. The law of karma may make you feel helpless, but how much more helpless would you be with no law, flung into life with good or bad qualities, under good or bad conditions through no reason?"

"What you say sounds good to me because I have a sense of justice, Huey. I feel it when things are unequal."

"Dutchman, the conscience, that small voice within, is developed from erring and learning and repeating the process in many lives past. Your intuition is the essence of all your lives. If you listen, it will speak truth."

John swatted at a mosquito. "Damn things."

"They're bad sometimes," agreed Huey.

John was beginning to understand how complex the whole subject was. "I really wouldn't care, probably," he said, "but this war . . . I've seen so much. Even my friend Roger turned strange on me. He's scared of dying, not because it hurts or anything but because he's done some things. He probably killed when he didn't have to, and other things. He's capable, the dumb bastard. Anyway, he was scared. . . ."

Huey sighed as if he had heard a lot in eighteen months. "Don't despair for your friend. No matter how bad his acts were or how bad he thought they were, the law of retribution will extract no more, no less, than is due, and afterwards he will be free from debt. A man can begin to turn things around in this lifetime by living as a useful, helpful citizen. Once acquainted with the law, a man is able to bear all and not fear the future."

John held his knees and shifted on the sandbags. The stars were out, and the camp was getting quiet as men went to their bunks. A balmy breeze blew in their faces. This man's words were strong. Here was power. How could one man have so many good answers when everyone else he asked could not answer even one question clearly?

"It's getting late," said John, "and I just remembered we have some kind of bed check. Can we talk again tomorrow?"

"Of course," said Huey. "How about after lunch sometime."

"Fine, two o'clock at the library be okay?"

"Two, then," said Huey, extending his hand.

In his bed, John lay on his back looking at the folds of the mosquito net caught in the dim light from the end of the bay. He was careful not to let his elbows rest against the net, a conditioned reflex he no longer thought about.

That night, he felt close to the answer he had been looking for since he was downed in Cambodia, since Arata died in his lap. He felt like letting the little word "Why?" out of the part of his brain where he kept it safely tucked. He now had a source of information for answering some basic questions. Why was he there? What was the effect of his contribution to the war effort? Was all this really necessary?

The next thing John was aware of was breakfast call. He didn't feel rested. All night he had dreamed that he couldn't sleep.

"Where were you last night at bed check?" It was pain-in-the-ass Lieutenant Bradshaw.

"I was sitting on a bunker talking to a friend."

"Do you want that to go into the report?"

"Yes."

"Very well."

John gritted his teeth. I don't want my karma mixed with hers anymore, he heard himself thinking.

"Colonel Ashton wants to see you, Mister Vanvorden."

"Thank you, lieutenant."

"Not at all." She walked away.

Nice-looking behind, thought John, wondering what the colonel wanted.

John got out of the hospital-issue blue pajamas and put on his fatigues. The pajamas, robes, and soft slippers made him feel locked in. This was a place for the sick, and he was no longer one of them.

He found the colonel making his rounds in a ward where a number of soldiers had missing limbs. John tried not to look too close.

"Colonel Ashton, did you ask to see me?"

"Vanvorden. Yes, how are the feet today?"

"Great."

"Good. I'm putting you out. I need the beds. There's heavy action up north. Your unit, the Sixty-first, has moved to Quang Tri, assigned to the Seventh Cavalry. It will be temporary, I am told."

John had already seen hundreds of helicopters on their way north the month before he left for Da Nang. The rumors were that they would take part in a secret operation known as Lamson 719. Invading Laos.

The sneak attack into Cambodia by the First Cav a year

before had caught the NVA by surprise. That meant record body counts and record finds of arms and rice caches. The U.S. generals had been convinced that the ARVNs could do the same in Laos, using ground troops and U.S. pilots. There was a difference. This was no quick hop over a border with total U.S. planning and troops. It meant a long, involved move up to the DMZ. The element of surprise did not exist. John guessed it was an unholy mess.

"Then I am joining my unit?"

"Not for a few days. I want you to be totally rested. You can stay at China Beach. The salt water will be therapeutic for your feet."

John had first heard of China Beach from the body snatchers he had flown out of Cambodia. But knowing his unit was up at the DMZ staging into Laos brought feelings of guilt. "Can't I just go back flying?"

"No. Not for a few days. Report to the desk this morning for your orders and assignment. You don't need any more medical attention unless something happens. Good luck.

A motor-pool bus made a scheduled run to China Beach every two hours. John caught a ride, wearing only swimming trunks, a shirt, and sandals. The bus headed out over the same beat-up bridge he had been on earlier.

China Beach reminded John of Cam Ranh. There was a main cafeteria with a juke box blaring nonstop tunes from the states. Somebody was getting rich setting up these joints, he thought. The beach itself was beautiful, curving gradually to the north until it met Monkey Mountain, the tallest landmark for miles. Monkey Mountain rose steeply out of the South China Sea. The U.S. forces had installed a high-capacity radar facility and dome on its top. Monkeys lived there, and rumor had it that the airmen and soldiers who worked on the mountain had taught the monkeys to flip the finger at anybody who drove up the switchback.

The sand was golden white and squeaked as he walked. The day was out of a picture book, with a warm, clear blue sea. Small pine trees on the land side whispered in the wind. John went up to sit in the shade under the pines.

Most of the soldiers lay on the sand, soaking up sun. There were no women to be seen.

Just down the beach, a group of soldiers were playing football. John was surprised at the ferocity of the game. They were doing full cross-body blocks and high-low tackles with no concern for injuries. Made sense, thought John. A broken collarbone could keep a man out of combat for a long time.

Two men sat out in the water on surfboards. John watched them riding the scarcely moving sea. There would be no waves caught today. He was unaware of anyone close by until a Vietnamese kid said, "You, GI; want number-one haircut?"

John focused his eyes on the boy. "I could use a haircut."

"My brother cut you hair; two hundred pi, okay?"

"One hundred," said John.

"One fifty."

"Okay."

The small youngster nodded, and a larger boy came over with a chair and a bag. "You want haircut one-hundred pi?" asked the older brother.

"One fifty," said the younger, with a look of warning. Then he said to John, "Brother good hair, no good business."

John laughed and sat on the folding wooden chair. While the older one cut and snipped, he watched the little guy, who was eating from a handful of small snails. With a pine needle, he poked into a shell and pulled a tiny snail loose by hooking it on the barb of the needle.

"You want one?" he offered to John.

"No, thanks."

When he had finished with the scissors and comb, the older brother took out a straight razor to clean up around the ears. This is nuts, thought John, letting a Vietnamese so close to my throat with a razor. He made no sudden moves as the boy carefully finished, shaving the fuzz on John's forehead and even making a pass on the bridge of the nose. Done with that, he took out a narrow tool with a wire loop on the end and started for the ear hole.

"That's it," said John, standing up and reaching for some money pinned to his towel.

"He clean your ear," said the little one.

"Thanks, anyway." John paid them and watched as the kids wandered off, the small one hunting for customers, the big one dragging his chair and bag along in the sand. Rubbing his hands through his hair to get the clippings out, John guessed that it was not a bad haircut. He would take a swim before having some lunch.

For the rest of the afternoon, as he lay on the beach, he could not prevent himself from thinking about Roger. What had he done that was so bad? Killed, tortured, raped? John remembered the interrogation incident when he was flying peter pilot for Roger. Roger could have done any of those things. But in a war, were not killings and other violent acts justified, warranted? When were they immoral? Basic military training did not cover that. They just taught you to kill. Religious treatment of the subject was ambiguous: Thou shalt not kill . . . Joshua fit the battle of Jericho . . . Religious leaders during wartime told people that God was on your side and you would be victorious. It came down to—well, you decided when to hold back the dagger by how you felt inside.

Suppose Roger's fears of punishment for what he did were for good reasons? Could there be a God keeping track? His religious relatives believed God was all ready to let you into heaven or send you to hell. Or was it as Huey had said?

Why didn't he just ignore such questions and get through his twelve months? He was there. Vietnam. The best and worst acts imaginable were taking place. He'd ask Huey that afternoon why he thought man went to war.

John suddenly got up and jogged south for about a quarter of a mile until he came to an off-limits sign and a wire barrier running into the water. Turning around, he ran back, using the firmest sand at the water line. It was half a mile to the north before he ran into off-limits signs again. He did the whole loop once more, stopping at the northern barrier. The salt water and sand were helping his feet, toughening them. The run felt good.

Up from the beach, he found an old stucco house. There was no sign, but the kids—there were always kids around—called it Maryann's.

"You come Maryann's have drink . . ."

"I left my money back there."

"No matter. You pay later."

"Well no . . ." Then he saw Maryann. Slightly built and pretty, she looked almost Spanish, the way her hair was done. She was wearing large, round earrings. He went up the steps and sat at one of the half-dozen tables on a wide concrete porch. Maryann lifted a Coke bottle from a chest filled with water. The cap was rusted.

John wondered from which war the bottle was left over and refused it politely. He sat there, watching Maryann, studying her delicate features and not thinking about anything much.

Two black marines in uniform came up and took chairs. Several Vietnamese kids followed them. The men drank the old Cokes and pushed the urchins away except for one. He had dark skin and curly hair and was obviously half Vietnamese and half black.

"Hey, Jeb, whatcha think we gone call this boy?" said one marine.

"I'm gone call this boy Clyde after my man Frazier. How you like that name, boy? Clyde. S'matter, don't you speak no American?"

"If this moe-foe part of the world had basketball, boy, you could be a star someday. Huh, boy?"

That thought tickled the two marines. The boy was an outcast in Nam, and they knew it, but were too tough to worry about it.

"Hey, Maryann, this boy yours?" They laughed again.

The boy tried to put his hand on one marine's M-14. The man gave the hand a sharp slap. The boy withdrew in pain but without tears. "That li'l nigger gook better stay away from my gun . . ."

His companion was trying to get Maryann to sit on his lap. She stayed out of reach.

John got up to leave. "So long, Maryann," he said.

The black marines looked hard at him and followed him with their eyes as he jogged back down the beach.

22
THE ANCIENT WISDOM

"WHY IS THERE WAR?" JOHN ASKED HUEY. "HOW COULD so many of us screw up so badly at the same time? Can Buddhism, or the ancient wisdom answer this?"

Huey spoke in a quiet voice. "The wisdom teaches that there is group karma as well as individual. A nation has its own karmic record, and through its progression, there is a cyclical pattern with high points and low points. War is a low point. All is a learning process."

"I don't quite feel like saying bullshit anymore, but your explanation for war seems weaker than when you talk on the level of the individual," said John.

The library was busy, and they were interrupted by a few men who wanted books. Then Huey went on. "In my opinion, Dutchman, this war is realigning our priorities as a nation, as a world power. If we learn from this war, which has driven many world citizens from our fold, including most of the South Vietnamese, then maybe we will avoid a more devastating war in the future."

"I understand you, but what if we are attacked?" asked John.

"You mean like the Gulf of Tonkin incident?"

"Something like that, maybe bigger."

"If every time an embassy is harassed, a boat is attacked, a statesman is killed, we respond in kind, what hope is there for the world? If the strongest country in the world cannot show restraint in the use of force, armed might, what hope is there? Our role on earth right now is to lead. A death or two, or even a few hundred, is not worth the hateful, wasteful karmic tangle of millions of lives that war causes. There is not time to continue in these old ways. Technology is too powerful. The rules of the game have changed, and the game must be done away with. You have only to look around you here to know it. America alone can lead the world's citizens away from this game."

"Your view is too idealistic," said John. 'Force will be necessary for a long time. The U.S. has to remain strong."

"I agree. Strength will be necessary for the foreseeable future. I'm saying that with this strength we take on a huge responsibility to use restraint. We have not used restraint in Vietnam, and it has hurt us. . . . Just a minute."

John waited while Huey checked out a bicycle.

"What about me, my job here?" John asked. "Will I be punished in future lives with negative karma?"

"Punished is the wrong word. You will have debts, responsibilities to the race for your role here. The debts may not be so great for you as for others here."

"But—"

"I know, I know. Don't say it. Let me just tell you this, Dutchman. For the rest of your tour, listen to your conscience. Be charitable when possible. Do your duty but avoid excesses."

"Excesses?"

"Like your friend. You know what I mean. Live the golden rule if you can, Dutchman, even in war. Every great religious leader—Confucius, Socrates, Gautama Buddha, Mohammed, and Jesus of Nazareth—has said to treat others as you would be treated. Listen to them, not me. They knew the law. They had the ancient wisdom."

Huey paused to take some book returns.

John thought about the power he himself had with one helicopter and its crew. He could transport himself with the flick of a wrist and rain death and terror on any one of those villages out there. In peacetime, those Vietnamese villages would just be hot, fetid, substandard housing for a portion of the world's poor. With the element of war added, the countryside became a place of intrigue. It was hard not to see enemy everywhere. It was hard not to rake a whole village after taking a round or two of small-arms fire. Excesses. The thought was disturbing.

"You say Socrates knew about Buddhism. I mean this wisdom that is in Buddhism," said John, getting back to the conversation.

"We know Socrates through Plato. Socrates was like Confucius and Christ: he spoke rather than wrote. Plato was Socrates' favorite and most brilliant pupil. He later wrote from memory the conversations he had heard between Socrates and other great men of the time. These writings are called the *Dialogues* and are grouped under the name of his teacher, Plato. Much of what is written is Plato's, however, who was probably a greater teacher than Socrates."

John listened.

Plato's *Republic* is a large part of the *Dialogues*. In the *Republic*, I think in book seven, Plato describes a hypothetical situation now known as Plato's cave. In this cave are people who have been bound hand and foot their entire lives, facing a bare wall and not able to turn their heads. Behind them is a light, a fire. Between their backs and the fire walk their guards and other servants all casting shadows on the wall above. The prisoners, having never seen the real people and objects, have names for the shadows. Can you see it?"

"I get the picture," said John.

"When a prisoner is released and allowed to turn around to face the fire, he is at first blinded and confused. Once everything is explained to him, he then understands that when he was fettered, he had not known the truth of the images, the shadows. Furthermore, if he is taken up the steep ascent out of the cave into the light of day and he sees the world outdoors, after an adjustment period, he understands how terribly limited the cave existence was.

"I follow you."

"Then Plato likens the story to ascending to the regions of the mind from a purely physical surrounding. He remarks how much more clearly the physical region is understood after having ascended to the mind region and then returned. He also points out how those in the cave might not believe the truth of what is revealed in the region of true light and would turn against the one speaking heresy. Some say that Plato is referring to the cycle of reincarnation and is illustrating how the most advanced spirits return to earth to teach."

"These are ideas I've never heard before," said John.

"The *Dialogues* are full of second meanings. For example, in the *Apology*, after Socrates has been condemned to death, he comments on his conscience. 'My familiar prophetic voice of the spirit in all times past has always come to me, frequently opposing me even in very small things, if I was about to do something not right.' "

"If these guys are referring to reincarnation, why don't they say it?" asked John.

"In the first place, there was no need for Plato to keep repeating the principle to his students. They were already trained in the wisdom. And secondly, people were persecuted for such beliefs. Plato says the people in the cave would kill the one who returns to tell them the truth. Freedom of religion is a recent development. It is part of what puts America in the lead."

John suddenly remembered the time and the need to catch a bus back to the beach. "I got kicked out of the hospital this morning, and I get to stay at China Beach for a few days before I go back to my unit. So I need to go while the buses are still running."

"China Beach," said Huey. "I bicycle there once a week."

"I still have some questions about this wisdom and

Christianity. Okay if I come back? Might be a couple of days."

"Come anytime, Dutchman. I'll be in the library during the day."

"Thanks, I'll see you later, then."

For two days, John stayed at China Beach, alternately reading, exercising, eating fast food, and resting. The distant, periodic explosions from artillery batteries served as reminders of the serious situation up north. He felt as if he were letting his unit down, although he knew that Laos would teach the men how to fly combat more surely than he ever could. He returned to the Ninety-fifth Evacuation Hospital to tell Colonel Ashton he was going north to Quang Tri.

Ashton was busy loading litter cases on buses for transport by C-141 to Japan and then on to the states. He signed John's release with no argument. Walking away, John thought he recognized someone sitting on the bus. He walked up to the window.

"Hey, Swede, is that you? You going on the plane?"

His old chess partner turned his head slightly. There was no recognition in his eyes. His hands shook.

"Don't you know me? It's the Dutchman."

"Yeah," said Swede. "Dutchman. How you doing?"

"You leaving Nam, Swede?"

The flight surgeon leaned toward him and said in a low, guttural voice, "And I won't fucking come back!"

"Where you been?"

"It's hell up there. This is my ticket *out*." He folded his arms and looked straight ahead.

John now guessed he had been moved to Quang Tri. "Where you going?"

"Canada," he hissed out of the side of his mouth, and would not look at John again. The Swede was through talking. He just wanted out of Vietnam. John no longer existed. John watched as the bus moved forward. So the flight surgeon is going to desert, he thought. I hope he recovers from this in Canada.

John put the flight surgeon out of his mind and started toward the library. He hoped Huey would be there so he could say good-by.

John found Huey at his desk and told him of his plans to go north as soon as possible. Huey's calm manner slowed John's impulse to make it a short good-by. They began to talk.

"I have to tell you, before I ran into you, I asked some chaplains and the like the same questions I asked you, and you wouldn't believe some of the answers I got."

"I had heard all the same answers, too," said Huey.

"You know, I think of reincarnation as Oriental. I still don't really feel it applies to the West, which is kind of stupid because if it happens in the East, it happens in the West," said John.

"It's true. We are conditioned more toward the concept of one physical existence. What you see is what you get. The way Western religion is taught in most instances, it is to the clergy's advantage to pin heaven or hell up as your eternal reward, depending upon whether you follow their advice or not. How many times have you heard some preacher telling you what the Lord wants you to do? Even if God told him personally, it's still secondhand when you hear it. Don't get me wrong. We need teachers and books and interpretations. But it's through the experience of many lives that your spirit recognizes where truth is.

"Yeah, but people like my aunt side with the preachers because they quote the Bible. At least I think so. She keeps quoting it to me."

"That is the beauty of the parable. It reaches all levels of understanding. In the beginning, getting people to do the right things for selfish reasons still brings about progress."

"But what kind of ammunition from the Bible could I use on her after she quoted ten passages to support her way of thinking?"

"Dutchman, you came to me and asked me for some books on Buddhism. I offered my views. I didn't go after you thumping a Bible. I showed you what I have found that answers my questions. For me, this wisdom is truth. There can be no religion higher than truth. Matching her quote for quote isn't going to prove your belief over your aunt's. You have to study Scripture yourself. Finish reading that book. After you have, certain passages in the Bible will take on more meaning. For example, the Book of Job is a mystery. In the thirty-eighth chapter, God says to Job. 'Gird up your loins like a man; for I demand that you answer me. Where were you when I laid the foundations of the Earth? Tell me if you have an understanding.' Later, He asks Job, 'Have the gates of death been opened to you? Have you perceived the breadth of the Earth, declare if you know it all.' And later He asks, 'Do you know it because you were born back then or because the number of your days are great?' "

"How do you remember all that?"

"If you read through it enough times, it sticks. My quotes aren't verbatim."

"What does all that about Job mean?"

"I told you it is a mystery, but do you think God would ask Job those questions if it weren't possible for Job to have lived in the past, and then again in the present?"

"I don't know." said John.

"My guess is that He is teaching Job the secrets of the kingdom of heaven that Jesus taught his disciples."

"You mean the law of karma and reincarnation?"

"Yes, put very simply," said Huey.

"Where does Jesus refer to these principles?"

"Karma is a Sanskrit word meaning action. All actions are effects coming from preceding causes and become causes of future effects. When you say this is my karma, you mean this event is the effect of a cause set going by me in the past. Jesus' disciple Paul said, 'Be not deceived; God is not mocked; for whatsoever a man soweth, that shall he also reap.' The Holy Bible is filled with this kind of reference to karma. When Jesus and his disciples passed a blind man, they asked Jesus, 'Who did sin, this man, or his parents, that he was born blind?' For them to ask such a question, could they be referring to anything other than a previous life and the forces set moving there?"

"You've really done your research."

"I've had a year and a half in a library with one question to answer: where is the justice in all this?"

"I've asked it, too, but does life have to be just?"

"If it is not, why is there hope? Why does this most natural of all human emotions exist?"

"You keep answering my questions with questions, Huey."

"It's because the answers to the questions you ask are already in you."

John continued questioning, "Are there other Christian references to reincarnation?"

"I know some others. In the book of Matthew, in chapter eleven, Jesus tells the people that John the Baptist is the former Elijah. And later, in Matthew, after John the Baptist has been beheaded, Jesus tells Peter, James, and James' brother John that Elijah had already come back to earth, that the Jews didn't know him, and they killed him, as they were soon to kill the son of man."

"That's in the Bible?"

"It is, and there is more, but Jesus cautioned the disciples against giving the people information they were not ready to hear. Many of Christ's teachings were in parable form, as you know. He told them not to give that which is holy to the dogs, nor to cast their pearls before swine. When they asked him why he spoke to the people in parables, he said that they, the disciples, were qualified to know the mysteries of the Kingdom of Heaven, but the people in general were not. He said, when speaking in parables, those seeing see not, and hearing, they hear not. He said, blessed are your eyes, for they see, and blessed are your ears, for they hear."

John spoke up. "When I was in Bangkok, a beautiful young woman told me some things about Buddhism. From what she and you have told me, the Orientals have more of the wisdom than us in the West."

"It's true, but their eyes see not, and their ears hear not! If they did, you and I wouldn't be here in this wretched little war. There'd be no war here."

"But we do have a war here. And I can't help it; I have to get back into it." John stood up. "I'm sorry to leave you, Huey, but I have to go get a plane out of here today. I won't forget you or what you taught me."

"I understand."

"Thanks, Huey, and good-by." John held out his hand.

"Good-by, Dutchman," said Huey, offering his hand.

23

LAMSON 719

An Son was practically deserted. A skeleton crew was still there, and a few ground troops remained to secure the base. An officer had stayed on in the operations building to pick up stragglers like John coming back from leave or R & R. He directed John to Qui Nhon to catch an MACV flight north.

In Quang Tri, John had trouble finding his unit. There were hundreds of slicks, and everybody was sleeping in or under them. All the men were red-eyed and white-faced from constant flying into battle the past two weeks. And everywhere there was a smell of fear. Nobody was partying, almost no one talking. The Dutchman had been their teacher before the Sixty-first left An Son. Now, in Laos, experience was the teacher.

John found Tex, who asked where he had come from.

"Convalescent leave. I just got back."

"You should have stayed, buddy. You should have stayed."

"Well, Tex, here I was all worried about you guys, and now you tell me I should have stayed."

"We missed you, Dutchman, but I wouldn't wish this on any man."

"Where's Samson?"

"I guess you ain't heard. He didn't get back two days ago. Someone reported a visual on him going down. Nobody got out."

"Christ! Anybody else?"

"We been hit pretty light. Second Platoon lost a couple."

"I better report to the CO."

"Him!" said Tex, sounding older. "You'll probably find him chewing out maintenance. The Junkman's changed things a lot."

"What's the Junkman?"

"New maintenance officer. Mister Solomon. He's on his fourth tour in Nam, and he's a real tough hombre. A W-3. He really knows Hueys."

"Be seeing you, Tex."

John found Captain Hayes, as Tex predicted, raising hell with a spec 5 and a private. Hayes had a thing against flying in any ship with over 500 hours on it, and his favorite helicopter was not operational.

"I tell you I want that helicopter ready to go at 0430 hours tomorrow morning if you have to work all night. I'm flying command and control. . . ."

"Junkman says this bird stays on the ground. Didn't he say so Shonebone?"

"Sure did."

"I say it flies," said the CO. "I'm the CO."

"Yes, sir. We know. But there's nothing you can do but court-martial us. The Junkman, he kill us, maybe." The mechanic pointed to another helicopter. "That'll be Command and Control tomorrow."

"How many hours?"

"Fourteen hundert thereabouts."

"That's no damn good. Where's Mister Solomon?"

"You know, Shonebone?"

"Sleeping in one of them, I expect," said the private. He

swept the hundreds of choppers with an outstretched arm. Maintenance got sleep when and where they could.

"I came to tell you I'm back," said John to Captain Hayes.

"Oh. Well, I can see that. Your feet better?"

"Good as new."

"I can't get any cooperation out of maintenance since that man they call the Junkman got here."

"What's the problem with that helicopter?" asked John, interested.

"That isn't any of your business, Vanvorden. Go talk to the XO and settle back in. He's in the shack they call the operations building."

Kant was glad to see the Dutchman back on flight status. "Sure missed my best pilot," he said warmly. "Tell me about it."

John told him about the hospital and beach, but he did not mention Huey. Kant filled him in on Lamson 719, the Laos affair. Entire companies had been wiped out. Every insertion was a Romeo Foxtrot (RF), translated rat fuck, the name given by flyers to doomed missions. The Sixty-first had been lucky—so far.

Two days later, flying into Laos, John understood the mood at Quang Tri. All hell broke loose around his ship. It was worse than anything he had seen in Cambodia with the 155th. In Cambodia, the enemy shot at the helicopters with 7.62 mm. and 12.7 mm. guns. In Laos, the slicks were shot at with 23-mm. 37-mm. and 57-mm. canon. The 12.7s were being used in multiple supporting positions.

Crippled slicks suspended from the bellies of Sky Cranes or Chinooks were a common sight during the day. At night, the camps were shelled by NVA artillery. When the eight inchers commenced coming in, most pilots went for their starters, and hundreds of helicopters began taking off. Everybody went for elevation at the same time, and midair collisions were common. The first night John's crew tried to make him go up, he refused. "Go back to sleep, damn it. I'm not getting up with all those crazy bastards. It's safer right here on the ground."

John still had the hammock he'd kept with him since Ban Me Thuot. He rigged it from a D-ring hooked onto the AC's handhold above the seat on one side and on the other to a piece of pipe he bolted into the ceiling over the gunner's seat. With a couple of sleeping bags for padding, he slept great. He and his crew waited out the incoming on the ground. Sometimes a ship got blown up, but the crew admitted it was safer than being the air. Besides, what went on at night wasn't half as dangerous as what they would be doing come daylight.

The missions were so bad that crews taped chicken plates down on the chin bubble and on the floor to stop the bullets. Door gunners wore chest and back armor plates and sat on pieces of armor. So many ships were shot down that replacement helicopters came into Quang Tri all day long. Damaged ships were sling loaded out if they could not be easily repaired. Nobody knew how many had been shot out of the air. John heard that over three hundred had not been recovered.

On his third mission into Laos, a 51-caliber bullet tore through the floor, shearing the peter pilot's collective pitch control in half. The fierce jolt broke the man's wrist. The dual control put a three-inch blood blister in John's palm. The wrench of the controls flipped the ship out of formation as if it were trying to do an inside loop. As it stalled over on its side, it missed the rest of the flight by pure luck. Feeling returned to John's hand, and he got things under control in time to abort to Lao Bao.

On his fourth trip, on the way out of Laos, an exploding round hit the ship somewhere high. Shrapnel riddled the roof, but missed the crew. Everything began to shake violently. John knew his rotor blade was hit by the way they were lumping along. He broke formation, and escorted by the next ship, turned back to Lao Bao again. As soon as they touched down, everybody scrambled away from the crippled helicopter. A hole a foot in diameter was visible in the main rotor blade. The projectile had missed the main spar by "no more than an ant's ass,'' said his crew chief. John and the men huddled together watching the ship. As the damaged rotor slowed down, it collapsed of its own weight and cut the tail boom off clean. The ship spun around and fell on its side, while the remaining blade took one last swipe and buried itself in the ground.

The U.S. pilots had it bad during Lamson 719, but the VNAF pilots were hopeless. They lost nearly everything they had, mostly because of poor flying skills. Sometimes they would not even go into battle but took their ground troops and went elsewhere.

Relations between the ARVNs and the U.S. soldiers worsened in Laos. The Americans would no sooner land several hundred ARVNs than they would be crying back on the radios to be picked up and retreated. The ACs argued against going back so soon, but the U.S. commanders always gave in to the ARVN commanders, and back the choppers would go. Those that did not get shot down due to the lack of cover from the disorganized ground troops were in danger of being pulled out of the sky before they could land. In their panic, the ARVNs mobbed the returning helicopters. The pilots learned to come in quickly and just hover. If the wild ARVNs grabbed the skids, they shook them off and tried again. When downed American flyers were to be picked up, they threw out the ARVNs aboard to make room.

John was shot down once in Laos with a knocked-out engine. By the time he had autorotated and landed, the ship that followed him down was kicking out ARVNs to make enough space for him and his crew. John himself picked up downed crews several times.

Before Lamson 719 came to its inconclusive end, the United States had dumped as many ARVN soldiers as possible onto the Ho Chi Minh Trail. The whole area had been pounded with every kind of artillery and aerial bombardment in the U.S. arsenal. After two and a half months, word filtered by grapevine that the Laos invasion was being abandoned. The NVA acted as if they knew this. During the last week, they cut loose with SAM-IIs as they never had before. At one insertion, pilots counted thirty SAMs fired at a flight of 100 helicopters, incredibly hitting none because the choppers stayed too low. It was terrifying, though, to see them, like telephone poles trailing a stream of white smoke and roaring by to explode somewhere overhead.

John was there for the last four weeks. He flew fifty-three insertions, taking hits every time. The only man he lost was a crew chief, shot in the face by a 51 caliber. As a whole, the Sixty-first had been more than fortunate, losing only six pilots and eight crew members. Captain Hayes seemed unchanged through the whole experience. He was as pompous as ever and had learned very little about air combat. In fact, he seemed disappointed when the commanding generals finally called it quits. He was the only one in the company who did not seem to understand why.

24

DFC AND BAD KARMA

BACK AT AN SON, THE ARMY SPRUNG FOR BEER AND STEAKS IN quantity. For a week, the company partied every night. People talked to each other again. Ranking officers began to catch up on the shaggy look the unit had brought back with them from Quang Tri and ordered men to the barbers. Situation normal, but John and a few other pilots vowed to keep their hair as a memento of what they'd been through in Laos.

Senior AC Vanvorden now listened to the voice inside as never before. He took it upon himself to plan the details of every combat assault. The harder he worked, the more lives he protected. Meeting enemy forces head-on was to be avoided. The soldiers he inserted were hunting—he couldn't change that—but he would do his utmost to get them inserted unannounced. To do that, he radically altered planning procedure.

Normally, when ground forces planned a CA, they gave helicopter companies a general area for their destination, allowing the companies a choice of landing zones. Past procedure had been to overfly the LZs several days before the assault to see which ones were adequate. John halted the overflights and made all his determinations from maps, including picking alternate LZs. The U.S. maps were so good by then that only in rare cases was an LZ's position or size misrepresented. In addition, he convinced operations to hold off all planning of missions until the night before a mission. This minimized the time during which information could leak out.

The operations building was locked up tight at 2200 hours. Then maps were taken out and every detail planned. None of the crews knew their helicopter assignments until the next morning when they were awakened for the OPS briefing. This change was unpopular. A pilot had always known a day or two before a mission whether or not he was flying or whether he could stay up partying if he wished. Now no one could plan his off hours. The Dutchman lost some of his fans.

As his final preparation, John personally arranged a prebombardment of the LZs they would use. When he couldn't get B-52s, he got fighter bombers. After the air drop came the artillery. There were few places in South Vietnam out of range of at least one artillery battery. If ground commanders wanted to go where the artillery could not reach, John talked them out of it. As a result, the Sixty-first began flying into very dangerous areas without taking casualties. During the whole time the Dutchman planned the missions, not one helicopter or one life was lost.

John finally did get his haircut, though. One morning, he happened to hear Bates being chewed out by a new top sergeant called Foghorn.

"Mister Bates," roared Foghorn. "You better have that hair cut before I see you again."

Bates glanced at his shoulder to see if his bars were still there. "C'mon, Top, you can't talk to me that way," he said good-humoredly.

The top sergant reached an enormous arm across the desk, grabbed Master Bates by the front of his shirt, and hauled him forward off his feet, scraping his knees against the edge of the desk.

John, watching from the doorway, felt his mouth drop open.

"Listen, you little fucker, you get a haircut or I'll bust your fuckin' head," the sergeant boomed, and tossed Bates back to his feet.

John left without being seen and went straight to the barber. Long hair wasn't all that comfortable, anyway. A few minutes later, Bates walked in.

"Dutchman, I didn't think I'd see you in here."

"No? Well, I kinda got tired of combing this mop. How come you're here? I thought you said they'd have to catch you first."

"Oh, well. My helmet doesn't fit right with all this hair. . . ."

"Can be a problem," said John without a smile.

"How about some chess later on, Dutchman?" asked Bates as he climbed into the chair John vacated.

"Good. Come on over this evening. Don't let your ears get cold," he added as the right side of Bates's hair came off under the clippers and fell down his shoulder.

John noticed that no one really complained about old Foghorn. Everybody started looking regulation again, and the only comments were offhand, such as, "This sure is turning into a rinky-dink outfit," or, "Doesn't the orderly room realize there's a war on?" The poker games started up again in the Dutchman's hootch; the only change was that Samson was gone. Nobody talked about him.

A glib, fast-talking fellow named Ernie Fisher from North Carolina replaced Samson. He told bad jokes. One of his favorites was "Roses are red, violets are blue, I like peanut butter, can you skate?"—and complained constantly about a girl friend back home who was talking about their getting married. She spent too much time at his mother's house planning grandchildren and things. The platoon overlooked

Fisher's irritating habits because he loved to play poker and always lost.

Master Bates collected a letter for him when Fisher was flying one day and noticed that it was from the girl friend. Her name was Susie. On the back of the envelope, he wrote in the best imitation of her handwriting he could manage, "Eat shit, Ernie."

Fisher said nothing for three days. He did not complain about Susie or even crack one of his lousy jokes. He just looked around at everybody suspiciously. He also looked troubled, and his card playing changed. He was now a morose winner rather than a good-natured loser.

"Hell, Fish, you tryin' to get even in one night?" asked Tex as he lost his last dollar to Ernie. "These good in this game?" He held up a "twee" dollar bill, a phony, printed to look like a greenback. The denomination was the number "three" spelled twee. And instead of a president, the bill had Alfred E. Newman's picture on it.

John held out his hand for it. The paper and ink were very real looking. "I'll lend you ten till pay day if you give it to me."

"It's a deal," said Tex. "Let's play."

"I'm out," said Fisher, standing up. "I'm tired."

"You look like you been eatin' shit, Fisher," said Master Bates.

Fisher did not say a word, and he ignored the barb, walking out of the room.

The next morning, there was a note taped to the door of Bate's room. Labeled the "Swamp Curse," it ran in one long sentence for ninety-three words. "May a dozen Pygmy women," it began, and described what they would do with all Bates's parts. Bates handed it around, and all that anyone said was "Wow" or "Geeze" or some such one-word expression of astonishment. Neither Bates nor Fisher ever admitted what they had done to each other.

Fisher flew with John for the first time in support of the 173rd Airborne Brigade. The day before, the Sixty-first had transported hundreds of GIs on a combat assault into the mountains northwest of Phu Cat.

"We're flying command and control for the 173rd today," said John. "A lot of brass'll be on board, so don't tell any of those terrible jokes, newby."

"Who's the brass?" asked Fisher.

"Colonel Palls, the brigade XO, and two majors, battalion commanders. One of them I don't know too well. The other is a good man, Major Decker. He calls himself the Flying Dutchman, too. Heard me use my call sign during a combat support about two months ago, and he came out in his jeep to see me when I landed. He's got Flying Dutchman written across the front of his jeep. His parents came from Rotterdam, like my grandfather did."

"We really taking 409? The CO's new bird?"

"Right. He lets it go for this harmless stuff, like CC and VIP flights."

"How many hours on it?"

"About a hundred, I think."

"Wow. I never flew in a new helicopter before."

"We better not mess this one up, or we won't fly one again. The CO really loves his new Huey."

Especially outfitted for command and control, the helicopter had an extra radio pack with four FM radios to talk to ground troops. At altitude, C & C flew well out of the range of ground fire and high enough to reach everyone by radio. Some visual recon was done, but most important was line-of-sight radio contact.

Major Decker walked up with the colonel and the other major, who got in. "How ya doing today, Dutchman?"

"Real fine, sir. Good day. No clouds."

"Hope it stays that way. I want you to stay at about eight thousand or so all day. We've got the XO, you know."

"Yes, sir. It's a big operation."

"It is that."

After going through the pretake-off check list with his peter pilot, Fisher, John took the ship up to two thousand feet as fast as it would climb, and then, heading for the area of operations, he began a slow assent to eight thousand feet.

These were VIPs, and there would be no excuses for any kind of a screw up. "Make sure you know where the needles are reading on the six-pack," he reminded Fisher, taking note himself of the exact oil pressures and temperatures.

Everything went smoothly, and they reached their station. From all the radio activity, it was obviously hot down on the ground. Several hundred men on both sides were shooting everything they had at each other. In about an hour, during which John responded to a few directions from the commanders, they lost medivac. Three of the four gunships assigned to cover the medivac helicopters were out. Two had taken hits from the concentration of antiaircraft fire, and one had mechanical problems. Medivac units were under orders not to go into a hot battlefield without escort, and one gunship was not enough. A second was necessary to suppress fire after the first made its gun run because the first was a sitting duck while turning back for the next pass. The rule had been installed late in the war because they were losing so many medivac ships. It was designed to protect them while making sure they would still go in under hazardous conditions.

Unlike medivac or dust off pilots, slick pilots were under no such orders. They were fully responsible for their ships, and a slick pilot could use his own judgment about going into any combat situation.

A young voice started hailing medivac over his radio: "Dust off, Dust off! This is Bravo Company. We got two hurt real bad. One gut shot, one sucking chest."

"We understand, but we can not come in. We lost escort" was the reply.

"Goddam it! These men are dying." The young voice was sobbing. "They are my friends. They're losing blood. You got to get them out now. Come get them. Please!"

John listened as the young man, calling medivac over and over, pleaded for his comrade's lives. Medivac would not go in. Bravo company was situated between two tree-covered escapements owned by the enemy. A deadly net of 12.7-mm. antiaircraft guns was hitting everything within range. Then the young man called command and control, John's ship. John felt the sobbing from the radio pound in his head, and he swore to himself about all the brass on board. He could not risk the lives of the commanders, but he automatically assessed the risk involved in saving those two on the ground.

"Dutchman . . ." Major Decker had unbuckled and come up between the seats, trailing his headphone wire. "What do you say? Can we go down and get those guys?"

"I want to, but I can't. I'm responsible for your lives."

"The colonel says its okay. He'll take the responsibility."

John's spirit soared. "Go buckle in and have the colonel tell base what you told me. We're going in!"

"Let's go," hollered the major over the intercom after the call was made.

John glanced back. The other major wasn't saying anything. He had the look of fear in his eyes, but there was no way he could overrule the colonel. The colonel himself looked grim.

From eight thousand feet, the Flying Dutchman flew his chopper into a high-nose attitude and peeled off into a single-ship approach. His passengers were looking straight down at the ground from the open doorway. Before anyone could blink, they were diving toward the ground at four thousand feet a minute, about as fast as a helicopter can come out of the sky with its main rotor still attached. The 12.7s opened up. Tracer rounds looked like basketballs zooming by. Supersonic bullets popped as they passed. When one found its mark, it felt like someone smacking the ship with a baseball bat. Fortunately, the bullets were armor piercing and not ball rounds. Neat holes were punched through the skin, the diameter of a thumb. Because of the rapid descent, most hits were in the tail section. The master caution light went yellow, and every chip light lit up. Metal fragments had hit vital components. Engine and transmission oil pressure began falling as John spiraled in overhead, flared out, and set down exactly between the two smoke markers.

As soon as the troops on the ground had hefted the two critical cases into each side, John blasted out at low level, all the while taking fire from the ground. He knew the Huey didn't have long before it became so much battered magnesium. He needed five minutes to reach the MASH unit set up close for just such emergencies. John held the helicopter at 140 knots, although VNE was 120. At that excessive speed the rotor blades border on retreating blade stall, making the ship feel like a car crossing railroad tracks with no tires on its wheels.

Every warning light was on. Broken glass was shaking out of the instrument panel. The gauges showed high temperature and no transmission oil pressure. The transmission was howling like a banshee, but the engine was still going strong.

Major Decker had checked the blood types on the dog tags of the wounded men while John called ahead to MASH.

"We got two bad hurts. Both lost a lot of blood. The one on my side, portside, has a sucking chest wound, blood type A positive. The man on the starboard door is gut shot, O positive. Be there in one or two minutes."

"Hear you, Flying Dutchman. We'll be waiting."

Bucking and jarring, with the noise from the transmission getting worse, they broke out over the trees and John flared hard, setting down on the MASH unit helipad. As soon as he rolled off the throttle, the transmission came to a screeching halt, torquing the ship's position forty-five degrees. Eight medics, four on each side, immediately began plugging blood into the wounded, running tubes from four bags into both arms and legs of each man.

John got out of the ship as the men were loaded onto stretchers and carried into the mobile hospital. When his feet hit the ground, his knees folded under him, and he sat down. His heart was pounding in his ears. He was surprised, because the whole time he was flying the rescue, he had felt calm, and his head had been so clear that it seemed like the action was in slow motion. From entering the descent to touch down at MASH had taken only seven minutes. He just sat there, afraid of passing out, while Fisher, as a precaution, went after a fire extinguisher. The second major staggered away, heaving his guts out. The colonel still sat in his jump seat, his face white as a sheet. Major Decker came running up to John, whooping.

"Wow, goddam, that's the greatest thing I ever saw! You're one hell of a pilot, Dutchman." He slapped John on the back and knelt down beside him. "Let me tell you, Dutchman, you can do no wrong from now on in the 173rd. You come by anytime. You get anything you want." The major squeezed his shoulder. "God almighty, what a damn fine show."

A little later, behaving normally again, they all walked around the helicopter counting holes. The ship had taken twenty-seven hits. The transmission was so hot it had burned off all the paint and turned purple. The engine exhaust area was burned black. There were holes in the nose, up through the instruments, floor, rotor blades, and tail section. The CO's new helicopter was a piece of junk.

John and the crew waited two hours after Decker and the others left for maintenance to bring another chopper. The two wounded men were successfully operated on and medivacked to the hospital in Qui Nhon. When maintenance arrived, the CO was with them. When he saw his helicopter, he went into a rage.

"Who do you think you are?" Captain Hayes yelled at John. "You've destroyed government property! You had no business going in there. You risked the lives of those commanders and your crew, and I'm sure those soldiers are going to die, anyway, so you saved nothing. Vanvorden, you're in for a courtmartial, and you're going to have to pay for that helicopter. . . ."

John let the captain's words flow right over him; then he interrupted to answer back. "I'll tell you what, sir. There aren't any hundred helicopters worth those two guys not having a chance of making it. What if that was you down there? Or your brother? Don't talk to me about government property!"

The captain was so furious he made a move toward John. Turning his left hip, John drew his right fist back. The captain stopped and turned quickly back to the helicopter. "I'm flying AC. You ride in back. That's where you belong. You're grounded, starting now!"

His grounding lasted exactly a day and a half, at which time Colonel Palls requested the Sixty-first to send John over to fly a VIP flight. When he heard the Flying Dutchman was grounded, he went to see Gen. Clark Willaby, the commander of the 173rd. That evening, General Willaby, Colonel Palls, and Major Stoddard met with Captain Hayes. The meeting lasted for one hour, and everybody in the company knew something was up. It was unusual for so much rank to call on a captain.

First to leave the orderly room was the general, a good-looking black man with a star on each shoulder. He smiled slightly as the men outside snapped to attention and saluted. "As you were, gentlemen."

Next, Colonel Palls came out, smiling broadly and returning salutes in a brusque, high-command manner. Major Stoddard, commander of the 7/17th Cavalry, came out not smiling, and Captain Hayes following, looking smaller than usual and stunned. The big brass left unceremoniously in their jeeps, and the captain went to his hootch.

At 0800 hours in the morning, Mister Vanvorden was reinstated as senior aircraft commander.

Colonel Palls was awarded a Silver Star. John was written up for one, but it was downgraded to a Distinguished Flying Cross, which was common practice. The two majors also got DFCs, and Fisher got a bronze star with a V device for valor. Both gunners were awarded air medals with Vs.

General Willaby himself came to the Sixty-first to pin on the medals and to pick John up for the awards ceremony. The notoriety embarrassed John, who knew well that such rescues were performed day in and day out by U.S. pilots. His recognition came only because a bird colonel had been on board.

The 173rd requested John from then on when they needed a helicopter. At their mess hall, he ate at the general's table. Also, after resupply missions, the 173rd would leave a case of the coveted freeze-dried LRRP rations in his helicopter. Major Decker had made good on his promise that the 173rd would treat John royally.

On the other side of the coin, Captain Hayes treated John worse than ever. Men that wanted to curry favor with the CO could do so by bad mouthing the Flying Dutchman. Furthermore, unannounced early-morning wake-ups continued to diminish his popularity, though maintaining that procedure was keeping men alive.

Since he was a short timer, there was little the CO could do to John. The goal that he could hold onto was to preserve lives by doing his job to the best of his ability.

Walking into operations one day at noon, he found Captain Hayes planning a mission without having consulted him. That struck a raw nerve. The OPS officer, Captain Medsker, looked helpless when John walked in. The maps and charts were all laid out, and the CO was making measurements on them.

"What's going on here? asked John.

Medsker kept quiet. Hayes went back to his maps without saying anything.

"I said what's going on here?"

"It's none of your business," said Hayes.

"Are you planning a mission?" There was no response. "What is it you're planning?"

"A new assignment came down from HQ," said Medsker.

Captain Hayes glowered at him.

John had heard through his own channels that the Sixty-first had been chosen lead company in the biggest CA since Laos. They had been picked because of the company's outstanding combat performance since their return to An Son.

John was responsible for that record, and he knew it. Now Hayes wanted to run the show, having ignored all the details of mission planning up to then.

"Is this the CA using Americans, Koreans, and ARVNs?" asked John.

"Who told you anything about it?" asked Hayes angrily.

"It's my job to know. I'm the senior AC."

"Senior AC means nothing to me," said the CO, rolling up the maps so John could not see them. "You think you're a big shot, don't you Vanvorden? Warrant officers are nothing in this army, and it doesn't matter who your friends are!"

"I'm helping to plan the CA," said John.

"You won't have time. You're going to Saigon tomorrow. You're ferrying a helicopter to Bien Hoa. Those are my orders."

"Are you sending me on some shit detail to get me out of the way . . . ?"

"You refuse to fly, I get your AC orders. It's the same difference."

Arguing was useless. John was had. Turning on his heel, he marched over to the XO's office. "Look, Kant, keep your hand in while I'm gone, will you? I'll get back, I think, before this thing kicks off, but if someone doesn't watch the CO, he's going to fuck it up."

"The CO knows what he is doing. . . ."

"Bullshit. You know it. I'm just asking you to watch what's going on while I'm gone. I should be back in three days, maybe four."

"Well, okay, Dutchman."

"Thanks, Cunt."

"Don't call me that anymore."

"Right. Nicknames are a sensitive subject with me, too. I'll see you."

Bates was the most loyal of all the pilots. He knew exactly why the Sixty-first wasn't taking casualties and hadn't forgotten that the Flying Dutchman had taught the unit to fly combat. The survivors of Lamson 719 had grown cocky after Laos. Nothing would be as bad as Laos. Furthermore, they figured the Dutchman was short and pretty soon would be playing it too careful. Bates no longer tried to defend the Dutchman.

John went to Bates's hootch. "Want to play?" he asked.

Bates looked pleased. "You're getting too good, Dutchman."

"Good, hell. You let me beat you last time." At first, John had never won. Now, on the average, he did win one out of ten. If he got past the middle of the game with equal forces, it was an even match. He had learned a lot of chess from the master. They set up the board.

"The CO is planning the biggest CA we've had since Laos, and he won't let me near," John said.

"What?" Bates was shocked.

"You know what he thinks of me. He's after glory, and this is a big one. Koreans, ARVNs, our guys. You know I never talk about what's coming up, but he's sending me to Saigon, and I want you to keep your eyes and ears open. When I get back, let me know what you know."

"Sure will, Dutchman. You can count on it."

John took a deep breath and rubbed his aching temples. "Maybe I'm upset over nothing. It's a feeling I have. I know the brass of the 173rd came down on him with both feet, and I just hope he isn't still so ragged about it, he gets somebody killed. It's bad karma."

"Bad what?"

"Uh . . . karma. The Buddhists think you carry a bad act with you, and you have to work it out in the future some way."

"Sounds hokey."

"Maybe so."

"Is that in the book I see you reading sometimes?"

"Yep. A friend gave it to me."

Bates held out his clenched fists, a pawn in each one.

''Left,'' said John.

''Black,'' said Bates.

They escaped together onto a battlefield of sixty-four black and white squares where the hurts were inflicted on the ego only, not the body.

25

TDY SAIGON

"So you're the Dutchman. You ain't too old, are you, Dutchman?"

"I'm as old as I can be," said John.

Solomon, CW-3, the other pilot on the mission to Tan Son Nhut Air Base near Saigon, thought that was funny. "I'm the Junkman. You probably heard of me."

"Heard about you a while back, in Laos."

Helicopters with 2,000 hours were sent to Tan Son Nhut for overhaul. Everybody wanted to fly these ash and trash missions because they could get into the capital city for a couple of days. John knew he was being sent so the CO could plan the big combat assault without his interference, but since he had to go, he might as well enjoy it.

"That place was hard on helicopters," remarked the Junkman.

"Screw the helicopters. What about the pilots?"

"Screw the pilots."

"Let's start over," said John, looking at the veteran maintenance officer, who was on his fourth tour. "Did I ever tell you guys what a great job you do for us clumsy bastards, who are always mucking up your helicopters?"

"Damn right we do a good job," said Solomon, grinning at him. "Some of you bastards are better'n others."

"Thanks—I think."

The flight to Tan Son Nhut took half a day. Crews usually spent two or three days waiting there for a replacement helicopter. When John and the Junkman arrived at the base, the military police demanded that they check in their M-16s and sidearms. The Junkman said you needed a weapon in Saigon because it wasn't safe, and John argued against checking his .45 automatic. That Colt was a popular weapon and could easily be stolen, even in MP custody. The MPs were adamant.

After registering for rooms at the BOQ, they took a bus with steel mesh over its windows in to the city. Saigon's streets were jammed with people, bikes, motorcycles, cars, and trucks. They all drove like the French. Getting into town was a slow business.

"Ought to get a couple of Rome plows on the street every night and let the traffic start over in the morning," said the Junkman.

"I don't think that would help." said John. The city was far larger than any of the northern ones.

"Fun to watch, though, by God. C'mon."

John followed Solomon off the bus. The Junkman appeared at home in Saigon and led him up a main street for a block, then into back streets that soon turned into alleys. Clothes and bedding hung from every window. Corner stands of vegetables and meat were everywhere. The crowd looked and sounded different.

"Cholon section," said the Junkman. "Chinatown." He stopped in front of a small restaurant with a sign in Chinese characters. "Best food in Saigon. The owner does the cooking hisself. He moved here from the big place he had when the police were looking for him. GIs didn't know where he went."

"How do you know?"

"Hell, I been comin' here since before you knew there was a war on, sonny. I killed my first gook while you were still playin' marbles."

John let it go. The old-timers he had met in Vietnam were all bitter. They talked about when the country used to be paradise, when the dollar went a long way and the people were friendly and the city was safe. Disturbances occurred in the countryside and once in a while in the city, but that was little bother. Then it changed. Old friends left the country or were put in prison or died. You had to sneak around just to find good food. . . .

In the restaurant, the Junkman was told the police had caught up with Mr. Chu. He had gone to prison for a bombing incident in his restaurant that had occurred years before. The Saigon police kept files on everybody, especially the Chinese population. The charge was that Mr. Chu had bombed his own restaurant. No official could say why. Solomon showed no emotion. He just looked tired.

Chu's daughter was now the chef. They sat drinking tea for a while. Then the food came. Appetizers were three kinds of meat dumplings. You sucked as you bit into them so the juices would not go down your shirt. Crisp fish came next, with a sweet delicious sauce. Then came barbecued spare ribs, dark in color, with a pungent sauce. John and the Junkman argued over the last of the ribs.

The dingy little restaurant had offered no clue that it served such good Chinese food, but the white tablecloths were immaculate, and the platters that continued to come from the kitchen were so delicious that John was sorry when he had to slow down. Spicy prawn with fried water cress, a chicken dish with crackling rice, eel, peppery bean curd. The Junkman ate everything with undiminished gusto. As a special courtesy, they were given one last dish of almond soup.

They hardly said a word during the meal. John tried the clear Chinese liquor the Junkman had been sipping during the feast. It smelled foul, but the taste was not bad. He felt a small glassful all the way to his belly.

"How was that, Dutchman? Better than C rats?"

"Great. Just great." The tastes lingered in his throat and nostrils.

"You'd have to come in here a month of Sundays to eat every kind of food they fix. Whatdya say we see what's happening at the New Yorker?"

"That a bar?"

"It ain't no teahouse."

At the New Yorker, the Junkman immediately disappeared up a stairway with the girl who had come running to him as soon as he walked in. John sat at the bar and ordered a beer.

"You buy me a drink?" An aggressive little bar girl plumped down beside him and put her hand on the inside of his thigh.

"Sure, what do you like?"

"Wicky Coke."

Whiskey Coke. She would. "Okay, but drink slow. I don't have much money." John had left most of his money in his room for fear it would be stolen. The bar reminded him of Bangkok. It was sleazier, but the music and the noise were the same. The girls were shorter and thinner and looked hard compared to the Thais. All of them wore short Western-style dresses or skirts with halter tops, and not many shaved under their arms. They did not have much hair, anyway.

Women pros were taking money from drunken GIs, a scene repeated thousands of times in hundreds of Nam bars every day. And there he was handing over his money to a drunken little broad. She was hitting him on the arm again for a third whiskey Coke. He caught her fist and told her to go away. When she would not, he got up and found a booth. Another one tried to sit by him. "Hello. My name Rose."

"No more whiskey Cokes," said John, refusing to move over. "Will you drink Saigon tea?"

"I drink."

He moved over then.

Her English was not good enough for conversation, but at

least Rose did not hit him on the arm, and after an hour and a half, she was only on her third Saigon tea, about half the price of whiskey Cokes. He was out of money now except for some green he kept in his boot.

"I like stay with you," said Rose.

"I'm out of money."

"You got money. You big-time officer. Officers got money." She started to go through his pockets, but he stopped her.

"I'll show you." He pulled out his wallet, which was empty except for the twee dollar bill with Alfred E. Newman's picture on it. It was the best phony money he had ever seen.

"You give me this."

He could not resist. With the twee dollar bill, she paid for another drink and brought back change in piasters. He told her a quick joke, and then he laughed until his eyes teared. She did not think the story he told was funny, but she liked his laughing.

"Go home with me," she said. "No money. No sweat. I take you free. Don't tell other GIs? Go get taxi, wait. I come out."

"Sure," said John, and walked through the noisy crowd to the door. Outside, he called a taxi and went back to the base. No way would he go with a whore who wanted to do it free. This was dangerous country for a great many reasons.

That night John's thoughts before sleep were as bad as his dreams. Captain Hayes would have it all his own way while his senior aircraft commander was gone. The OPS officer was a lifer and would never raise objections. The CA was to take place in an area with twelve bare hill tops capable of holding two helicopters each, and John was certain that Hayes would make daily tours over them, taking with him group commanders he wanted to impress. That would alert the enemy that something big was coming. Further intelligence was certain to filter out, and when they got there, the enemy would be waiting.

The Junkman took John sightseeing the next day. He wanted some snapshots of the Saigon Cathedral, a large, European-style church that looked out of place in its tropical setting. It must have been the French that built it. The arched doorways were thirty feet high, and inside among the altars, the art work, the quiet, they could have been in Europe. John felt the familiar discomfort about organized religion that always afflicted him.

"I've had enough of this place," he said to the old warrant officer.

"I was ready to go before we came in," said the Junkman.

"Well, get your pictures and let's go."

The next stop was a street where Solomon said they could get good fish and rice. On the street, shopkeepers were busy selling baskets, sandals, food, and clothes; an old lady swept a portion of the sidewalk with an ancient broom. The exhaust fumes from cars and motor scooters fouled the air. They walked side by side down the crowded street, two officers in jungle fatigues with expensive cameras hanging from their shoulders, towering over the black-haired people brushing by them.

Suddenly, two men jumped out of the crowd toward them and began yelling in bad English. One pointed a gun, while the other stripped their cameras, watches, and wallets. They stood perfectly still while the man with the gun hollered, "No move! No move! I shoot! *Dung lie*! I shoot!"

People passing took little notice of the mugging. It was like a business transaction to which they were accustomed. As the robber stripped off John's watch, his long dirty fingernails gouged his victim's arm. Pain turned John's fear to anger, but he remained still. A few passing Vietnamese looked amused—two more GIs were getting no more than they deserved. The two robbers, with the cameras over their shoulders and watches and wallets in their hands, turned to run away.

"Watch this," said the Junkman, dropping to his knees and pulling up his pant leg. With a practiced move, he snatched a small 32-caliber automatic pistol from the top of his boot. It had been scotch-taped to his calf.

With total accuracy, he shot both thieves in the back of the head. Fifteen yards away, they dropped to the pavement like dead weights. One was out cold, the other writhing, and both were bleeding profusely. John stood there stunned. The crowd reacted. Women were screaming; people were running. Shopkeepers kicked customers out and slammed metal gratings shut. Solomon picked up their possessions from the two prone bodies and yelled at John, "Let's go!" As they took off running, he handed John back his things. It was easy getting through the crowd now because everyone was ducking for cover. A block away, they caught a cab and went back to the base.

"You don't tell nobody what happened there," said the Junkman as they walked through the gate to the BOQ. "Them gooks got justice a little quicker than they expected, that's all. Next time, maybe they shoot us."

"Don't worry, I won't say shit."

In his room, John slowly reviewed what had happened. He did not feel guilty. Maybe they should not have run, but they were not supposed to have a gun in the first place. He was still somewhat scared. There was not a thing he could have done to prevent the shooting . . . No court in the states would convict you for killing a thief, gun against gun. Self-defense. It had to be bad karma, though. Huey had warned against excess. Better to let them have the stuff than risk a future debt for killing somebody. But how did you decide when to use force? He could not solve that big riddle, but he had to conclude that the killing had been excessive. It was too final.

John did not go back into town with the Junkman that night. Instead, after evening chow, he went to the officers' club where two airmen singers were entertaining. One had a nasal voice but played the guitar very well. The other, a redhead, had a beautiful Irish tenor. When he sang, the audience was quiet. The singer with the nasal voice made them noisy again, including one country boy up front who kept yelling, "Shut the fuck up!" The final song was in free verse and set to a nonrepeating tune that ended on an agreeable note: "Vietnam is a nice place to visit, but I wouldn't want to die here."

In the morning, he and Solomon picked up their weapons from the MPs and walked to the flight operations building to fill out papers for a new helicopter. The Junkman told John he was lucky he had not come in town the night before. Rose was looking for him. She was mad at him for passing bad money.

In the air on the way back to the Sixty-first, the Junkman was talkative. He trusted the Dutchman now. "You should have been here in sixty-two," he said. "I was a W-1, like you. Flew H-19s. I liked it so much I extended another year. Vietnam was the best-kept secret the army had in them days."

"What do you mean?"

"This place was heaven. I was stationed near Monkey Mountain. We only had a couple choppers, and I spent most of my time shackin' up with a girl that already had a kid by some Frenchy. No Vietnamese man'd have her so long as she hung onto the brat. I kinda liked the kid. She looked like her mom. Then I went back to the states."

"What happened?"

"I thought I could leave, and that'd be it, but I couldn't. I got myself reassigned back here. It was easy. They needed all the pilots they could get. I went right back to Monkey Mountain, which is what I got for volunteer'n, and the girl was waiting for me. I'd wrote her every week I was gone. Then, a month after I got back here, her and her daughter was dead. She'd gone to visit her folks for a couple of days, and the VC walked in, shot half the village t'show the other half who was runnin' things."

"Jesus. I'm sorry."

"Long time ago. The rest of that tour was hard. I never wanted to see this place again. I never wanted to see another gook again. Then, back in the states, I couldn't stop thinkin' about it, and I couldn't stay away. I came back just in time for Tet."

"The Tet Offensive," said John.

"That's what they called it. It was bloody hell for a while. After that, I got into maintenance. I don't like flying combat anymore. Lose too many friends."

John was surprised at the Junkman's sensitivity. "Didn't it bother you any yesterday, shooting those two guys?" he asked cautiously.

"Why should it?"

"It's not like combat . . ."

"The hell it isn't. It's worse. Anytime anybody points a gun at you, it's combat. Don't forget it, or you'll be dead."

"But they were running away."

"That's their hard luck. Shoulda picked a different profession."

"What made you come back this time?"

"Dunno. I think I can stay away after this tour. I hope. It's not a good place anymore. They all hate us, the North and the South. The gooks're so fucked up they don't know what they want, what to do. They'll go Commie probably. Commies have their shit together, and they're the only ones that do. Half our troops are on drugs and won't fight. What's more, I can't think of a reason why they should."

"How'd you get the name Junkman?"

"Not from drugs, I can tell you that. It's from dealin' in helicopter parts and whatever I need t'keep the birds flyin'."

John then told him about the green market, what he had done for his old CO at the 155th in Ban Me Thuot, and all about the arrangements with Sergeant Jameson. It was good telling him about it, and it felt good to earn the old warrant officer's respect.

26
THE CO'S BIG SHOW

WHEN HE GOT BACK FROM SAIGON, JOHN SENSED A CHANGE in the company, a nervousness. Everyone knew that the CO had been overflying the area of operations several times a week, and John found out from Bates that Hayes had been showing his friends in infantry command how the plan would work. It was practically advertising the real estate they were planning to invade, and all the seasoned pilots now feared that enemy observers on the ground would begin preparing a reception party.

Six days before the CA, Captain Hayes held an operations briefing with uncommon ceremony. All sixty pilots were called to the briefing, which would normally be given by the senior AC and OPS officer. When the first sergeant hollered, "Atten HUT!" everyone snapped to their feet.

"At ease," said Captain Hayes, striding in. "Take your seats." On the podium, he surveyed his audience in silence. No one could speak before he did.

"Gentlemen." He paused and looked down at them. "The Sixty-first Assault Helicopter Company has been chosen to lead the largest combat assault in II Corps since Tet in '68. We have been chosen because of our outstanding combat record. This is a proud moment for our company." He paused again. "This history-making event could be a turning point in the war."

Someone said "bullshit" and disguised it with a cough so that only the men around him could hear.

"I have spent long hours meticulously planning this mission, and I know it will be successful."

"Rat fuck." This was muffled in a sneeze, but most of the pilots got the message.

"Whoever you are out there with that cold, please get up and leave so the rest of us don't get sick and miss the mission!" The pilots broke into stifled laughter, and the CO smiled as if his wit had been appreciated.

The OPS officer and his assistant passed out instruction packets containing maps, radio frequencies, and call signs for artillery, tac air, command and control, company and ground troops.

"If you open your maps, you will note the area of operation outlined in red. Blue marks the LZs, twelve of them, lettered A through L. There will be seventy-two slicks and sixteen Charlie models coming from four assault helicopter companies. The seven-seventeenth Cav's providing eight cobras and eight Chinooks from Big Windy." There was a satisfied, important look on his face as the pilots frowned over the maps.

"The slicks are broken down into twelve flights of six each. You will land and unload, two at a time, at three-minute intervals. Each flight of six will have a gun team covering it. When the LZs are secure, we'll bring in the Chinooks. The first insertion will take place at 0700 hours in each LZ. Any questions so far?"

"Sir!" John spoke up, and all the pilots looked at him. "With three separate landings within each flight of six, the gun teams can't cover the slicks both in and out of the LZs."

"That's right, sir," chimed in the gun platoon leader quickly. "By the time the first pair is on the ground, we will have to leave them to pick up the second pair coming in, and the same goes for the third pair. We can't escort the ones going out."

"You don't need to cover them out unless they take fire. . . ."

"No, but sir, if we do have to cover the pair out, it leaves the two coming in uncovered. . . ."

Hayes interrupted the gun platoon leader, who was also a captain. "Listen, captain, I don't want to hear what you can't do. Just do as you are told. If you don't think you can handle it, we'll get someone who can. Understood?"

"Yes, sir."

"That's that. We will be inserting nine South Korean battalions, four U.S. battalions, and five ARVN battalions, in that order." He pointed to the wall map. "At 0430 hours, we load in the PZ here." The pickup zone was next to the Korean fire-support base, Binh Khe. "Lift off is 0600 hours. We fly up the Song Con River to the IP at ground coordinate 15660264." He indicated the initial point and went on. "At IP, we break into twelve separate teams and pick up armed escort. The gunnies will lead the slick teams to the LZs, and en route each team will divide into three flights of two. Coming back, you will form up again at IP and return to the pickup zone the same way you left. The gunnies will stay on station, giving support to the ground troops until the slicks return reloaded."

The seasoned ACs were frowning. John hated the plan so strenuously that the beginnings of a new plan were already forming in his head.

"Every second trip, the gunnies will return to refuel and reload. The slicks will make a total of fifteen insertions. Starting with the seventh, the Chinooks will join in and make nine. By that time, each LZ will have 216 troops to provide adequate covering fire for the Chinooks. In fact, since the slicks will lead the seventh insertion, there will be an additional thirty-six troops dropped off in each LZ just prior to the Chinook landings. The round robin from liftoff to liftoff at the PZ will take an average of forty-eight minutes, including fuel stops every second trip."

Hayes looked pleased, but the pilots were unnaturally silent. A number of them were looking at John, who normally gave the briefing.

"Any more questions?" The CO was forced to acknowledge that the attention of the men had shifted to John. "How about you, Flying Dutchman? We haven't heard much from you. Perhaps you think I've stolen your show?"

No one snickered. The room was silent. John stood at attention, all eyes on him.

"Sir, what I have to say about this CA I want to say to you in private."

"You just forget that," said Hayes. "If you can't say it now, I don't want to hear it."

The tension in the room magnified sounds.

John cleared his throat. "Who's on AMC?" he asked.

"Myself and the battalion commander, Major Raeburn, and we—"

"How are you going to keep track of twelve flights of slicks, eight Chinooks, and twelve gun teams . . . sir?"

"You let me worry about that, Mister Vanvorden! Your ship and crew assignments are on the board. The Sixty-first will fly the lead two ships of the first nine flights into LZs A through I. *We* are the lead company, and we are going to lead."

John did not sit down. "Sir. You haven't given us the artty barrage ending times."

"There will be no artillery barrage or tac air," Captain Hayes admitted brusquely. "They'll be available, but we want to surprise Charlie. We aren't going to wake him up with a lot of artillery warning them to dig in."

Now, it was certain. Everybody knew this was a rat fuck.

"Sergeant," said the CO, leaving the podium.

"Atten HUT!"

Captain Hayes followed the first sergeant, passing along

the rows of pilots. Stopping by John, he said without looking at him, "See me in my office in fifteen minutes!"

As soon as he was gone, John was surrounded by the pilots. What did he think about this badly planned mission? they asked. What would he say to the CO? Even the pilots close to the CO were all scared now. There was no time to stand around. John pushed his way through the door without saying anything and exactly fifteen minutes later walked into the CO's office.

"Mister Vanvorden reporting as ordered, sir!"

"Stand at ease," said Captain Hayes. "Well, now. Just what don't you like about my CA plan?"

"I don't like any of it, sir. We have only four ACs capable of leading a formation, especially if they have to lead a flight out of such a huge formation, find their gun team, and then find the correct LZ. After insertion, the flight leads have to join up with eleven other teams, which is the most difficult part of all. The way you have mixed companies and platoons, most of them will be flying with strangers . . ."

"Is that your only complaint?"

"No, sir. We have to land in LZs where the enemy will surely be waiting. Those twelve LZs are the only possible landing zones in the whole sector. But you won't give us Arc Light, Tac Air, or artty. Besides, you have not arranged gunny protection flying out. You know that we take fire going out as often as going in, and since you've been scouting the AO every day, they are bound to know we are coming. You know they watch for us. . . ."

"Goddam you, Vanvorden. That's enough! I will take no more from you. I've shown my plans to the 173rd Airborne and the Koreans, and both have given me the okay!"

Hayes's defense of himself was too shrill, John thought. He must know that he should be listening. In a way, John blamed himself for this mess. That reprimand Hayes had gotten from the 173rd after he tried to court-martial John had wounded his ego, and he had taken this opportunity to show his military prowess.

"Did the other helicopter companies okay the plan?" asked John, knowing they had not but trying to give the CO an out.

"They have nothing to say about it. Group made me AMC and ordered all the other flight commanders to do as I tell them to."

"Sir," pled John. "It won't work. It will be a disaster. *Please* let me work on the plan. I won't tell anyone that I did. I'll say whatever you want me to. Just let me help."

"There will be no changes. The ground commanders have okayed it. It's set and that's that."

"They don't know enough about airmobile. They'd agree to anything."

"Mister Vanvorden, this conversation is over. Dismissed!"

"I am not flying this mission," said John.

"Fine. I'll have you up for desertion."

John walked out.

For two nights, he barricaded himself in his hootch, yelling at anyone who knocked to go away. He planned an alternative combat assault. There had to be a way he could persuade Captain Hayes to substitute it for the rat fuck. Meticulously, he made fresh calculations, reshaping flight numbers and the time schedule into something that could be managed by air mission command. On the third night, it was done. When Bates banged at his door, John admitted him.

"I have to talk to you. Everybody's jumpy. They keep asking me why you aren't talking about this Romeo Foxtrot that Hayes dreamed up. They think you can do something."

John was feeling better. His revised plan was finished, and the CO should finally listen to reason. It was to the CO's advantage, after all. "I'm working on it."

"Everybody says you refused to fly it. You know it's supposed to be you, me, and Sergeant Pulaski and that gunner—what's his name? The one we like from Arkansas."

"Coombs."

"Right. Coombs. All of us on the same ship."

"I did refuse. Anybody in country six months can see it's a disaster on paper. But I've replanned the whole thing."

"Think he'll go for it?"

"I don't know. If he's smart, he will."

"Can I see it?"

"No. If Hayes says no, it won't do you any good."

Just then, Coombs peered through the slightly open door. "Can I come in a minute, sir?"

"Not now," said John.

"Just for a minute, sir?"

"You mind?" John asked Master Bates.

"I'll go and come back later."

"Sure," said John. "Come on in, Coombs. What's on your mind?"

"I just want to ask you to fly AC Saturday."

That was the day of the big CA. John had almost forgotten the date.

"Why me? What's so big about that day?" As if you could keep information about a Romeo Foxtrot from the enlisted men.

"Because, Mister Vanvorden, if you're the AC, I know I'll get through it. I wouldn't ask, sir, but I got a new responsibility now. I gotta make it through the next four months." He carefully took a small photograph out of his wallet and handed it to John.

A wave of emotion hit John. There in the palm of his hand lay a newborn infant. A GI had made him responsible for his baby. The Vietnamese came to you with their babies now and then, and you did what you could, thought John; got them to the medics, got food or something. Now our side is holding up its babies. Jesus God, what are we doing here?

"I'll fly," he said, handing back the photograph. "I'll do my best. Now you put that in your locker and don't think about your kid for the rest of the tour. Don't think about anything but doing your job."

"Right, Dutchman, sir." The young man was grinning. "Good night, sir." He closed the door softly.

John sat on his bunk and looked at the rude wooden flooring. He felt as though a barbell was on his shoulders, as if he were doing squats. He looked up and rolled his head to get the crick out of his neck. He would fly as he had promised the gunner, as the voice within now commanded, even if the CO would not accept the new plan.

There had been many other times when going in meant possible death. Before this, he had always felt confident. Even when he earned the DFC against those heavy odds, he was sure he would make it in and out. Now he did not have that confidence. Well, all he could do now was to try his best with Hayes.

"You still awake?" Bates called at the door.

"Come in."

"Want to play some chess, Dutch?"

"Not now."

"What'd Coombs want?" Then he added, recognizing that it might be private. "None of my business."

"I told him I'd fly the CA."

"That's it? You're going?"

"That's what I said."

Bates looked so relieved it was almost comical. He had just made AC and had been afraid he would have to fly AC on this mission and not copilot with the Dutchman's lead ship. He began to talk about home, which he had never done before.

"You know, my mom's the only one there now. My aunt lived with her, but she just got married and moved away. I'm hoping Mom finds someone to marry. You think that's unfaithful or anything?"

"No, I don't," said John. The guys sure were shook up. "What happened to your dad?"

"He died when I was little, and my ma waited so long, she got out of the habit, I guess. I'm the only kid she has. Only child."

John had no idea what Bates was getting at.

"Once my cousin Danny came to stay with me for a week. His mother—she was my mother's brother's wife—had a complicated pregnancy and had to spend a while in the hospital. After that, I was glad I didn't have any brothers."

"Well, why?"

"It seems stupid now, but one afternoon we were playing and Danny rolled over some dog shit. Got it in his hair. He had to take a bath, and Mom put me in the tub, too. I guess I decided I didn't like sharing. You know?"

"I guess so. I have three brothers.

"Now I wish I did have a brother," said Bates. "I think I missed a lot."

"You missed a lot of fighting, I'll tell you that," said John.

"Yeah, but you really got people who know you, people you can depend on. Brothers."

Something about that word brother makes it catch the ear, thought John. It jumps out at you.

"Maybe I don't know what I'm talking about," said Bates after a minute. "It's hard to talk like this. Anyway, I'm sure glad you're going with us now. See you tomorrow."

"Wish me luck, with the CO tomorrow."

"You got it!"

John approached the interview with determination and hope. He walked right in on Hayes, who was drinking coffee, and put his papers on the desk. "I made some changes, sir, I want you to see."

"Suppose I don't care to listen to you, Vanvorden."

"It's my job as senior AC to advise you, so please just listen." Before the CO could object, John rushed into an orderly explanation. "With three flights of twenty-four slicks and three flights of three Chinooks, you can still assault twelve LZs, but three landing zones at a time instead of all at once. As air mission commander, you can control three LZs much easier than twelve. Then, instead of twenty-four separate radio frequencies, you need only six—"

"Hold a minute! Now just who do you think—"

"I don't have a minute, and neither do you, sir. Hear me out. With twenty-four slicks in a flight instead of six, you can bring in the Chinooks on the third sortie instead of the seventh. When the Chinooks come in, there'll be four hundred thirty-two troops to cover them instead of two hundred fifty-two. After they leave, the three LZs will have enough men to secure the area so that the gunnies and slicks can begin assaulting the next three LZs while the Hooks finish up, and so on, until all twelve have been assaulted. You can get the ninth Chinook from Big Windy. I checked. They have two more ready to go if you need them."

At least Hayes was listening now.

"Six of the twelve gun teams can escort helicopters into and out of the three LZs while the remaining six gun teams stand by at the pickup zone to support ground troops or replace other gunnies during refueling. Also, they can be used to reinforce any LZ that gets hot or cover medivacs—"

"Is that all?"

"No. Using three different initial and release points will cut down the flight times and eliminate forming up into a huge flight over one point. I can give you three good lead pilots who will lead into every LZ—"

"Your way would take two days," interrupted the CO, scorn in his voice.

"No, sir. It would not. It'll take less time because the Chinooks are used sooner and round robins are shorter with three initial points and recovery points. It will take seven hours and nineteen minutes from start to finish. See, here are the calculations. Shorter trips and larger troop insertions will give a much better chance of survival on the ground. Spread over twelve LZs, your plan leaves only thirty-six soldiers in each LZ for forty-eight minutes in an area known to have thousands of enemy. My way puts one hundred forty-four troops into the LZ with a thirty-five-minute wait. That finally puts seven hundred-and-two troops in each LZ, and the twenty-four extra squads can be held in reserve as replacements to be brought in with medivac where needed most."

"Are you quite finished?"

"No!" John raised his voice. Surely the man had to see

that this way was better. "You must prep the LZs before first insertion, sir. If you don't, they'll blow us away. The artillery can hit the first three, and Tac Air can bomb the others as we get ready to go on. That'll prevent cannon shells from hitting ships in the air . . ."

"We do not have time to change. Even if your plan were better than mine, which I don't think it is. Everybody's briefed, it's okayed, and everything is going as scheduled."

"But two days is plenty of time," protested John.

"Furthermore, there will be no prebombardment. We want to surprise them, as I informed you."

John had tried to sound reasonable and respectful, but this was too much. "Are you crazy? We need everything we can throw at those LZs! The way it's laid out this CA could kill God knows how many. There's no way in hell you can control twelve simultaneous insertions if things go bad. . . ."

"Mister Vanvorden! I am overlooking your insolence. You will be part of this CA, which will go exactly as I planned it because I need you for one of my leads."

John felt sick. He turned and walked out.

The day before the mission, John was so uneasy he did everything he could to take his mind off the CA. Filling his idleness, he sunbathed, read from Huey's book, and finished off three bags of freeze-dried spaghetti left over from LRRP packets. Avoiding the other pilots, he thought about going home, about getting into college, about his friends in Utah. But that evening he made one more try to warn Captain Hayes that the enemy might be expecting them. Hayes did feel worried enough to move the CA up one hour, but that was all.

In the predawn, as the pilots of the 268th took off for Fire Base Binh Khe in the Korean sector, the sky was filled with stars. There would be clear weather for the big show. At 0430 hours slicks by the dozen began descending on the pickup zone like a plague of monster dragonflies.

While trying to form up into the complicated flight of

seventy-two, two of the helicopters had rotor strikes. No one was hurt, but the two ships were out of action. The companies did their best but could not manage better than a loose crowd of helicopters all going in the same direction. In the first flight, which John was supposed to lead, he saw at least two helicopters ahead of him, out to the right.

"This is lead," he radioed. "Whoever the hell is out in front on my starboard side, get back in formation."

"Can't, Dutchman. Those bastards want to chew me up in there" was the reply.

John let it go. Any possibility of surprise would be lost if there was too much radio chatter. The radio was very quiet because the other pilots were also aware of the danger. It was eerie to fly in with no Arc Light preceding them to mark the objective, with no artillery speaking. Anxiety pervaded the flight.

At the IP, they broke into ten flights of six and two of five, since they had already lost two choppers. The twelve flights and their gunships headed to the twelve LZs.

As the first flights approached for landing, the shooting started. Every LZ was hot! Pilots on all twenty-four VHF and UHF radio frequencies were demanding instructions. It was total chaos.

John gritted his teeth. Would Captain Hayes and Major Raeburn have the sense to abort immediately, to hold back until Tac Air and artillery could blast the LZs? No such instructions arrived. Swamped with radio communications, they lost track of time.

The enemy had set up mechanical mines in every LZ. Surprised by the early arrival of the slicks, they weren't completely ready. So, fortunately for the first flight crews, only four ships were blown up as they touched down. Three LZs were rendered unusuable. During the first insertion in each LZ, no Korean ground troops survived the waiting reception, and three more helicopters were shot down.

No one stopped the CA, so flights kept going in to dump troops. They were like buffaloes following each other over a cliff. The small number of surviving troops on the ground prevented artillery or Tac Air strikes now. The South Koreans were already in a blood bath. It would be total suicide to pull out because troops on the ground were providing the only covering fire the helicopters had.

John's flight of six made it out, but one ship was losing engine oil and deadheaded for the nearest recovery point. Twelve aircraft on the first insertion were lost or damaged sufficiently to put them out of action. The loss of helicopters and the ensuing confusion slowed the time schedule.

The second insertion, consisting of fifty-eight slicks, each carrying its load of men, fared somewhat better. With some friendlies on the ground, the reception was less devastating. John's flight went into LZ Alpha, which was now littered with the remains of a gunship. John led as the two ships approached in tandem. Knowing it was hot, he came in fast. Chalk Two could barely keep up. Jungle rushed at them as they descended to treetop level and began to zigzag. John homed in on Alpha, using his senses of direction like radar, flared out, and set his ship down close to the trees to allow room for the slick behind him. Ground fire rang out immediately. The ship shook as volleys of armor-piercing bullets destroyed the engine.

"Engine's gone!" shouted Master Bates.

"Two, lead is down, need a lift out," shouted John as he unbuckled.

Fifteen feet in front of the helicopter, a Viet Cong soldier appeared, pointing an AK-47. John was looking directly into the eyes of his executioner. Combat changes seconds to minutes, and John could see every feature, every movement of the VC. He was young. He wore black pajama pants and a green shirt crossed with an ammo belt. He was hatless, and his hair needed cutting. He must have been on the move for a long time.

The VC moved his AK, and John felt thunder on his chest as if he had been hit by a Mac truck. It stunned him. When he slid his hand in behind the chicken plate to feel his chest, the front of his body was wet. He withdrew his hand, expecting to see it dripping red. It looked perfectly normal. He felt again. His chest was wet, but his hands were not red. It was sweat, not blood. But he could not breathe. He had not been breathing for a long time. He tried to speak and could only grunt.

Master Bates was at his left side, trying to help him out of the chopper. The way he looked frightened John all over again. Bates put his hand to John's throat to wipe away blood. Porcelain bits from his chest plate, shattered by the two AK-47 rounds, had cut him on the throat. He jumped into Bates's arms while the South Koreans defending the crew laid down good covering fire with M-16s.

Adrenalin flowed into John's veins, miraculously enabling him to run and to try to get his wind back at the same time. Steadied by Bates, he reached the second chopper. His diaphragm would not yet inhale, and he exhaled in low groans. All he could hear was automatic weapon fire and exploding rifle grenades. Then the helicopter whine penetrated his ears. The two gunwales were blazing. Dangerous, he thought, and managed to climb in behind his own gunners, who had got there before him. When the first breath came, it was as if someone had turned the lights on. Another breath came. Good. Now a big one. He scrambled to the middle and sat facing the doorway. Bates, last to get in, did a slow-motion swan dive next to John as the ship blasted off. He turned on his side. There was a faraway look in his eyes, a look John had seen too many times before.

"Oh, no! You hit?" he yelled.

Bates dragged on his elbows for a few inches to his AC. John felt the bloody hole in his back and yelled emergency instructions to the pilots. Returning to his friend, he took off both of their helmets. Bates's eyes were clouded, and he was trying to say something. John put his ear to Bates's lips.

"I wish you was my brother, Dutchman," whispered Bates.

They both knew he was dying. John put his lips to Bates's ear. "I am your brother. I always will be."

Bates closed his eyes as John spoke. Perhaps he could no longer hear, but John kept talking to him. Coombs and the crew chief sat watching as John said good-by. "It's the end of shadows, Bates; that's all. You'll get plenty more chances. Don't fear anything. I'll see to your mother." Tears were running from the dying man's eyes. He must have understood. John tried to think of more to tell Bates, more from the book, but he was choking up. No time remained for tears. This was a corpse. The man had gone. The body would be bagged and shipped out back to native soil. Earth to earth.

Anger came in place of tears. How, he did not know, but he would fix the CO for this. When he had, Hayes would be finished. No more men would die through his incompetence. Pain began to register after Bates died. John hunched forward to relieve the pressure on his battered ribs. The helicopter was hurrying to a MASH unit.

The MASH medics gave John a quick check-out and sent him back to the Sixty-first with orders to rest for several days. Everybody who came into his room would see the chicken plate he propped on his wardrobe. Most of the porcelain had fallen off in big chunks. Two dents on the front of the armor plate marked where the bullets had hit. On his chest were two dollar-sized bruises the color of black cherries. Little bits of porcelain were embedded in his throat, shoulders, and arms. He worked the fragments out with his fingers one at a time.

Darkness came, and John lay in his bunk listening to the ships coming back to the unit. He did not want to hear anything about it. Seeing one friend die that day was enough. From the sound of the Chinooks, he knew damaged ships were being sling loaded back.

When a black private from maintenance named Bradley dropped by to report, John was not glad to see him.

"Man, that chest ain't looking too good."

"I'll be all right."

"I thought you'd like to hear about the rest of the mission today. It was just like you said it would be."

"You thought wrong," said John, wincing as he turned on his side away from Bradley. "I don't want to hear. Turn the light out on your way out, please, Bradley."

"Mister Vanvorden," the private said, making no move to leave. "Mister Holihan got killed. Him and Mister Bates was the only two from the Second Platoon."

John rolled back and swung his feet to the floor with an effort. He sat up, pushing with his arms to avoid using his stomach muscles.

"Holihan, too."

"Yes, sir. Like you said, Charlie was dug in. The Koreans are up there dying like flies. They still don't have all the U.S. and ARVN ground forces in, so we got to resume the CA tomorrow. They stopped now because everybody's too tired to fly."

"You on recovery?"

"Yes, sir. Most of them ships took hits. Every LZ was hotter than a firecracker."

"I saw, Bradley. I saw. Who else got killed?"

Bradley named five men from other platoons. John knew them all. "I'm real tired now, Bradley. I need to sleep."

All that night he was awakened by bad dreams and by his painful ribs. The dreams restarted each time he dozed off. He was in the helicopter looking into the eyes of the young VC. He would try to fly away, but the controls would not respond. The VC would shoot him, and the pain would wake him up.

He lay awake in a cold sweat. After eleven months, he had finally realized that he could die here. That young VC had not been shooting at a helicopter. He knew he had blown John away. He wasn't shooting at anything else. He was looking right at John.

Remembering his close calls over the past months, he considered that he should have been more careful. Perhaps he should quit now. It would be the natural thing to do. Find a quiet corner and lick his wounds, maybe quit altogether, as

Huey had done when he got his first honest look at the situation. Old age had come upon John late, but as surely as the delivery of that round from the AK-47.

There was something he had to do first. He had to get the CO, remove him, bust him. The only way was the hard way, up through the chain of command.

27

CHAIN OF COMMAND

JOHN'S RESOLVE KEPT HIM GOING. HIS CHEST HAD TURNED THE color of dark blue denim, with the bullet marks a deeper color. The crews flying back into battle left him alone in the barracks. He spent the next day dozing. After that, he walked around naked from the belt up. His skin was so tender to the touch, he could not wear even a T-shirt. For once, the mess sergeant did not throw someone out for coming to chow without a shirt.

The hootch maids avoided him. They thought anyone with a purple front must have some very bad sickness. He walked up on two of them eating rice and roared. They spilled their bowls, turned tail, and ran for the gate.

That made him laugh, but nothing helped much during the three remaining days of the CA. It was called off when the commanders realized there was no chance to make headway against the well-entrenched VC and NVA. The ground forces had to retreat out of the hills on foot, while every day for a solid week after it was over, half a dozen Chinook-loads of dead bodies were brought out. Most of the dead were South

Koreans. Lost aircraft added up: nineteen slicks, 5 gunships, and 2 Chinooks. Many more were disabled, and most had taken hits. The CA was a total failure.

The more reports came in, the angrier John grew. The camp was like a ghost town. In the Sixty-first, twenty bunks were empty, vacated by the dead or seriously wounded. Few people left their rooms or socialized. The loss of life filled John with such rage that he wanted to grab the CO and throttle the life out of him. John had seen it coming, and the CO had refused to listen. Now Hayes was lying low.

Although John's skin still burned to the touch, he decided he must start up the chain with Major Raeburn, with or without a shirt. Putting on clean fatigue pants and his go-to-hell hat, he went to the battalion commander's office.

"Major Raeburn, Mister Vanvorden requesting permission to speak, sir."

"Come in, Mister Vanvorden." When he saw the purple chest with its two black marks, he refrained from chewing John out for not wearing a shirt. He could not take his eyes off the ugly markings.

"Sorry, sir. It's too tender to cover up yet. Maybe in a couple more days. I took two AKs in the chicken plate on that—rat fuck CA."

The major had obviously wanted to forget the CA. He was part of air mission command, and an investigation might taint his military record. John knew that, but he wondered if the major's conscience was bothering him, if he could sleep nights. Some commanders learned early how to bury conscience. "Just what are you doing in my office?" Raeburn asked.

John went into a formal report of how he had tried to stop the CA plan, how he had been excluded from the planning process, and how Hayes had turned down the alternate plan John had proposed, which he described to Raeburn. All this took some time, and as he talked, the major stared at the black spots.

"Boy, you're a fool to come in here. You know perfectly well I was up there with your CO, don't you? I am telling you to keep your mouth shut from now on, or you will be in a hell of a lot of trouble. You get out of my office, boy, and don't come back."

That was that. He had done the correct thing. Now he would go over the major's head. Chain of command regulations said you must ask to see the next higher up. You cannot be refused, but you must first ask before you go.

"I request permission to go to group, major," he said, standing as straight as his ribs would allow.

"You are not going to group. Where you'll go is to jail. I warn you, I'll get you for anything and everything."

"Does that mean you refuse me permission?" John knew the major had to give it.

"No. I'll get you to group. But from now on, boy, you are in trouble."

John got himself to group headquarters two days later. He was able to wear a shirt when he faced Colonel Freeman, the new group commander with only five weeks in the country. The colonel, a tall stork of a man with nearly white hair, looked at John with unblinking eyes. The press in the colonel's clothes was so sharp, the man must have ironed his own uniforms. Only men with devout military minds looked quite like that in Nam.

He permitted John to tell his story.

"Yes, Mister Vanvorden, I am familiar with the fiasco. It was indeed a tragedy. However, I must tell you that your undertaking as a W-2 to remove a captain is impossible."

"Why, sir?"

"If your commanding officer merited removal from office, his superior officers would know it. You are simply not qualified to judge your superior."

"You don't think the mission was run ideally, do you, sir?"

"Obviously not. But missions cannot always be expected to be ideal."

"The U.S. Army has had a lot of experience in Nam, sir.

Do you think when something like this happens, it's all to the credit of the NVA and VC?"

"Now, Mister Vanvorden, I know what you are trying to lead me into, and I will not be led. I have said all I will say."

"You can't—or won't—do anything, then?"

"There is nothing to be done."

"Then I would like to go to brigade headquarters, sir."

The stork stared at him for a full minute. "You have my permission, of course. But you should be warned that word will precede you. All you will accomplish is to arouse my ire as well as that of those below me. And furthermore, I shall be surprised if the general even talks to you."

"I still want to go."

"Mister Vanvorden, you have bitten off more than you can chew, but it's your choice."

As soon as he left the office, John headed for Long Binh with the objective of seeing General Plummer at brigade headquarters.

He took his place in an outer office where two clerk typists worked steadily and an orderly spent his full time answering the telephone and placing calls for the brigade commander. The general himself walked in or out several times, never paying the slightest attention to John.

John had heard about him. He was an academy man, and his goal had always been to become a general. He had a gruff voice, a lined face, and a flat-top haircut that made him look more like an old soldier risen through the ranks than a West Pointer, as if he should be wearing stripes and hash instead of stars. John thought of such men as Wallace Berry types. Vietnam was their Hollywood set, only bigger and better. Still, these old war horses could be pretty great, some of them.

The office functioned steadily as John sat there waiting. He took no lunch, but waited between 0800 hours and 1700. The general went in and out, and the general's visitors came and went. At first, John turned his head every time a door opened and pestered the orderly every hour or so. His attempts to attract the general's attention were in vain. In the evenings at the officers' club, he reminded himself that at some point the general would have to see him.

The second day was the worst. The two ceiling fans endlessly moved stale air from one corner of the room to the other and back again. The GIs at the typewriters dealt with mountains of paper work. They might as well have been in Nebraska instead of Vietnam. Only a chance direct hit by a VC 122-mm. rocket would bring the war to them. His chair seat was hard.

By midmorning, he was thinking back over the events that had brought him there. Not getting in right away had unnerved him a little. Perhaps he had made some mistake the brigade commander already knew about, but if that were the case, he'd have been disposed of in a hurry. He felt imprisoned in the chair, but if he left, he might have to start all over again. It was a survival test.

The hours dragged. When the clock reached 1700, he got up and left. The end of his second day came without so much as a nod from the general.

The third morning, there was no sign of the brigade commander. John spent his time analyzing his motives for trying to get the captain busted. It was an action bound to have a reaction according to the law of karma. Doing nothing, though, would also have its result, probably more wasted lives. John knew that the chosen action must not violate the voice within. The voice was clear. No choice. He had to get the captain for the safety of other men. Revenge had been a motive before, but it was not now. All that time had made him think.

"What the hell do you want?"

It was noon, and the general had arrived and was standing beside him. John leapt to attention. "I'm waiting to see you, sir."

"I know that! What do you want?"

"I have a serious problem with my company commander."

"Oh, you do, huh?"

"Yes, sir. It's a long story—"

"I'll give you a couple of minutes. Come in." His voice was gravelly and accustomed to command. He strode into his office and pointed to a chair opposite his desk. His face was like granite and showed no emotion.

"To begin, sir, my name's Vanvorden. I'm the senior aircraft commander from the Sixty-first Assault Helicopter Company in An Son. I was told you knew I was coming. . . ."

"Well, go on."

As he had rehearsed, John outlined how the Sixty-first had earned the right to plan the big CA, and he went through the safety record compiled after he made changes as senior AC.

General Plummer picked up the phone. "Cancel my twelve-thirty lunch with General Aikens. Bring in sandwiches and coffee. I'm busy here." He turned to John. "Keep talking, Mister Vanvorden. I'm listening."

John described in detail how he had learned to surprise the enemy by keeping all plans secret until the last minute and then prepping the LZs with everything at his disposal. The general nodded approval several times, but then commented, "But you never did respect your CO, did you, Vanvorden?"

"Not Captain Hayes."

"Why not?"

"He's no combat pilot, sir. He had under three-hundred hours when he took over, and he never learned the basics. Most of his experience came from grinding up men and helicopters a week ago."

The general frowned. "What does your CO think of you?"

"Not much. A while back, the 173rd put me, two majors, and Colonel Palls in for commendation. Captain Hayes wanted to court-martial me."

"For what?"

"We pulled out two of their boys over near Phu Cat when they couldn't get dust off. The colonel okayed it. We'd been flying command and control . . ."

"Palls got a silver star as I recall."

"That's right, sir."

"So what was the offense?"

"We were in the captain's new helicopter. It took twenty-seven hits. It was totaled. He wanted to get me for destroying government property."

The general threw back his head and laughed, and John joined him, although he didn't think it was that funny.

"What happened next?"

"General Willaby of the 173rd came to my company with Colonel Palls, and they had a meeting with my CO."

"I bet they did. Clark's a good commander. So, no court-martial, right?"

"No, sir."

"Now I remember. Palls called you the Flying Dutchman. Said that was the prettiest piece of flying he's seen. How did those two boys make out?"

"I heard they lived."

"Good. Good. Got to win some."

Sandwiches and coffee came in. John was surprised that there was some for him. He began to relax.

"Now tell me about that rat fuck CA," said General Plummer, using the phrase he knew was used by the men. "All I have heard were excuses. Tell me just as you saw it, Dutchman."

"Yes, sir." The general had let him stew outside the office for a couple of days, maybe to see what kind of stuff he was made of. Now he was listening intently to the senior AC.

John watched the general's controlled anger growing as he recited the whole story, the story of a disaster that would upset any commander—How there had been month-long over-flights that gave away the AO and Hayes's refusal to prep the LZs. He gave every detail of the captain's plan, delivered at the premature briefing.

"Man's a fool," said Plummer between his teeth and picked up the phone. "Cancel all appointments this afternoon." Then he half squinted at John and leaned forward. "Got any cigars, Dutchman?"

"No, sir."

"Wait a minute. I'll get one from Bailey." He went out and returned a few seconds later puffing on a cigar. "Helps me think."

After puffing a few streams of smoke toward the ceiling, he asked the question John was anticipating. "Why didn't you stop it before it happened? You were senior AC."

"I tried. He did most of the planning after he sent me to Saigon on some ash and trash to get me out of the way. When he revealed the plan, I spent the next two days replanning the entire mission."

The general nodded encouragingly. John recited the details of his revised plan, the time changes, prepping of LZs, simplification of control procedure by changing assault tactics. The general nodded sharply several times. "But he told me to get the hell out of his room. Then I told him I wasn't going to fly lead. I wasn't going to fly period."

"You flew, though."

"Yes, sir. Damn right I did." He lifted his shirt and showed his chest. "Two AKs in the chicken plate at close range."

"Christ. What did that feel like?"

"Sledge-hammer. Took my wind. I'd have taken ten more, though, sir, if I could have protected my copilot. He was killed helping me into Chalk Two. Our engine was shot up."

"Why did you fly when you knew what it would be like?"

"Everybody knew. Every combat-seasoned AC knew for sure. They had to follow orders. Me, I was, well, too short to care about orders from a man that doesn't know shit from shinola, but my gunner came to me the day before, and he showed me a picture of his new baby, and he said he knew he'd make it if I flew. . . ." The general cleared his throat, and John hurried on. "What could I do? The enlisteds all know what's going on. Half the time they know better than the pilots. They got no say-so at all." John realized that the general had withdrawn immediately behind tradition. Enlisted men follow the officers' lead. He shouldn't talk about that. Nevertheless, the general picked up the phone again.

"Get me some records, Bailey. Captain Hayes. CO of the Sixty-first. What's his first name, Vanvorden?"

"Courtland."

"Courtland Hayes." He hung up. Leaning back, he contemplated the young man sitting in front of him. "I'll tell you something, Dutchman. I don't have five men in the brigade who would do what you have done. I think it's damn fine. Why aren't you an officer?"

"I am, sir, I'm a W-2."

"No. I mean an RLO. We need men like you in the officer corps. I can make you a second lieutenant by tomorrow morning."

Gratified and feeling very at home with this man, John blurted out, "With all due respect, sir, I don't want to be no fucking butter bar."

They both began laughing. In the army, a butter bar was the worst thing you could be, worse than a private.

"Can't say I blame you, Dutchman!"

They both laughed so hard now that the men in the outer office must have heard them and wondered what in hell a W-2 was doing, laughing in there with the general.

"Doubt if I can make you a regular officer by tomorrow, but I'll see what I can do. And I'll make a decision about Captain Hayes. So I think I'd like you to spend the next two or three days here in case I need you. Come and have dinner with me tonight. See you at the officers' club at eighteen hundred hours for drinks."

"Thank you, sir. I'll be there."

The next three days were very strange. He did not talk privately with General Plummer again, although he was invited for dinner with him and a few other officers every night. Because Plummer outranked the others, a brigadier and some colonels, they were cordial enough to John, although they obviously felt unnatural having a warrant officer along. The officers played no cards or chess but drank away the evenings and talked. Most of the talk was was about World War II, of which they were all veterans. All such veterans of any rank, John had observed, did not consider Nam their war.

Plummer had introduced John as one of the finest pilots in Vietnam, and the brigadier had said to him, "You young pilots have it pretty good here, whether you know it or not. Back in Bari, Italy, during the big one, it was hell. We had to carve airfields out of nothing. Our B-24s didn't have any of the stuff you boys have in airplanes now."

"I fly Hueys," John had responded.

"Those B-52s never get close to ack-ack. We got torn up by it all the time."

"So do our helicopters."

"Got you there, Jack," said General Plummer.

"And when we weren't flying over Germany, we were doing our best to survive on the ground in Italy. We had no barracks, no entertainment. Here you have television, all the booze you want, women, and you only have to stay twelve months."

"We're lucky, all right," John said with a straight face, and clammed up. It was all pretty boring in the evenings, standing around or sitting in O bars while they threw down whiskey and talked about the days before Vietnam, but boredom was a small price to pay to accomplish what he had come for.

Before he left to return to the Sixty-first, General Plummer shook hands and told him "things had been fixed" without explaining what that meant.

28
OLD AGE

NOTHING SEEMED TO HAVE CHANGED AT THE SIXTY-FIRST. What had he expected? Trumpets? A firing squad? John headed for his room to park his stuff, but no sooner had he got there than the XO appeared at his door.

"Dutchman! Welcome back."

This unusual visit set John's heart pounding. "How are things, Kant?"

"Couldn't be better. As if you didn't know."

"Didn't know what? What's happened?"

"Yesterday. Major Raeburn came and met with Captain Hayes for two hours. Then they called me in and told me I was acting CO, and it probably would be permanent."

"No shit!"

"I can't believe you don't know what's going on."

"I know a few things. So what else happened?"

"They acted like old friends with a bit of bad luck, but every time Hayes said he wanted to talk to group, the major just held out his new orders from General Plummer."

"Where'd he go?"

"Back to the states. Raeburn waited for him until he was packed. He's gone. It's the quickest I ever saw the army move."

John felt a glow inside, a kind of awe. He felt rather as he had the first time he had ordered Arc Light. One phone call from him and a piece of Vietnam's real estate had disappeared under a wave of explosions. One talk with a general and a captain disappeared with all his belongings.

"What did you do at brigade, Dutch?"

"Talked to General Plummer."

"You talked to General Plummer? Just like that?"

"Not just like that. I waited three days, sitting there, until he finally called me in. Then it was great. He's really down to earth. I told him everything Hayes did to lose all those men. He was mad as hell about that rat fuck already, so he ordered up the CO's, I mean Hayes's, personal records."

"You went through Hayes's records with the general?"

"Hell, no. He wouldn't do that kind of shit, not with a warrant. But that reminds me. I might be getting promoted one of these days. Seems like General Plummer wants me in the regular officer corps."

"I got you to thank I'm CO."

"Well, for getting rid of Hayes, anyhow."

"What else did you do there?"

"Three nights the general took me out drinking with a brigadier and three colonels. I looked around Saigon two days with my own jeep and driver. They were very decent."

"Damn! I don't know how you do it. Sure glad you're back, Dutchman. The 173rd's been asking for you for a VIP flight."

"Okay."

"And I need you to take over mission planning. I know you're short, but you can help me before you D-ROS. I've only been CO for a day, and I got more problems than I thought. You will, won't you?"

"Sure. See you later."

With only three weeks left in Vietnam, John could have

started slacking off, but he stayed busy instead, working long hours helping Kant learn how to run operations.

With Bates gone, John spent his free time mostly by himself. Now, with full cooperation from the CO in discharging his duties as senior AC, the invisible wall of authority was lodged more firmly between him and the other pilots.

Newbys passed legendlike stories among themselves about the Flying Dutchman. Some even came close to the truth. By this time, the seasoned ACs of the Sixty-first had done a lot of hard flying themselves. They no longer seemed to be as impressed with John as they had been when he first came to the unit. Still, they would probably admit he was the best pilot. What really impressed the ACs, especially the ass kissers, was the Dutchman's elimination of Captain Hayes.

John found that his concerns had narrowed in his old age. As a newby, he had thought about U.S. progress in the war, and notions about making the place safe for democracy had occurred to him now and then. Maturity brought concern for the success of his unit. A leader was judged by his unit. In old age, you covered your own safety first and then thought about the larger picture. Men who served multiple tours stayed in the mature phase longer than others, but they, too, eventually got old.

The fear he could not shake, of again being shot point-blank, could affect his performance as lead, so he flew trail instead. It was the best position for teaching, anyway. When an ARVN operation to retake a fire-support base came up, Kant promised this would be his last. The ARVNs had lost the base to a single company of NVA.

Located west of Kontum in the triborder region, the base perched atop a mountain. As planned, the Sixty-first inserted two battalions of ARVNs to the west and southwest of the mountain. Under strength, both battalions still totaled about one thousand men. It took sixteen slicks half a day to move them from the staging area fifteen minutes away to the bottom of the mountain. The 129th AHC ferried one ARVN battalion to the east of the mountain.

All three battalions looked store bought. Each troop had a new camouflage uniform, new steel pot, new boots, new weapon, and enough ammunition and food to last five days.

On signal, one thousand five hundred South Vietnamese soldiers began walking up the mountain in broad daylight with battalion commanders in the lead. Halfway up, the two battalions west and southwest started taking extremely heavy fire from the fire base on top. The NVA were throwing everything they had.

First to turn tail were the ARVN officers leading the troops up the mountain. The panic spread. In minutes, the two battalions had retreated in full flight, leaving dead and wounded behind, and a trail of weapons, ammo, and supplies. Then an incredible thing happened; the panic-stricken ARVNs stripped off their uniforms.

In the meantime, the battalion to the east was outflanked by a large number of North Vietnamese. With heavy fire at their backsides, the battalion charged up the mountain and captured the fire-support base, driving a decimated NVA company back into the jungle.

John and the other pilots, surprised at being called in to evacuate the ARVNs only one day after insertion, were flabbergasted to see most of two well-equipped battalions waiting for them in cheap-looking, loose-fitting jocky shorts.

The scene was so bizarre and the ARVNs so disorganized that the flight leader chose not to go in. After getting the full story from American advisers on the ground, US headquarters decided to make the dishonored ARVNs walk out.

On the way back, John got a call from Lucky Star Base, asking him to fly some artillery specialists and some advisers to the top of the mountain just recaptured.

EPILOGUE

IT WAS ON THE FOLLOWING DAY THAT JOHN HAD BEEN HIT BY an armor-piercing bullet that came up through the helicopter seat and collided with the Colt .45 automatic pistol he wore between his legs. The pistol absorbed the remaining force of the bullet and saved his life by the narrowest margin. MASH doctors stopped the bleeding from John's leg arteries and stabilized his condition; then they transferred him to the Ninety-Fifth Medivac Hospital in Da Nang.

Very slowly, John awakened. Gradually, a dark mist cleared, and he could see that it was a sunny day. He lay on his back with IVs in both arms. His legs were propped up and spread-eagled, and there were bandages on the inside of each thigh. When he turned his head, he saw that he was in a hospital bay for the seriously wounded. It reminded him of Da Nang. . . .

The last thing he seemed to remember was flying a helicopter. He could not recall when or where. Feeling the bandages on his legs, he reached two . . . big things the size of grapefruit. My God, he thought, are those my balls? He felt the cathether running out of his penis. Beginning to panic, he yelled, "*Help*!"

A nurse came running. "What's the matter?"

"What happened? What happened to my crew? What's wrong with me?" He put both hands on his testicles. Then the pain hit him.

"You'll be all right," said the nurse. "In a few days, the swelling will go down."

"Tell me what happened!"

"I don't know anything. Ask the doctor. Now you have to put ice on them."

"I hurt," said John. "No ice."

She was a tough-looking nurse and not very pretty. "You have to put ice on them. If we don't get the swelling down, you'll see how it hurts."

They were short of ice bags and she came back with a surgical glove that had been filled with water, tied off and frozen. The ice-cold hand on his balls distracted him from the other pain.

For three days, he could do nothing but lie there, sleeping as much as he could and awakened by pain when they would give him no more drugs. He wanted to get up and walk around and yell, but he could not stand.

The soldier on his right was a double amputee who had lost both his legs at the knees in a fire fight. When they wheeled him out and did not refill the bed, John took it as a good sign. On his left was a fellow helicopter pilot recovering from a shoot down. He had lost his left arm and suffered some intestinal damage. He was lucky to be alive. The whole bay was nothing but amputees, and John became irrationally fearful that they were fixing to cut him. Whenever one ice bag gave out, he ordered another one. Nobody was able to tell him what had happened to the others in his helicopter, so he shut the question out of his mind. When he felt a little better, he tried to cheer up his neighbor. Tommy had played baseball for two years at Arizona State and only joined the army because he was flunking out. He had not wanted to go into the service, but without student deferment, he would have been drafted as a ground pounder, so he joined the warrant-officer program. It was good duty, and he had played some baseball for his army post team. Now he was morose. He loved the game he could never play again.

"Hey, Tommy, you awake?" John whispered one morning. It was very early.

"What do you want, Dutchman?"

"That nurse. The one coming down the aisle. I think I know her."

"From the states?"

"No. When I was in here before. You know her name?"

"Yeah. Lieutenant Bradshaw."

"That's her! Bradshaw." John leaned over to him and recounted his battle with Nurse Bradshaw. Tommy laughed, the first time he had so much as smiled.

"She work this floor?"

"I think they rotate around. I can't figure it out," said Tommy.

They were quiet as the nurse approached and reached their beds. She picked up Tommy's chart.

"Well, we're feeling chipper this morning, aren't we, gentlemen?"

"I guess," said Tommy.

"Back again, are you, Captain Vanvorden?"

That was a mean kind of joke, thought John. Typical of Bradshaw. "Mister Vanvorden to you, lieutenant."

She took John's chart off the hook. "It says here captain."

John stared at the chart and then looked at his wrist ID bracelet. It read captain. "What the hell's happened?"

"I'm sure I can't say," said Nurse Bradshaw. She looked suspicious that he was making a joke at her expense for Tommy's benefit.

"Why can't I find out? What the hell goes on? Is this a prison?"

Bradshaw reacted with cold fury. "I do not know anything at all about you. We have several hundred men a week coming through here.'' She consulted his chart and pulled back the sheet.

John tensed. ''What are you going to do?''

She took hold of his penis. ''This is going to hurt,'' she announced as she yanked the catheter out.

His agonized yip came out before he could stop it. ''Did you have to do it that way?''

''That is the way it's done, sir,'' she said as she cleaned up and swished away on her rounds.

John looked at his penis. The poor thing was bent right instead of the usual left. He reached for the ice glove and pulled the sheet up under his chin. ''Remind me to watch my mouth around that one, Tommy. She's got all the trump cards.''

Tommy laughed again.

In the afternoon, John's personal effects were delivered to him. He checked first to see that the book was there. Then he opened a letter that had arrived. It was dated June 20, 1971 and was from Kant.

''Dutchman,'' he read, ''this letter is to explain what is going on and to wish you well on your way back to the world.

''After you were shot, Rosen took you to a MASH unit where they patched you up and kept you for a day before sending you on to Da Nang. You were the only one hit. I wrote you up for a Heart.

''The hospital says you are recovering. A lot of guys have started wearing their sidearms to the front. You've got something going for you, Dutchman. That same day, orders came from Washington promoting you to captain. I still don't believe it. How did you do it?

''I'm giving you an extra set of my own captain's bars so you can wear them home. With the kind of pull you have, you should never get out of the army. You're a natural career officer.

''Good luck, Dutchman. The hospital will handle your transportation and medivac you if you want. Thanks for the help and the promotion to CO. Your friend, Captain Bob Kant.''

The bars were in the envelope pinned to a copy of the promotion orders. General Plummer must have pulled some strings for the promotion to captain. He must have wanted to influence John to stay in the army. It was an unusual jump, no matter how good his military record looked on review. ''I'll be damned,'' John said to himself. ''Who would've thought?'' He felt like throwing a promotion party, but this was too sad a place. He would keep it to himself.

In the days remaining, while his injuries healed without complications, he spent time reading his book, comparing it to what he remembered of his talks with Huey, and thinking about the new wisdom he was discovering. He wanted to find words to comfort men like Tommy. What could he say to a young veteran with no legs? It's just the physical body? Your spirit is unharmed, and in future lifetimes, all will be as it was?

How could he? He was not sure that he himself believed. His need to believe was not immediate because his body was still whole, and he would come out of all this intact. He did know that the voice inside him never spoke against this wisdom.

John opted for a commercial carrier flight home. He wanted no more of hospitals or nurses and as little as possible of the army. He wanted to go back to the real world.

When he left the hospital, he went to say good-by to some of the soldiers on his floor. He wished them well, wanted them to take heart.

At the air terminal in Da Nang, John had mixed emotions. There were the crowds of grunts straight out of the field waiting for a call to load the states-bound airliners. Wearing freshly laundered summer class-As, he felt overdressed.

A few new replacement troops were still trickling into Nam, including some helicopter pilots. A young warrant officer in a clean uniform caught his eye and came over.

''Sir, I'm new here. Can you tell me how I find my unit?''

"Just stand over there somewhere. Some noncom will be along and call a list of names."

"Thank you, sir."

"Listen, over here you don't call warrant officers sir, no lieutenants and damn few captains."

The wobbly one moved quietly away. He did not want to sound like an FNG by asking more questions.

John walked slowly through the busy terminal. Leaning on a wall to wait for the loudspeaker to give his boarding call, he realized it was the same wall where, when his feet and hands had been infected, he had thrown his crutches, and hit the big marine.

So much had happened in one year. Would he be able to explain to anyone other than a Nam vet what it was like? Could his family even begin to understand? How could he ever describe the secret thrill of combat, the clarity of mind, and at the same time his revulsion to it all, knowing how the body and the mind could be ravaged? From the upper air, with a flying machine strapped to his back, he had been brought low. In the peace to which he looked forward, one day real old age would inevitably bring him down for good.

He did not yet fully understand or value spiritual freedom more than the physical freedom he had felt flying a helicopter, but he suspected it would gain in importance. Huey had said he must work hard to learn from words that sounded so simple. Back in the real world he would have time. He could be young again.

ABOUT THE AUTHOR

Jay and David Groen are brothers who both served in the Vietnam war. As a U.S. Air Force Intelligence linguist, specializing in Chinese Mandarin, Jay Groen spent two-and-a-half years in Asia, including a total of twelve months in Vietnam, stationed in Da Nang, and three months on temporary duty in Bangkok, Thailand. Jay, who has an M.A. in Economics, worked nine years for the CIA as a China Specialist in their Office of Economic Research. In recent years he has worked as a business consultant to companies doing business in China.

David Groen dreamed from childhood of being a pilot. At fifteen he sent away for the plans to a gyrocopter kit, and was crushed when his high school's machine shop wouldn't let him build it. David joined the Army's warrant officer flight training program in helicopters three days after his high school graduation. Upon successfully completing flight school, he volunteered for Vietnam because his brothers Jay and Martin were there—and he wasn't going to be left out. As a warrant officer flying Hueys, he earned the nickname the Flying Dutchman. After his discharge from the Army, he flew helicopters commercially until 1982.

The authors both live in Salt Lake City, Utah, where they grew up. They are both married and each have three daughters. Jay and David have just formed a new company, which is building and marketing homebuilt gyrocopter kits. They describe their autogyro, which David helped to develop, as a new generation rotary aircraft.